GERMANY AFTER THE 2013 ELECTIONS

Germany After the 2013 Elections

Breaking the Mould of Post-Unification Politics?

Edited by

GABRIELE D'OTTAVIO
Italian-German Historical Institute-FBK, Italy and
University of Trento, Italy

THOMAS SAALFELD
University of Bamberg, Germany

ASHGATE

Published by
Ashgate Publishing Limited
Wey Court East
Union Road
Farnham
Surrey, GU9 7PT
England

Ashgate Publishing Company
110 Cherry Street
Suite 3-1
Burlington, VT 05401-3818
USA

www.ashgate.com

British Library Cataloguing in Publication Data
A catalogue record for this book is available from the British Library

The Library of Congress has cataloged the printed edition as follows:
D'Ottavio, Gabriele.
  Germany after the 2013 elections : breaking the mould of post-unification politics? / by Gabriele D'Ottavio and Thomas Saalfeld.
    pages cm
  Includes bibliographical references and index.
  ISBN 978-1-4724-4439-4 (hardback) – ISBN 978-1-4724-4440-0 (ebook) – ISBN 978-1-4724-4441-7 (epub) 1. Germany. Bundestag – Elections, 2013. 2. Elections – Germany – History – 21st century. 3. Political parties – Germany – History – 21st century. 4. Germany – Politics and government – 1990- I. Saalfeld, Thomas, 1960- II. Title.
  JN3971.A95D36 2015
  320.943 – dc23

2014039543

ISBN 9781472444394 (hbk)
ISBN 9781472444400 (ebk – PDF)
ISBN 9781472444417 (ebk – ePUB)

Printed in the United Kingdom by Henry Ling Limited, at the Dorset Press, Dorchester, DT1 1HD

Contents

List of Tables

List of Figures

Acknowledgements

This volume is the result of a truly collaborative effort which was made possible by a number of people and organizations. First and foremost, we would like to thank the Istituto Carlo Cattaneo in Bologna for launching this project and asking us to make it real. A workshop at the Johns Hopkins University School of Advanced International Studies (SAIS) in Bologna, two months after the German election of 22 September 2013, allowed all contributors to meet and discuss their work and interpretations of the election. We would like to thank the Johns Hopkins University SAIS Europe, the Department of Political and Social Sciences of the University of Bologna, the German-Italian University Centre and the Italian-German Historical Institute-FBK in Trento for their generous financial support in making this workshop possible. We are also grateful to Erik Jones, Winrich Kühne, Hanns W. Maull and Salvatore Vassallo for acting as chairs and discussants offering their valuable insights. Special thanks are due to Elisa Piras for her generous assistance during the preparation of the manuscript. We are also grateful to Anne Hudson for the final proofreading of the volume, and to Brenda Sharp, Rob Sorsby and Philip Stirups at Ashgate. Johannes Geiger, Lukas Hohendorf and Fabio Rössler assisted us in compiling the index. Last but not least, we would like to thank each contributor for their participation in this project and their efficiency in delivering their essays 'at relatively short notice' after the election.

Gabriele D'Ottavio and Thomas Saalfeld

Notes on Contributors

Gianfranco Baldini is associate professor of political science at the University of Bologna. In 2007 he founded the book series 'Elections, governments, democracy' ('Egd') at the Istituto Cattaneo Research Foundation, also in Bologna. He was deputy-director of the Cattaneo Research Foundation in 2010–11. The 'Egd' series, which he has directed since 2012 as sole coordinator, publishes volumes in Italian and English on the political systems of the biggest European countries after relevant general elections (a corresponding volume on Germany is forthcoming from Il Mulino). He has published extensively comparative works on representation, elections, electoral systems and territorial politics. Among international publications are the following: *Italian Politics. Governing Fear* (co-ed. A. Cento Bull), Berghahn Books, 2010; *Elections, Electoral Systems and Volatile Voters* (with A. Pappalardo), Palgrave, 2010; and *Coalition Britain. The UK Election of 2010* (co-ed. J. Hopkin), Manchester University Press, 2012. He has published in, among others, *West European Politics*, *Government and Opposition*, and *Regional and Federal Studies*.

Silvia Bolgherini holds a PhD in political science (2003) and is assistant professor at the University of Naples Federico II (Italy) where she teaches comparative politics and public policy analysis. She was research fellow at the Istituto Carlo Cattaneo, Bologna, and named Ladislao Mittner Laureate for political science in 2007 by the German-Italian University Centre/German Academic Exchange Service (DIH/DAAD). In addition, she was visiting scholar at the University of Granada (Spain) between 2012 and 2013; at the Freie Universität Berlin and at the University of Potsdam (Germany) in 2008 and 2012; and at Sciences-PO/CNRS, Paris (France) between 2004 and 2006. She has published widely on comparative politics, electoral studies, European studies and local government. Her recent books include *Oltre le Province. Enti intermedi in Italia e in Europa* (Padua University Press, 2014, co-edited with P. Messina); *La Germania di Angela Merkel* (Bologna: Il Mulino, 2010, co-edited with F. Grotz); *Come le regioni diventano europee. Stili di governo e sfide comunitarie nell'Europa mediterranea* (Bologna: Il Mulino, 2006).

Gabriele D'Ottavio is research fellow at the Italian-German Historical Institute-FBK in Trento and teaches international and European history at the University of Trento (Italy). He holds a PhD in contemporary history from the University of Bologna. He was DAAD-visiting fellow at the Humboldt University (Berlin) between 2005 and 2006, visiting fellow at the European University Institute

(Florence) between 2009 and 2011, and visiting fellow at the Goethe-University (Frankfurt am Main) in 2015. He is a member of the editorial board of *Ventunesimo Secolo. Rivista di Studi sulle Transizioni* and a member of the editorial secretariat of *Annali dell'Istituto storico italo-germanico/Jahrbuch des italienisch-deutschen historischen Instituts*. His main areas of research are German history, the history of European integration, and German and Italian intellectual history. His publications include *L'Europa dei tedeschi. La Repubblica Federale di Germania e l'integrazione europea 1949-1966* (Bologna: Il Mulino, 2012) and *Entscheidungen für Europa. Die Bundesrepublik Deutschland und die Europäische Integration, 1949-1966* (Berlin: Duncker & Humblot, forthcoming 2015).

Kenneth Dyson is professor of politics at the University of Cardiff. He holds a BSc and MSc in economics from the University of London and a PhD from the University of Liverpool. He started his career as lecturer (subsequently senior lecturer) in politics at the University of Liverpool and was later professor of European studies at Bradford University. Visiting professorships have included the Free University of Berlin (DAAD Distinguished Research Professor), Konstanz University, McMaster University (Distinguished Hooker Professor) and Siena University. He chaired the (UK) Association for the Study of German Politics (ASGP), of which he was a founder, and the Standing Conference of Heads of European Studies (SCHES), of which he was also a founder. Professor Dyson was awarded the German Federal Service Cross ('Bundesverdienstkreuz' First Class) for services to Anglo-German relations, and in 2003 given an honorary doctorate of letters by Aston University for services to European studies. In 1997 he was elected a fellow of the British Academy. He was also elected an academician of the Learned Societies of the Social Sciences, a fellow of the Royal Historical Society, a fellow of the Royal Society of Arts, and, in 2010, a founding fellow of the Learned Society of Wales, of which he is a council member.

Simon T. Franzmann is currently assistant professor (pro tempore) for comparative political science and methods at the Heinrich-Heine University Düsseldorf and member of the steering committee of the Manifesto Project on Political Representation (MARPOR) conducted by the Science Centre in Berlin. In 2004 he finished his studies of economics and political science at the University of Cologne. He holds a PhD in political science from the University of Cologne. His dissertation dealt with the ideological and programmatic change of contemporary party systems. In 2010 he worked at the Institute for Data Analysis and Data Archiving in Cologne. Then he moved to the University of Potsdam and became a lecturer at the Chair for German and European Politics. In 2011 and 2012 he was a substitute professor for comparative political science at the University of Greifswald before moving to his current position in Düsseldorf. His research focuses on the empirical study of party systems, political sociology, comparative empirical studies of democracies and theories of party competition. He is a specialist in analyzing party strategies, political ideologies and the content analysis of political texts. Together with André Kaiser he has written 'Locating Parties in Policy Space', published in *Party Politics*. His work has also been published in journals such as *West European Politics*, the *Journal of Theoretical Politics* and *Politische Vierteljahresschrift*.

Margret Hornsteiner is a doctoral student at the University of Bamberg. She obtained her MA in political science from the University of Bamberg in 2009 and worked there as a temporary lecturer in political science between 2009 and 2014. She is now completing her doctoral thesis on 'Manifesto Formation and Its Consequences for Representation'. This project focuses on the intra-party dimension of parties' election programmes (manifestos). Her publications so far have focused on the German party system and include 'Parties and Party Systems' in Masamichi Sasaki, Jack Goldstone and Ekkart Zimmermann (eds) *Concise Encyclopedia of Comparative Sociology* (2014, with Thomas Saalfeld), and 'Parties and the Party System' in Stephen Padgett, William E. Paterson and Reimut Zohlnhöfer (eds) *Developments in German Politics 4* (2014, with Thomas Saalfeld).

Simon Jakobs has been a research fellow in political science at the University of Trier since October 2013. From 2008 to 2013 he studied political science, German studies and philosophy at the University of Trier. He graduated in 2013 with a 'Staatsexamen' (State Examination in Education) and an M.A. (Magister Artium). Although he enjoyed various school placements during his studies, he decided not to pursue the career of a school teacher but to continue his research on party organizational transformation and political participation. In his doctoral dissertation project, he investigates the reasons why people do not join political parties and the impact of these factors on party organizational resilience.

Uwe Jun is professor of political science (German and comparative politics) at the University of Trier in Germany (2005 to date). His research focus is on political institutions in Western democracies, in particular party politics and political communication. He is the chairman of the standing group on party politics within the German Political Science Association and has published widely on political parties and on contemporary developments in the German political system. Professor Jun began his professional career at the University of Goettingen in Germany. Afterwards he taught and conducted research at several universities, among others Harvard University in Cambridge (USA), the University of Potsdam (Germany), the Free University of Berlin (Germany) and Södertörns University in Stockholm (Sweden).

Matthias Mader is a research fellow at the Chair of Political Psychology, University of Mannheim, and a member of the Bamberg Graduate School of Social Sciences (BAGSS). His research interests include political psychology, public opinion, electoral behaviour and security studies. He has made contributions to *Electoral Studies*, *German Politics*, *International Journal of Public Opinion Research* and *Zeitschrift für Internationale Beziehungen*.

Alister Miskimmon is head of the department of politics and international relations at Royal Holloway, University of London where he co-directs the Centre for European Politics. Miskimmon is the author of a number of books including (with Ben O'Loughlin and Laura Roselle) *Strategic Narratives: Communication Power and the New World Order* (New York: Routledge, 2013). Miskimmon has also published the following in the field of German politics: (with Simon Green and Dan Hough) *The Politics of the New Germany*, Second Edition, Routledge; (with William E. Paterson and James Sloam) *Germany's Gathering Crisis: Germany and the Grand Coalition since 2005*, Palgrave; and *Germany and the Common Foreign and Security Policy of the European Union*, Palgrave. Miskimmon's main research interests are German foreign policy and strategic narrative in international relations.

Luuk Molthof is a PhD student in the department of politics and international relations at Royal Holloway, University of London. His thesis examines the strategic use of ideas in Germany's policy on European monetary affairs. He holds an MSc in modern Chinese studies from the University of Oxford and an MA in international relations from the University of Warwick.

Thomas Saalfeld is professor of political science at the University of Bamberg and the founding director of the Bamberg Graduate School of Social Sciences (BAGSS), an institution funded under the German Excellence Initiative. Before joining the University of Bamberg he was professor of political science at the University of Kent (Canterbury, UK). He also held visiting professorships at Boğaziçi University, Istanbul, the Institut d'Études Politiques de Lille and the University of Mannheim. Professor Saalfeld is a fellow of the (UK) Academy of Social Sciences (AcSS), managing academic editor of *German Politics* and a member of the advisory board of the *Italian Political Science Review*. His research focuses on representation, legislative behaviour, parliamentary accountability and coalition government in European democracies. His work has been published in academic journals including the *European Journal of Political Research*, *International Studies Quarterly*, the *Journal of Legislative Studies*, the *Rivista Italiana di Scienza Politica*, *Parliamentary Affairs* and *West European Politics*. His most recent publications include *The Oxford Handbook of Legislative Studies* (jointly edited with Shane Martin and Kaare Strøm, 2014) and *The Political Representation of Immigrants and Minorities* (jointly edited with Karen Bird and Andreas M. Wüst, 2011).

Harald Schoen holds the chair of political science, especially political psychology, at the University of Mannheim. After having been a professor of political sociology at the University of Bamberg for five years, he joined the University of Mannheim in 2014. His research interests include political attitudes and political behaviour, political psychology, political communication, and social science methods and methodology. He has published widely on these topics. Publications include articles in *British Journal of Psychology, Electoral Studies, European Union Politics, Internet Research, Journal of Conflict Resolution, Political Behavior, Political Psychology* and *Public Opinion Quarterly*.

Reimut Zohlnhöfer is professor of political science at Ruprecht-Karls-University, Heidelberg, Germany. In 2001, Professor Zohlnhöfer received his PhD from the University of Bremen where he also worked at the Centre for Social Policy Research. He spent his postdoctoral years in the political science department at Ruprecht-Karls-University, Heidelberg, and at the Center for European Studies at Harvard University. From 2008 to 2011 he was professor of comparative public policy at the University of Bamberg before returning to Heidelberg. His research focuses on economic policy and the welfare state in Germany as well as in comparative perspective, with a focus on the OECD countries. He has published and edited numerous books and special issues of academic journals, most recently *Developments in German Politics 4* (Palgrave, 2014, co-edited with Stephen Padgett and William Paterson) and a special issue of the journal *German Politics* on the second Merkel government (co-edited with Thomas Saalfeld, published in 2014). Furthermore, he has published articles in many leading journals, including *Comparative Political Studies, Journal of European Public Policy, Governance, West European Politics* and others.

Introduction

Breaking the Mould of Post-Unification German Politics?

Gabriele D'Ottavio and Thomas Saalfeld

On the surface, the German election of 22 September 2013 seems to indicate an extraordinarily high level of stability. Compared to the election of 2009, party-system fragmentation in the Bundestag was reduced. According to Laakso and Taagepera's (1979) measure of party-system fragmentation, the 'effective number of parties' in the Bundestag dropped from its post-unification peak of 4.7 in 2009 to just below 4.0 in 2013 (Hornsteiner and Saalfeld 2014, 86). Led by their popular chancellor, Angela Merkel, the Christian Democrats (CDU/CSU) achieved a remarkable 41.5 per cent of the popular vote and returned to an electoral position they last held in the 1980s under Chancellor Helmut Kohl. In fact, the Christian Democrats had the highest share of the vote and the highest number of Bundestag seats since 1994. In their contribution to this volume, Matthias Mader and Harald Schoen show that the CDU/CSU's success was multi-faceted but had a strong base in Merkel's considerable personal popularity. After admittedly protracted negotiations, on 16 December 2013 the Christian Democrats formed a grand coalition with the Social Democrats (SPD), commanding a huge parliamentary majority in the Bundestag with approximately 80 per cent of the votes in the chamber.

Table I.1   Result of the 2013 Bundestag election (compared to 2009)

	2013 (%)	2009 (%)
Turnout	71.5	70.8
CDU/CSU	41.5	33.8
SPD	25.7	23.0
Left Party	8.6	11.9
Greens	8.4	10.7
FDP	4.8	14.6
AfD	4.7	–
Pirates Party	2.2	2.0
NPD	1.3	1.5
Free Voters Association	1.0	–
Parties with less than 1% of the national vote	1.8	2.5
Parties not in the Bundestag	15.8	6

Source: Bundeswahlleiter (2013).

Nevertheless, the 2013 election may well be considered as a watershed in the future. As in 2009, turnout was relatively low by German standards (71.5 per cent compared to 70.8 per cent in 2009). Almost one-third of eligible citizens did not exercise their right to vote. Aggregate volatility – that is, the net changes between the parties' electoral strength – reached its highest level since the early 1950s (Hornsteiner and Saalfeld 2014, 87). The high levels of aggregate volatility, showing net changes in the strength of the parties between two elections, are a result of the recovery of the CDU/CSU by over 7 per cent, the sharp decline of the Liberals (FDP) by approximately 10 per cent and the rise of the Alternative for Germany (AfD) from zero to 4.7 per cent. The combined share of the two main parties' electoral strength was a mere 67.2 per cent of the vote. This was slightly up from the postwar low-point of 56.8 per cent in 2009, but remained the second lowest level of aggregate support for the two catch-all parties since 1949 (Hornsteiner and Saalfeld 2014, 87).

Table I.2   Second votes of the main parties (percentage), 1949–2013

	CDU/CSU	SPD	FDP	Grüne	Linke	Others
1949	31.0	29.2	11.9			27.9
1953	45.2	28.8	9.5			16.5
1957	50.2	31.8	7.7			10.3
1961	45.3	36.2	12.8			5.7
1965	47.6	39.3	9.5			3.6
1969	46.1	42.7	5.8			5.4
1972	44.9	45.8	8.4			0.9
1976	48.6	42.6	7.9			0.9
1980	44.5	42.9	10.6	1.5		0.5
1983	48.8	38.2	7.0	5.6		0.4
1987	44.3	37.0	9.1	8.3		1.3
1990	43.8	33.5	11	5.1	2.4	4.2
1994	41.4	36.4	6.9	7.3	4.4	3.6
1998	35.1	40.9	6.2	6.7	5.1	6
2002	38.5	38.5	7.4	8.6	4.0	3
2005	35.2	34.2	9.8	8.1	8.7	4
2009	33.8	23.0	14.6	10.7	11.9	6
2013	41.5	25.7	4.8	8.4	8.6	11

Source: www.election.de.

The percentage of smaller parties not represented in the Bundestag rose from 6 per cent in 2009 to 15.8 per cent of the vote, with the FDP (4.8 per cent) and the AfD (4.7 per cent) narrowly missing the five-per-cent hurdle. For the first time since 1949, the FDP failed to overcome the five-per-cent hurdle of Germany's electoral law (see Table I.2). It was eliminated from the Bundestag after 64 years of uninterrupted representation in the chamber, including 49 years in government. This left the CDU/CSU as the only party on the right and centre-right side of Germany's political spectrum. However, at least one new right-wing party seemed on the ascendancy, although it narrowly missed the five-per-cent hurdle: the Alternative for Germany. Founded only a few months before the election, its 4.7 per cent of the national vote put it only slightly behind the well-established FDP with its nationally well-known federal ministers. Although they are only 'second-order elections', the elections to the European Parliament on 25 May 2014 showed that the AfD may well become the CDU/CSU's main competitor on the right, replacing the FDP: in the elections of May 2014, the anti-euro party polled 7.0 per cent of the national vote, more than twice the number of votes cast for the FDP (3.4 per cent). Gianfranco Baldini and Silvia Bolgherini's contribution to this volume will examine the extent to which the AfD's strength at the polls can be seen as an expression of strong popular discontent with Angela Merkel's management of the euro crisis during the 2009–13 parliament.

The fate of the parties of the left and centre-left was less spectacular. The SPD (25.7 per cent) enjoyed only a small increase in its vote share compared to the disastrous result of 2009, which had been its worst since 1949. As Table I.1 demonstrates, the Greens (8.4 per cent) and, to a lesser extent, the Left Party (8.6 per cent) suffered losses following their relatively strong results of 2009. The 2013 result was particularly disappointing for the Greens. Following the Fukushima disaster they had temporarily experienced a huge increase in popular support in the polls during the 2009–13 Bundestag. In 2011, the party swept into government in the state of Baden-Württemberg, leading a coalition of Greens and SPD under the new Green state minister president, Winfried Kretschmann. The trajectory of the Piraten (2.2 per cent) meanwhile seems that of a new party perhaps fated to disappear from the German political stage.

Table I.3   Distribution of seats in the 2013 Bundestag (compared to 2009)

	Seats 2013	Seats 2009
CDU/CSU	311	239
SPD	193	146
FDP	–	93
Left Party	64	76
Greens	63	68
Total	631	622

Source: Bundeswahlleiter (2013).

If this trend continues, the dominant pattern of alternating centre-right (CDU/CSU–FDP) and centre-left (SPD–Green) coalitions may no longer be feasible in the future. The election result left party leaders with a complex task. The distribution of parliamentary seats is shown in Table I.3, comparing the 2013 Bundestag to the chamber elected in 2009. Due to the large number of parties failing to clear the five-per-cent hurdle, the CDU/CSU's result of 41.5 per cent of the votes in the country translated into 49.3 per cent of the seats. In other words, the Christian Democrats narrowly missed an overall majority in the chamber. The coalition negotiations following the Bundestag election of 2013 demonstrated that the CDU/CSU had begun to reach out to the Greens, seeking to create more competition among potential coalition partners on the centre-left (chapter 10). In the future, the SPD may no longer be the party of choice for the CDU/CSU when a centre-right government is no longer feasible. Formed in the autumn of 2013, the CDU–Green coalition in Hesse – a major state in which Christian Democrats and Greens had had a problematic relationship fraught with personal invectives – was generally read as a clear signal to this effect. This rapprochement had become possible because of the Green Party's move towards a pragmatic foreign and security policy in the years of the SPD–Green coalition under Chancellor Gerhard Schröder (1998–2005), the Merkel government's decision to phase out nuclear energy in Germany in 2011 and Merkel's social modernization agenda in her own party.

At the same time, the SPD gave up its refusal in principle to consider any cooperation with the Left Party. This change was based on a decision of the SPD Annual Conference in November 2013 when the party delegates decided to enlarge the leadership's options when it came to coalition negotiations. With the AfD considered non-coalitionable because of its anti-euro position, the Bundestag election of 2013 and its aftermath thus seem to have opened up opportunities for new patterns of coalition government, ranging from the grand coalition of the two major parties ('black–red') to a 'black–green' and 'red–red–green' coalition (SPD, Greens and Left Party). This may be of great significance for policy making in the future. It also has implications for the credibility of the information contained in so-called 'coalition signals' or pre-electoral commitments towards particular coalitions. The German voters may face a much more difficult strategic situation in the future. The present volume, however, is about the election of 2013 and some of the events, developments and general factors that shaped it in the years prior to 2013.

A number of authors in this volume are also clear that the German election result of 2013 had wider European implications. The contribution by Alister Miskimmon and Luuk Molthof suggests that the domestic strength of the Merkel government is not replicated in its foreign and security policy. Thus the German vote and its outcome took place under the close scrutiny of the EU's other member states, some of which had hoped that the election would result in a government that was willing to review its European policy and, in particular, its politics of fiscal rigour, accepting more financial relief for the indebted countries. Germany is the country that – at least till now – has been shown to have a sufficiently realistic and adequate (at least for German interests) basic idea of how the problems linked to the growing integration of financial markets may be governed (chapters 2 and 3). In Germany (until recently) there is no crisis or, if so, it has not been perceived. Which does not mean that the crisis does not touch Germany as well. The economic and financial crisis has precisely brought to the surface an increasing assertiveness in expressing national interests, but also a growing impatience with Angela Merkel's Germany in some other euro-area countries and the US; an impatience further aggravated by the perception (whether grounded or not) that the recipe adopted by Germany is greatly benefiting Berlin, but also harming fiscally less virtuous countries.

Although Germany has the credentials to aspire to political leadership in Europe, it still lacks the capability to convince other European countries to follow its model. Even the most recent international crises – from Libya to Syria – have once again brought to the surface some of the limits, difficulties and contradictions of Germany as 'civilian power' when it comes to exercising a leadership role at the international level (on security and military issues). Germany faces a paradox, which has been reinforced by Angela Merkel's successful re-election: it is the European country that, at least till now, has performed best in managing the economic crisis since 2007, but it is also the European democracy that is most challenged by the problem of international governance in times of crisis.

The contributors to this volume will first examine the domestic as well as the international context of the German election of 2013 and then deal with the political parties and voting behaviour as a second step. In the first part, a number of scholars analyse the policy environment in which this election took place. Economic and social policy is the most important dimension of partisan conflict and has a huge influence on the voters' perception of the government's competency. Reimut Zohlnhöfer seeks to provide answers as to why the coalition of CDU/CSU and FDP under Chancellor Merkel (2009–13) did not implement some of the far-reaching liberal market reforms they had advocated in the mid-2000s. He argues that, first, the window of opportunity for a Christian–Liberal reform project in economic and social policy closed when the financial crisis and the euro crisis reduced the government's budgetary leeway for a larger income tax reform, as well as a more prominent role for a per capita premium in the funding of health care which would have necessitated large tax transfers to the health system. Second, the management of the euro crisis occupied policy makers' attention continuously during most of the legislative period and left them little time and political resources to invest in domestic reforms. Third, electoral considerations stopped the government parties from rolling out their original Christian–Liberal reform agenda.

The European dimension is a further important determinant of German politics. Gabriele D'Ottavio provides an analysis of Germany's relationship to European integration from the Treaties of Rome to the euro crisis. He critiques the widespread narrative based on the idea of a supposed clear-cut distinction between Germany's past and present attitudes towards European integration. He argues that Germany's increase in actorness in European affairs preceded German unification.

D'Ottavio points out that Germany's attitude in the last years has revealed an increasing national assertiveness within a more general 'domestication' of its EU policy. However, he argues that it is highly unlikely that this supposed 'new course' might lead to the relinquishment of the tenets of the Federal Republic's foreign and European policy. The continuity appears even stronger if recent findings on popular support for the euro are taken into account. These data do not support the argument of declining trust in the euro among Germans. D'Ottavio points out that until February 2013 one of the main differences with other member states was that Germany had not witnessed a relevant and outspokenly euro-critic political formation. He argues, however, that, compared with the bigger hold that Euroscepticism is gaining in other national contexts – for example in France or in the United Kingdom – the AfD should (so far) not raise too much concern. Whether the new grand coalition led by Angela Merkel will be called upon to reconsider its European policy will depend more on external factors than on domestic ones.

Kenneth Dyson's contribution extends this analysis and compares a number of German 'narratives' of the euro crisis and connects them to relevant policy choices. In one narrative of the crisis, the logic of the euro-area is the 'hollowing out' of democracy in the member states. It reduces the domestic scope for political choice and for fruitful and meaningful political discourse, leading to a democratic deficit. This 'hollowing-out' narrative and portrait of a dysfunctional euro-area generates two fundamentally different political choices. One solution is to re-establish political democracy and accountability at the EU level, where relevant decisions can be made about fiscal rules, banking supervision and regulation, and structural reform priorities. The second narrative is one of a dysfunctional euro-area and advocating the abandonment of the euro in its existing form. The solution is to opt to reverse back to the EU of 1998. Dyson himself offers a different narrative of the logic of monetary union, one that finds strong support within German elites. In this narrative, democracy in member states is not being 'hollowed out'. The creation of a European 'stability union' – as suggested by Merkel – offers a functional framework for ensuring sustainable economic, fiscal and monetary policies in member states. Nevertheless, this narrative, too, is fraught with policy problems as it requires adjustments in macroeconomic, social and labour-market policies. However, competitive, partisan, democratic politics has serious difficulties in factoring in negative externalities for other states, so-called 'beggar-thy-neighbour' policies. It faces also the problem of social justice with respect to future generations. Last but not least, this promise of an EU 'sustainability union' leaves open the political question of whether such a rational and technocratic vision can acquire and retain legitimacy. According to Dyson it remains uncertain whether the German elite will find answers to the policy problems arising from the necessary adjustments.

Alister Miskimmon and Luuk Molthof's chapter seeks to identify Germany's foreign policy challenges and opportunities after the 2013 election. Looking at continuities and changes, the authors conclude that the new German government, Merkel III, will continue to be faced with pressures to take more responsibility in a changing world characterized by greater competition for influence. Germany's predicament, they argue, is that the dominance of the euro-zone crisis in the minds of German politicians coupled with the potential risks which this exposes Germany to has exacerbated an already existing trend towards greater caution in foreign and security policy among German elites. Nevertheless, influencing the transformation of the international liberal order in the face of the rise of China and other powerful new voices has been a priority area for German elites. Germany's foreign policy remains limited outside of the multilateral contexts in which it has invested so much energy since 1949, despite the incentives to exploit closer relations with China and Russia. Germany remains tied to NATO and the EU. Miskimmon and Molthof predict that Germany under Merkel's third cabinet will focus on stabilizing the euro-zone and, in the face of calls to undertake greater international responsibility for the maintenance of the liberal order, continue to avoid expanding the use of military force in its foreign and security policy.

The second part of this volume deals with voters, parties and leaders' strategies in the run-up to, and aftermath of, the 2013 election. In their chapter, Matthias Mader and Harald Schoen provide an analysis of voting behaviour in the 2013 election. Using the latest available data, they seek answers to the question of whether it was the 'candidate effect' of Chancellor Merkel's personal authority, the European debt crisis or the AfD that shaped the behaviour of German voters in September 2013. Their multivariate analyses suggest that attitudes towards the euro crisis were the least effective predictor of voting behaviour for the CDU/CSU, the SPD, the Greens, and the Left Party. However, opposition to a continuation of German financial aid to EU member states affected by the debt crisis was the single most important explanatory factor of vote choice for the euro-critic AfD. Furthermore, the analysis revealed that it was not so much the economic liberals who found this issue especially important but rather the sociopolitically conservative. It thus appears that it was a latent ethnocentrism and exclusive solidarity that drove those attitudes and vote choices, and not pragmatic economic reasoning. The analysis demonstrates that, in line with the Michigan School, party identifications and candidate preferences were still the most important determining factors. Nevertheless, the analysis also shows how a new party such as the AfD is able to quickly win considerable ground on the electoral map if it offers an issue position that no other party offers and if at least some voters find this choice to be attractive. In addition, the authors show that the top candidates matter. They find that the popularity of Angela Merkel made it impossible for the SPD to draw attention away from the candidates to the issues.

Margret Hornsteiner's chapter on the role of the parties' election manifestos as an important element of representative democracy provides deeper insights into the parties' campaigns. By conducting quantitative analyses of party manifestos she demonstrates that German parties still hold distinct positions on key dimensions of political space: on a socioeconomic dimension defined by economic and welfare policies, as well as on a social-liberalist dimension defined by policies in the fields of home affairs and justice. In contradiction to some of the media, she finds that EU issues were less salient in 2013 because all major parties shared a pro-European consensus. Only the newly founded AfD held a distinctly anti-EU profile, but has (so far) not been able to alter the fundamental structures of German party competition. Hornsteiner additionally shows that those parties offering members a say in the process of manifesto formulation are also more responsive than other parties.

Uwe Jun and Simon Jakobs examine the programmatic change in the two main parties, the CDU and the SPD. They look at the manifestos of the two major parties, focusing on the two main axes of party competition in Germany: social and economic policies on the one hand and a libertarian-authoritarian dimension on the other. In particular, the two parties' strategic moves on the social and economic dimension paved the way for the coalition. Both parties moved to the left between 2005 and 2013. They discuss the CDU/CSU's steps towards programmatic renewal and analyse the SPD's strategic readjustment following the years under Chancellor Gerhard Schröder's leadership (1998–2005). Despite the SPD's return to more interventionist and social-democratic social policies, they argue, the move was moderate as the party did not entirely abandon former SPD government policy of the Agenda 2010. This facilitated coalition building with the CDU/CSU. While the SPD was in opposition, party leader Sigmar Gabriel managed to close the gap between modernizers and traditionalists in the party, generating the necessary unity within the Social Democrats. Even though this move of integrating the different party factions led to intra–party consolidation, it did not help to significantly increase the amount of electoral votes for the party in the elections of 2013. At the same time, Chancellor and CDU leader Angela Merkel's strategy of programmatic reform of the CDU/CSU also led to more extensive commonalities with the Social Democrats. Despite misgivings on the party's conservative wing, the CDU's programmatic renewal increased the party's electoral attractiveness. This strategy was successful in 2013 when the party extended its electoral support base significantly. In addition to the programmatic readjustment, however, Jun and Jakobs point to the popularity of Chancellor Merkel as a major factor in the CDU/CSU's success. At the same time, they argue, this programmatic move left enough space for other competitors such as the national-conservative AfD or the liberal-economic FDP to maintain or develop a niche in the electoral 'market'.

While Jun and Jakobs provide insights into the strategic discussions within the two main parties (CDU and SPD), Simon Franzmann's contribution focuses on the smaller parties, the Left Party, Greens and FDP. He interprets the smaller parties' declining electoral performance in the election of 2013 as the result of different – but generally failing – strategies either for political office or for particular policy positions. In Franzmann's view, both FDP and Greens pursued an 'office-seeking' strategy in the run-up to the 2013 election. If this is right, he argues, the paradox of German party competition in 2013 for the small parties was that they responded in different ways to the major parties' strategic moves (as described by Jun and Jakobs) by moving further to the more extreme ends of the ideological space. The FDP realized the limitations of its strategy of seeking a niche to the socioeconomic right of the CDU/CSU (in competition with the AfD) and unsuccessfully sought to switch to a strategy of attracting strategic CDU/CSU voters late in the campaign. At the same time, the FDP faced stiff competition in classical liberal fields such as civil liberties and education from the Greens. Franzmann expects that a fight for the pivotal position in the German party system will occur during the next years between Greens and the FDP. Whereas the FDP and the Greens are described as strategic 'office seekers', AfD and the Left Party are seen as responsive 'policy seekers' taking over neglected issues of the larger parties. Therefore, Franzmann predicts, these parties will stay at the ideological wings and maintain their successful strategy. Being the small party closest to the political centre, he argues, the Greens will be the most likely occupants of a pivotal position in the ideological space of German party competition. He sees the party as getting ready for a coalition with the CDU/CSU, with or without early elections before 2017. Much depends on the success of the major parties in the grand coalition. A failure of the grand coalition under Merkel, he suggests, will open a window of opportunity for the right wing of the Greens to convince sceptics in the party to join the Christian Democrats in government. In this case the office-seeking strategy of the reform wing of the Greens would be successful in future despite the electoral defeat in 2013.

Gianfranco Baldini and Silvia Bolgherini's contribution focuses on two parties that rose to prominence during the 2009–13 Bundestag, Alternative für Deutschland and the Pirate Party. Both parties are analysed as an expression of the changing relationship between citizens and the political system and an emerging 'third wave' of party-system change after the rise of the Greens and the addition of the PDS/Left Party after unification. Both the AfD and the Pirate Party are interpreted as protest parties mobilizing voter sentiments against the way traditional parties deal with the public (and how they managed the economic crisis and its effects on the weakest social groups), rather than by an effective appeal of their own programmatic platforms. In addition, the Pirates offered a very participatory model of membership involvement. The AfD challenged traditional politics, too, especially the permissive consensus on European issues. Despite some similarities, Baldini and Bolgherini identify a number of important differences between the two parties, including a different organizational model, the different programmatic inspiration and the different profile of the parties' top candidates. They observe that the AfD seems to be set to attract a wider electorate. Post-electoral developments inside the Pirates confirm their organizational problems, as the party looks still absorbed in a self-referential debate. By contrast, the AfD's potential of attracting voters seems higher. The party has already acquired some sort of blackmail potential on the euro issue. The European elections in May 2014 have shown that AfD has the potential to become a relevant party in the longer run.

In a final chapter, Thomas Saalfeld provides an analysis of cabinet formation after 22 September 2013. It starts with the observation that the election of 2013 brought a radical change to the German postwar party system as the FDP disappeared from the Bundestag. Given the likely need for more coalitions across the traditional divide between centre-left and centre-right (for example, grand coalitions of CDU/CSU and SPD or new coalitions between CDU/CSU and Greens), the chapter focuses on mechanisms of conflict management. Based on the comparative literature on the issue, he analyses coalition governance in the new grand coalition under Merkel. After the traditional bargaining between party elites, the SPD conducted a vote of all party members for the ratification of the bargaining result. This was an insurance policy for the party leadership vis-à-vis its rank and file, a reassurance for the CDU/CSU that the SPD was really committed to the new coalition, and a relatively successful bargaining tactic on the part of the SPD as it lent credibility to the various 'red lines' formulated by the SPD prior to the negotiations. One key aspect of coalition governance was the allocation of portfolios. Both parties secured control of those ministries whose jurisdictions were crucial to their attempts to claim issue ownership vis-à-vis core voters. After some initial support for the grand coalition, the negotiations were accompanied by growing public scepticism. One key point was that the legislative strength of the new coalition would be overwhelming (with around 80 per cent of the seats in the Bundestag), and that the two opposition parties, the Greens and the Left Party, would be too weak to mount a sustained and effective parliamentary opposition. In addition, media commentators missed the 'big projects' which the new government, Merkel III, would tackle. However, the deal the parties agreed on in 2013 seemed more like a package of small, if socially costly, policy measures reminiscent of the collective result of log-rolling. Saalfeld also argues that the new coalition is in a precarious situation. Whether it will last its entire term (until 2017) will depend on a number of factors, especially any 'exogenous shocks' that it may be subjected to. In particular, however, it will depend on the parties' constant evaluation of the electoral risks arising from the coalition.

References

Bundeswahlleiter. 2013. *Endgültiges amtliches Ergebnis der Bundestagswahl 2013*. Wiesbaden: Statistisches Bundesamt. Available from: http://www. bundeswahlleiter.de/de/bundestagswahlen/BTW_BUND_13/presse/w13034_ Endgueltiges_amtliches_Ergebnis.html (accessed 26 May 2014).
Hornsteiner, Margret, and Saalfeld, Thomas. 2014. 'Parties and the party system'. In *Developments in German Politics 4*, edited by Stephen Padgett, William E. Paterson and Reimut Zohlnhöfer, 78–102. Basingstoke: Palgrave Macmillan.
Laakso, Markku, and Taagepera, Rein. 1979. 'The "effective" number of parties: a measure with application to West Europe'. *Comparative Political Studies*, vol. 12, n. 1: 3–27.

PART I
Policy Environment

Chapter 1

A Coalition Whose Time Had Already Passed … The Economic and Social Policies of the Second Merkel Government

Reimut Zohlnhöfer

Introduction

The reform output of the Christian–Liberal coalition under Angela Merkel in economic policy has been criticized as disappointing by many observers (Hulverscheidt 2013; faz.net 2013).[1] This is a surprising finding given that both parties that eventually formed the government in 2009 had aimed at this particular coalition (Saalfeld 2010a). Contrary to its predecessor, the grand coalition of Christian Democrats (CDU) and Social Democrats (CSU), the coalition of CDU/CSU and Liberal Democrats (FDP) was not a consequence of an electoral result that did not allow for other majorities. Rather, both parties had campaigned for this coalition, which was labelled the 'coalition of choice' (*Wunschkoalition*). Nonetheless, the coalition did not seem to have a common policy project – or that project had disappeared before the coalition formed.

This chapter argues that there did exist a common Christian–Liberal reform project in economic and social policy during the middle of the first decade of the 2000s. The CDU in particular had moved its policy position in a markedly market-liberal direction with its proposals for tax and health care reforms adopted at the party conference in Leipzig in 2003. Thus, at that time, broad agreement existed between Christian Democrats and Liberals about the direction of economic and social policy reforms. Therefore, a common policy project would have existed had CDU/CSU and FDP won the 2005 Bundestag election. Four years later, when the election result allowed for the formation of a coalition of Christian Democrats and Liberals, the time of a common understanding of which reforms in economic and social policy were necessary was already over. The Christian Democrats (and the chancellor in particular) had responded to the 'shock of 2005', when they failed to win an election that was almost impossible to lose, with a social-democratization of their economic and social policy position (Zohlnhöfer 2010; Zolleis and Bartz 2010, 57–8). Therefore, the Christian Democrats were unwilling to pursue further some of the reform projects they themselves had embraced at the party conference

---

1   This text is a revised and updated translation of Zohlnhöfer 2014.

in Leipzig in 2003. This unwillingness was further reinforced by the fact that the problem load in economic policy decreased continuously as both the number of unemployed and the budget deficit shrank substantially and talk about a 'German employment miracle' began (OECD 2012, 10; Reisenbichler and Morgan 2012). This meant that reforms appeared less urgent for the time being, while it would have become particularly difficult to communicate the reforms as necessary and appropriate to the voters. Moreover, the federal government's agenda was dominated by the euro-crisis, which left little time and resources for other projects. Finally, given the enormous amounts of money the country had to spend to fight the financial crisis in 2008–9 and the even higher sums which the euro-crisis could make necessary, the government, and the minister of finance in particular, were unwilling to spend a lot of money.

I will develop this argument in three steps. I will first summarize the programmatic positions of CDU/CSU and FDP regarding economic and social policy prior to the general election in 2005 and show that these parties shared many market-liberal economic policy ideas. In the next step, I will discuss the most important economic and social policy reforms of the Christian–Liberal coalition with a particular focus on those areas which could be labelled the core of the Christian–Liberal policy project in economic and social policy, namely health care, tax reform and dismissal protection. Finally, I will explain why these projects failed to be adopted or were adopted in a much more moderate way than originally envisaged.

A Christian–Liberal Policy Project in Economic and Social Policy?

After the defeat in the 2002 Bundestag election, the Christian Democrats had aimed at a programmatic renewal, with a particular emphasis on economic and social policy (Zohlnhöfer 2007; Schmid 2008, 74 ff.). The party appointed an expert commission chaired by former federal president Roman Herzog in the spring of 2003 which paralleled a similar commission appointed by the then incumbent coalition of Social Democrats and Greens under the chairmanship of Bert Rürup. The Herzog commission was supposed to work out proposals for the recalibration of Germany's ailing social security systems for the CDU. The report the commission came back with included a number of comparatively unpopular reform proposals, including an increase in the statutory pension age to 67 years, the elimination of the pay-as-you-go funding of long-term care insurance, and the abolition of job-creation measures (*Arbeitsbeschaffungsmaßnahmen*) in West Germany, as well as a new form of funding the health insurance system. Rather than funding health insurance funds entirely out of social security contributions, paid by employers and employees, the commission suggested that health insurance contributions be frozen at the 6.5 per cent of gross wages they amounted to at the time and be supplemented by a lump-sum amount payable by every insured person. Low wage earners and children could be exempt from that per capita premium (Hartmann 2010, 331–2).

What is more, the CDU, more specifically the vice chairman of the parliamentary party of CDU and CSU, Friedrich Merz, also put forward a rather market-liberal tax concept. Merz suggested introducing a new income tax scale with only three tax rates at 12, 24 and 36 per cent. Among other things, that would have meant a further reduction of the top income tax rate, which had only been reduced to 42 per cent in 2000 (coming into effect in 2005, that is, after the reform proposal had been put forward). At the same time, many tax expenditures were supposed to be reduced, including the tax concessions for wage surcharges for Sunday-, holiday- or nighttime-work, which there were plans to cut.

Although both of these projects were unpopular among the voters as they were perceived as unfair, and although both were controversial in the CDU, they were adopted by the CDU party conference in Leipzig in December 2003. The CSU, in contrast, was concerned that both projects might put the social balance of the parties' policy programme in question and was thus unwilling to accept these policies; thus, an open conflict between the sister parties emerged. Regarding the tax reform, the conflict was settled by a less ambitious compromise for the manifesto for the 2005 elections. According to that compromise the old – so-called linear-progressive – tax scale was maintained but tax rates (including the top income tax rate) were supposed to be lowered. As Angela Merkel invited the former judge at the Federal Constitutional Court, Paul Kirchhof, to join her competence team – that is, the shadow cabinet – as the spokesman for fiscal policy, and as Kirchhof entertained rather radical ideas about tax reform, more far-reaching proposals (including the introduction of a flat tax) remained on the agenda, however. Regarding health care funding, the idea of a 'health premium' was maintained in the election manifesto, although in a modified version. In addition, the election programme also included a number of other unpopular pledges, including a liberalization of dismissal protection or an increase of value-added tax (VAT). According to the weekly paper *Der Spiegel* (14 November 2005, 24), Angela Merkel thus had campaigned on 'the most radical reform program a people's party has ever proposed' in 2005.[2]

This programmatic stance of the Christian Democrats was met with strong approval by the liberal FDP, which took a very similar economic policy position – with the exception of the VAT increase (Vorländer 2008, 143). The FDP traditionally sees itself as a party of tax cuts and it demanded a tax scale very similar to the one originally proposed by Friedrich Merz with tax rates of 15 (or 10 in 2009), 25 and 35 per cent. The Liberals also agreed with the Christian Democrats that the funding of health care should be decoupled from wages, although their proposals in their 2005 (and also 2009) election manifesto were more radical than the ideas of the Christian Democrats (Bandelow and Schade 2009, 65–6). Finally, the FDP also

---

2   The translation from German here and elsewhere in the chapter was provided by the author.

approved of the CDU/CSU's demand for a liberalization of dismissal protection, although again the Liberals proposed more far-reaching changes than the Christian Democrats (Vorländer 2008).

Despite a large lead in the opinion polls until shortly before the elections (Zohlnhöfer 2007, 135), the 'coalition of choice' between Christian Democrats and Liberals failed to win a majority in the Bundestag in the 2005 election. As a coalition of Social Democrats and Greens did not gain a majority either, a grand coalition of Christian Democrats and Social Democrats was formed. The lion's share of the CDU/CSU's election pledges regarding economic and social policy were not enacted by the grand coalition as the SPD rejected these policies and blocked their adoption (Zohlnhöfer 2010; Egle and Zohlnhöfer 2010). Only two of those projects found their way to the statute book during the coalition of CDU/CSU and SPD: first, the increase of VAT (by three rather than two percentage points!), which, however, did not belong to the core of the CDU's programmatic ideas but rather was a pragmatic way of reducing non-wage labour costs and consolidating the budget; and, second, the increase of the statutory pension age to 67 years. The reform of corporate taxation the grand coalition adopted also mirrored the CDU/CSU's ideas, but the necessity of substantially reducing business tax rates was uncontroversial among the tax experts in all parties. Regarding income taxation, health care reform or dismissal protection, on the other hand, the Christian Democrats were hardly successful at all in getting their Leipzig agenda enacted. Dismissal protection remained untouched during the grand coalition (Dümig 2010, 290). Similarly, income tax rates remained unchanged until late in the term with the exception of the top income tax rate, which was even increased (rather than reduced). Income tax cuts were only adopted at the end of the term as part of the stimulus packages that were to mitigate the effects of the financial crisis on the real economy. What is more, these cuts did not change the tax scale with the exception of a cut to the minimum tax rate of one percentage point (Grasl and König 2010, 222). Finally, concerning funding of health care, the Christian Democrats also basically failed to get anywhere near their election pledge of a per capita health premium because the SPD had put forward a model diametrically opposed, called 'citizens' insurance'. The compromise the grand coalition ended up with, called the 'health insurance fund', can be seen as a step towards the health premium only with reservations. According to the reform of the grand coalition a health insurance company that needs more money than the amount allocated to it via the health insurance fund must levy extra contributions on the insured, the amount of which, in principle, does not depend on the insured person's income. At the same time, the insured were granted a legal right to change their insurance company in the case of the latter levying extra charges, and regulations prevented the insured from having to pay too much in extra charges. Although this is a far cry from what the health premium was about originally, the health care reform of the grand coalition at least 'opened a loophole' (Hartmann 2010, 336) for the CDU's ideas because the reform made it easier to adopt its preferred option in the future – provided its coalition of choice won a majority in the Bundestag in the next election. This goal was reached in 2009. So in the next step we will need to analyse what the main reforms of the Christian–Liberal coalition were after 2009. Did the parties take the chance to adopt their liberal-economic and social policy project after 2009?

The Policy Profile of the Christian–Liberal Coalition

Labour Law: The Absence of Reform

Regarding employees' protection against dismissals, the second Merkel government remained inactive between 2009 and 2013. A relaxation of dismissal protection, which had been part of both coalition partners' 2005 election manifestos, did not come about. Neither did the government tighten employment protection legislation, however, despite pressure from the opposition to do so. In reaction to a number of cases in which courts had ruled that employers had the right to let go employees even for minimal offences – cases that were much debated in the media – the opposition had introduced bills that would have strengthened dismissal protection in these cases (Bundestag printed matters 17/648 and 17/649). The government did not vote for these bills, however, and did not present similar proposals either (Parliamentary Debates, Bundestag, Session 17/99, 24 March 2011, p. 11397).

On the other hand, the minister in charge of labour law, Christian Democrat Ursula von der Leyen, did not seem to deem a relaxation of dismissal protection necessary. In a preface to an official brochure on the subject, she underlined the advantages of dismissal protection in terms of long-term planning horizons and greater motivation of employees with secure jobs. Furthermore, she emphasized the special provisions for small companies as well as other already existing sources of labour market flexibility for larger enterprises, like temporary employment and fixed-term work contracts. Thus, she concluded: 'Dismissal protection is an important factor of stability in our Social Market Economy. Therefore, I am sure that it still has a long future ahead of it' (Von der Leyen 2012, 6). Interestingly, even an extension of the instruments that provide some flexibility on the labour market was not adopted despite a pledge in the coalition agreement (CDU/CSU/FDP 2009, 22).[3]

Instead of adopting the labour market part of the Christian–Liberal policy project, the main issue in labour market regulation during the second Merkel government focused on the introduction of minimum wages – a policy instrument diametrically opposed to the liberal ideas of the coalition parties' election manifestos of 2005. When the debate about minimum wages started under the grand coalition, the CDU/CSU was still highly sceptical about this instrument,

---

3   It should be noted, however, that a decision by the Federal Labour Court led to a certain liberalization concerning fixed-term work contracts (cf. Bandau and Dümig 2015, 389).

although it eventually accepted it in some sectors (Dümig 2010, 290; Schroeder 2010, 192). In line with this thinking, the Christian–Liberal coalition initially agreed not to introduce a general minimum wage; what is more, according to the coalition agreement, the coalition even contemplated revoking the existing sectorial minimum wages (CDU/CSU/FDP 2009, 21). These ideas were never put into legislation between 2009 and 2013, however; on the contrary, the coalition increased the number of sectors in which minimum wages had to be paid. Moreover, both coalition parties passed resolutions for specific forms of minimum wages at party conferences in the second half of the legislative period. Although these resolutions fell short of the general minimum wage the opposition parties had in mind, and they were never put into law, they still mark a remarkable departure from what the Christian–Liberal policy project in labour legislation would have looked like.

Tax policy: Much Ado About Very Little

According to the coalition agreement, the Christian–Liberal coalition wanted to reduce the income tax burden of lower- to middle-income citizens and families with children by about 24 billion euro. This was to be achieved via a change of the tax scale (CDU/CSU/FDP 2009, 10). Nonetheless, the coalition agreement also stipulated that all future reforms (including the tax cuts) were conditional upon financial feasibility (Saalfeld 2010b, 96). And, indeed, a substantial income tax reform was not adopted under the Christian–Liberal coalition. Even though the very first bill the Christian–Liberal coalition adopted (*Wachstumsbeschleunigungsgesetz*) dealt with tax issues, this bill did not include elements of a structural reform (Moog and Raffelhüschen 2011, 248–50). The most important measure of that bill concerned an increase of the children's tax credit (or an increase in child benefit) which cost around 4.6 billion euro. Companies received a tax relief of more than 3 billion euro. The relevant measures included a revocation of some of the revenue-increasing provisions of the business tax reform of the grand coalition (particularly regarding the so-called interest brake provision which was supposed to fight tax evasion via thin capitalization), as well as a highly controversial reduction of the VAT rate for hotels. As can be seen from these measures, this law certainly was not a structural reform – and it was not supposed to be one as its main aim still was to mitigate the effects of the financial crisis and the great recession (Bundestag printed matter 17/15, p. 1).

Nonetheless, the coalition had a difficult time agreeing on further tax measures (for the following Sturm 2012). Only in the autumn of 2011 was a compromise reached according to which income taxes were to be reduced by 6 billion euro in order to correct for bracket creep, that is, for the effects of inflation on the tax system. Technically, this was supposed to be achieved by a minimal change to the tax scale (Bundestag printed matter 17/8683). But even these limited tax cuts failed to make it to the statute book. The only tax reduction the coalition was eventually able to pass was an increase of the basic tax allowance of 350 euro, phased in over 2013 and 2014, worth 2.6 billion euro (Bundesministerium der Finanzen 2013, 10). This adaptation of the income tax code hardly went further than what would have been constitutionally mandatory anyway as, according to the Federal Constitutional Court, the subsistence level must not be taxed at all (Decisions of the Federal Constitutional Court vol. 82, p. 60).

Health Care: Really the Beginning of Flat-rate Financing?

Since the second Schröder government (2002–5), the most salient issue regarding health care had been a reform of health care funding. Thus, the opposing alternatives of health premium versus citizens' insurance had been prominent in the election campaigns since then, particularly in the 2005 election campaign. The coalition agreement of the Christian–Liberal coalition stipulated that health care funding should become decoupled from non-wage labour costs. Thus, the employer contributions to the health fund should be frozen. Moreover, in the long run a system was to be introduced that would be based on employee contributions irrespective of income, with a compensation for people with very low incomes (CDU/CSU/FDP 2009, 86). Despite this general consensus, the coalition partners were unable to agree on a more substantive reform proposal in the coalition negotiations. Therefore, a commission was supposed to be appointed to work out proposals for the reform (CDU/CSU/FDP 2009, 86).

The health care reform that was adopted by the Bundestag and Bundesrat in November and December 2010 included several elements (Pressel 2012, 207–10). Health care contributions were increased by 0.6 percentage points of gross wages. Interestingly, this meant employers' contributions to the health care funds also went up by 0.3 percentage points. Nonetheless, the reform stipulated that employer contributions would be fixed at this level (7.3 per cent of gross wages) for the future. Employee contributions also went up by 0.3 percentage points, reaching 8.2 per cent of gross wages, at which level they, too, were frozen. Increasing health care expenditures were thus to be borne by the insured alone in the future via extra charges unrelated to income. As an increase in regular contributions was supposed to be precluded in the future, this provision was expected to lead to a growing importance of extra charges in health care funding, which in turn could have meant that a substantial share of health care spending was going to be funded by a premium not related to income in the medium term.

At the same time, the compensation mechanism for persons with low incomes was reformed. The grand coalition had set a limit on the extra charges at 1 per cent of the income that is subject to social security contributions. According to the new provision, a person was entitled to compensation only if the average extra charge of all health insurance funds (not the extra charge of the respective person's insurance fund!) was going to be above 2 per cent of the gross income of the insured person according to forecasts. This provision implies the possibility that insured persons who have to pay an extra charge of more than 2 per cent of their gross income may have to pay the full extra charge as long as the average extra

charge is below 2 per cent of their gross income; similarly, people who are charged
an extra premium of less than 2 per cent of their gross income by their insurance
company may still be entitled to compensation if the average extra charge is above
the 2 per cent. The coalition's idea behind this regulation was to create incentives
for the insured to switch to the most economic health care insurers.

The reform of funding was not all there was to the Christian–Liberal health
policy, however. Rather, the coalition also adopted a rather surprising reform
regarding spending on pharmaceuticals (Gerlinger 2014). Prior to the reform, the
pharmaceutical industry had enjoyed enormous freedom with regard to its price-
setting for patented drugs – a privilege that had been protected more than once
by the Christian Democrats and the Liberals in the past. Nevertheless, the second
Merkel government curtailed the industry's leeway quite substantially. Since
2011, the additional benefit of new pharmaceuticals is being tested. If the result is
negative – that is, the drug is judged not to deliver an additional benefit compared
with existing pharmaceuticals – the same procedure for price-setting is applied that
is used for non-patented medicines. If the new drug delivers additional benefits,
negotiations about the price start between the authorities and the pharmaceutical
company. If these negotiations fail after one year, an independent regulator sets the
price. Even though this new provision leaves the pharmaceutical industry some
price-setting leeway during that first year, this reform is a quite remarkable and –
given the partisan complexion of government – quite surprising policy change.

Another policy change, enacted in 2013, was also quite unexpected against
the background of the Christian–Liberal project in economic and social policy –
the abolition of the so-called treatment fee (*Praxisgebühr*), a (very unpopular)
charge of 10 euro payable every quarter for a visit to the doctor. This instrument
had been introduced by the Social Democrat-led government with the approval
of the Bundesrat, then controlled by the Christian Democrats, in 2003 in order to
improve health care finances and to strengthen the individual responsibility of the
insured (Bundestag printed matter 15/1525, p. 83). As the treatment fee was an
element of co-payment it fitted nicely into the original Christian–Liberal project in
social policy; this, of course, makes its abolition all the more puzzling. It was not
for programmatic reasons, however, that the treatment fee was abolished. Rather,
the reform aimed at an improvement of the disposable income of the voters in
an election year, and was argued to be justifiable given the large surpluses the
health funds had accumulated over the previous years (Bundestag printed matter
17/11396, p. 18). Nonetheless, the abolition of the treatment fee is another clear
indicator that the second Merkel government had abandoned its economic and
social reform project from the mid-2000s.

Summary: An Implementation of the Christian–Liberal Project
in Economic and Social Policy?

The evidence so far shows that the second Merkel government failed to adopt
the core elements of what had been the common programmatic ground between

the Christian Democrats and the Liberals in the mid-2000s. The coalition at least moved in the expected direction regarding the funding of the health care system – even though with little immediate impact. Instead of introducing an outright health premium the CDU/CSU/FDP coalition only expanded the extra charge that had already been established under the grand coalition. What is more, at the time of the 2013 Bundestag election no health insurance company actually levied an extra charge! It thus remains to be seen whether the reform does indeed signify the beginning of a decoupling of the funding of the German health care system from income-related contributions. In order for that to happen, future federal governments would need to hold on to the freezing of employment-related contributions even in the face of growing health care spending, and thus also increasing extra charges. Given the intensity of electoral competition and the high frequency of relatively important elections at different levels of government in Germany, it may well be doubted that future governments will be willing to see these policies through. The fact that the Christian–Liberal government has drawn upon the pharmaceutical industry in its cost-containing efforts in the health sector is, by contrast, surprising, but not in contradiction with the core ideas of these parties' policy project of the mid-2000s. Things are very different with regard to the abolition of the treatment fee, which clearly contradicts the market-liberal ideas of both parties' election manifestos of 2005.

The coalition adopted even less of its 2005 policy project in the areas of tax policy or dismissal protection. The latter did not even make it onto the government's agenda after 2009 and had to give way to a debate on the introduction of minimum wages, which are difficult to reconcile with the market-liberal reform agenda the CDU and FDP in particular pursued in the mid-2000s. Although tax policy, at least, was constantly discussed during the second Merkel government and some tax changes were adopted, these were a far cry from the structural reforms of income taxation both parties had campaigned for previously.

Taking a look at the Christian-Liberal coalition's reform output in social and economic policy beyond the core elements of the policy project of the mid-2000s does not alter my conclusions in any substantial way. There were some noteworthy policy changes like the reform of labour migration, which 'put Germany among the OECD countries with the fewest restrictions on labour migration for highly-skilled occupations', as the OECD (2013, 15) noted. The coalition also liberalized long-distance bus transportation, a market that was previously closed in order to shield the railways from competition. These changes notwithstanding, the Christian–Liberal coalition adopted only very moderate reforms, if reforms were adopted at all. They fell way short of what might have been expected from both parties' common programmatic positions in economic and social policy in the mid-2000s. How can this abandonment of the Christian–Liberal economic policy project be explained? It is to this question that I turn in the next section.

A Coalition whose Time had Already Passed: Explaining the Christian–Liberal Coalition's Economic and Social Policies

A fundamental difference between the situation a coalition of CDU/CSU and FDP would have been confronted with in 2005 and the situation the actual coalition of these parties faced in 2009 was the political agenda. In 2005, public discourse still centred on the country's economic problems; in particular, unemployment had reached new record-breaking levels in early 2005. Although this was essentially an artefact of the new way of counting the number of unemployed, introduced by the Hartz labour market reforms that came into effect in January 2005, the fact that the number of unemployed had surpassed the 5 million threshold for the first time in postwar history was alarming for policymakers as well as a major part of the population. At the same time, it was clear that Germany would be unable to meet the deficit criterion of the Maastricht Treaty – for the fourth consecutive time! Thus, despite the far-reaching reforms of the former Social Democratic government, the perception of a deep economic crisis was prevalent among the voters, the media and policymakers. The even more far-reaching economic and social policy reforms the bourgeois parties were proposing thus seemed necessary – and it seemed possible to adopt them. Four years later, the situation had changed dramatically. Economic policy still played an enormously important role and it is impossible to deny that a sense of crisis dominated public opinion – which was not entirely unsubstantiated as the German economy shrank by 5 per cent in the election year, that is, it suffered the deepest recession in its postwar history. But the crisis of 2009 was not perceived as homemade by either voters or policymakers; rather, it was seen as a result of the financial crisis which was not related to a lack of domestic reforms – in stark contrast to the weak economic performance during much of the 2000s, which was blamed on a reform logjam (*Reformstau*). On the contrary, the grand coalition reacted rather swiftly and comprehensively to the financial crisis, spending amounts of money previously unheard of to prevent a breakdown of the banking system and to mitigate the effects of the recession (Enderlein 2010; Zohlnhöfer 2011). What is more, the coalition of Christian Democrats and Social Democrats had adopted reforms that filled the remaining gaps in the previous government's reform agenda. Examples include the reform of business taxation, budget consolidation, and an increase in the statutory pension age. Finally, the economy had developed in a markedly positive way in the years between 2005 and the outbreak of the financial crisis: unemployment had gone down continuously, as had the budget deficit, and the labour market was hardly affected by the crisis at all.

These developments had two important implications for the economic policy agenda the Christian–Liberal coalition could pursue after 2009. On the one hand, problem pressure was comparatively minor. In the most important policy fields, from the labour market to business taxation, rather far-reaching reforms had been adopted within the last few years, and these reforms seemed to work, as could be concluded from a glance at the development of the unemployment figures and the budget deficit. On the other hand, government debt and potential future burdens on the budget had skyrocketed as a result of the crisis: the bank rescue package alone was worth up to 480 billion euro, while the two stimulus packages added another 75 billion euro to the bill (Zohlnhöfer 2011). Thus, the budgetary leeway of the new federal government was seriously circumscribed by the different rescue packages – even before the European debt crisis had started in earnest, necessitating financial warranties which amounted to multiples of the figures that had been utilized to fight the financial crisis and the recession that followed it. Moreover, as a reaction to the jump in public debt because of the financial crisis, the grand coalition had introduced a new debt brake into the federal constitution which was supposed to enforce a reduction of the budget deficit – implying that the budgetary leeway was even more limited.

The euro-crisis itself also substantially circumscribed the Christian–Liberal coalition's room to manoeuvre in economic and social policy. On the one hand, this was due to the shrinking financial means the government had at its disposal. On the other hand, the euro-crisis dominated the government agenda to an extent that did not leave much room for other reform initiatives. Processing capacities and political resources of central government are limited anywhere (Jones and Baumgartner 2012) and it would have been necessary to invest substantial political resources and processing capacities to get the large-scale reforms the Christian Democrats and Liberals had initially planned in the mid-2000s adopted. In the case of the Merkel II government, however, these processing capacities were completely absorbed by the euro-crisis during most of the parliamentary term, so only a very small number of domestic reform projects could be processed. It is evident that economic policy reforms were not among these projects as the government decided to invest its remaining political resources in other projects, like the phasing out of nuclear energy or the introduction of a new benefit for families that do not take their 1–3-year-old children to day care (*Betreuungsgeld*). Thus, the question remains why the federal government did not invest more of its – particularly scarce – political resources in the market-liberal economic policy reforms the CDU and FDP had been so fond of only a few years previously.

Indeed, it seems that the Christian Democrats had lost interest in these reforms after 2005 while the FDP continued to pursue them. For example, during the coalition negotiations, substantial programmatic differences arose between the future coalition partners precisely regarding tax policy and health care policy – that is, in the very policy sectors which belonged to the core areas of the Christian–Liberal policy project in economic and social policy (Saalfeld 2010a, 191, 205–6). The FDP, for a short period of time, even suspended negotiations over a new Christian–Liberal coalition in Schleswig-Holstein, held in parallel with the coalition negotiations on the federal level, in order to stress its demand regarding tax cuts (Saalfeld 2010a, 191). Nonetheless, an agreement was not forthcoming – rather, the pledges concerning taxes and the funding of health care in the coalition agreement were very elusive and postponed many substantive decisions until later in the parliamentary term (Saalfeld 2010a, 191, 202–3).

Against this background it did not come as a surprise that the policy-making processes in both policy areas were highly controversial. Regarding taxes, the FDP had succeeded in including some more specific statements in the coalition agreement which would go beyond the tax cuts adopted immediately after the formation of the government (*Wachstumsbeschleunigungsgesetz*); the FDP's problem, however, was that all reforms were conditional upon financial feasibility according to the coalition agreement. Minister of finance, Wolfgang Schäuble (CDU), and a number of Land prime ministers from the CDU were not interested in tax cuts they deemed unaffordable, and had an easy time blocking them. The FDP tried very hard to keep the issue of tax cuts alive but the reform proposals the Liberals came up with grew ever smaller (for the following Sturm 2012, 268–9). A proposal put forward in April 2010 suggested a tax cut of 16 billion euros (which would have added up to the 24 billion euro envisaged in the coalition agreement when the 8 billion euro from the *Wachstumsbeschleunigungsgesetz* were taken into account) – while the FDP election manifesto had proposed tax cuts worth 35 billion euro. But not even this melted-down version of tax reform was accepted by the coalition partner. In the face of a growing perception that budget consolidation was of prime importance, together with an extensive public debate on tax increases, the FDP became even more defensive, declaring budget consolidation without tax increases the new policy of tax cuts (Sturm 2012, 269) – while the tax reform that the coalition agreement had stipulated would enter into force in 2011 failed to be adopted, the Christian Democrats fearing that the funding of the reform would cause too many problems.

In the end, the FDP was able to secure at least a (very) partial success. The tax reform that made it to the statute book was not a structural reform, however, as it only took care of bracket creep – that is, it was supposed to give back to the tax payers the extra tax revenues caused by inflation. Even in this field, the coalition partner, and the minister of finance in particular, were reluctant to back the reform, which led to a substantial reduction of the volume of the tax cuts. But not even the tax cuts the coalition partners eventually were able to agree on, worth 6 billion euro, were finally adopted. As the opposition of Social Democrats and Greens had secured a majority in the Bundesrat, the second chamber of parliament, they were able to block any changes to income taxation. The centre-left majority in the Bundesrat, however, was unwilling to approve of tax cuts that went beyond an increase of the basic tax allowance. They, too, argued that neither the federal government nor the Länder could afford to forego the respective tax revenues. The Green prime minister of Baden-Württemberg, Winfried Kretschmann, for example, justified his government's rejection of further tax cuts in the Bundesrat by arguing that tax cuts that led to an increase in the public deficit were unacceptable; thus he demanded further tax cuts would need to be funded by an increase in taxes for the better-off, for example in the form of an increase in the top income-tax rate (Parliamentary Debates, Bundesrat, 896th Session, 11 May 2012, p. 185).

A similar policy-making pattern could be observed with regard to health care reform. The federal health minister at the time, Philipp Rösler from the FDP, tried to push through a per capita premium, even though in a somewhat diluted form, but failed due to the resistance of the coalition partner. On the one hand, the minister of finance, Wolfgang Schäuble, opposed the bill. If an increasing share of health care funding came from non-income-related sources, this would necessarily go hand in hand with a growing volume of the compensation mechanism, which would need to be funded out of general taxation. Thus, a per capita premium would have led to growing government expenditure, which the minister of finance was desperate to avoid (Pressel 2012, 205). Thus, the severely limited financial room to manoeuvre played an important role in this respect.

On the other hand, the CSU, and the Bavarian health minister Markus Söder, in particular, fiercely attacked Rösler's proposal. Söder argued that Rösler's plans were 'systematically and socially the wrong way to go' (Pressel 2012, 204). Apart from programmatic differences, electoral reasons may have played a role in this assessment, with Söder remarking that even nuclear energy (seen as highly unpopular among the voters) had a higher acceptance rate among the German population than the per capita health premium (Pressel 2012, 204).

This latter observation points to a general pattern. The result of the 2005 Bundestag election had been very disappointing for the Christian Democrats. Although they had led in the opinion polls by a large margin until shortly before the elections, they had failed to win the election and form the coalition they had campaigned for. Many in the party argued that this weak result in the 2005 election had been caused by the market-liberal election manifesto, which had kept voters from voting for the Christian Democrats (Zolleis and Bartz 2010, 51–68). This 'shock of 2005' had led to a social-democratization of the Christian Democrats already in the grand coalition (Zohlnhöfer 2010); but even under the politically more favourable conditions of a coalition with the FDP, the Christian Democrats were unwilling to take the risk of deterring voters with far-reaching market-liberal reforms in economic and social policy. Söder's remark shows that these considerations did play a role in the reform of health care – on the funding side of the health budget as well as on the expenditure side, as can be seen from the reform of price-setting of patented pharmaceuticals (Gerlinger 2014). Given that the extra charges levied by some health insurance companies – as introduced by the health reform of the grand coalition – rose, and the government discussed a strengthening of the element of health care funding that was not related to income, which could possibly burden people with low incomes in particular, the government came under pressure. It needed to push through some spending cuts on the supplier side of the health system in order to falsify the accusation that its policies were biased against low-income earners. In this particular case, the concern that a socially unbalanced policy might deter voters away from the Christian Democrats seems to have triggered a reform that curbed health spending by substantially cutting back the profits of the pharmaceutical industry. Similarly, the abolition of the treatment fee sought to prove the social balance of the Christian–Liberal coalition's social policy, which it was hoped would help win the 2013 election.

The deliberate abandonment of the plans to liberalize dismissal protection can be explained along the same lines. This reform would in all probability not have been popular; what is more, the trade unions would have fiercely opposed it. For electoral reasons, the second Merkel government was keen to avoid such a mobilization against its economic policy – particularly given the fact that the Christian Democrats had won the 2009 elections after a campaign that was described as deliberately de-mobilizing voters of the Social Democrats (Zolleis and Bartz 2010, 64). Moreover, problems on the labour market were diminishing at a rapid rate as the number of unemployed people went down almost continuously and even experts started talking about a German employment miracle (Reisenbichler and Morgan 2012; OECD 2012). Under these circumstances, it would have been particularly difficult to communicate a highly unpopular labour market reform to the voters; therefore, the government did not pursue the policy further and rather turned to the issue of minimum wages. This turn again was mostly motivated by strategic concerns. Opinion polls regularly found broad majorities in favour of minimum wage legislation, which was a pet policy project of the Social Democrats and the Left Party. Thus, it is highly likely that the coalition's failure to revoke sectorial minimum wages (despite a pledge in the coalition agreement to at least consider doing so) and the expansion of minimum wages to more sectors, as well as the willingness of both governing parties to consider an enactment of a general minimum wage in some form in the next legislative period, were an effort to absorb the impact of this popular SPD initiative in the upcoming election.

Conclusion: The Coalition that Assumed Office Too Late

While both Christian Democrats and Liberals had embraced a rather far-reaching market-liberal reform project in economic and social policy in the mid-2000s, they only implemented a very few elements of this project during their time in government between 2009 and 2013. This chapter has sought to explain the reasons for this development.

I have argued that the time for the Christian–Liberal reform project in economic and social policy was already over before the 'coalition of choice' even came to power in 2009. Had Christian Democrats and Liberals been able to form a coalition in 2005 they might really have tried to adopt far-reaching reforms with regard to dismissal protection, income tax reform and the funding of the health care system. But when the necessary Bundestag majority had finally been won in 2009, the Christian–Liberal reform project was already obsolete. The financial crisis and the euro-crisis had reduced the budgetary leeway of the government to such an extent that the minister of finance blocked a larger income tax reform as well as a more prominent role for a per capita premium in the funding of health care, which would have necessitated large tax transfers to the health system. In addition, the management of the euro-crisis occupied policy makers' attention continuously during most of the legislative period and left them little time and political resources to invest in domestic reforms. Interestingly, the core elements of what had been the Christian–Liberal reform project in economic and social policy were not among the few domestic policy projects the government pursued. One of the most important reasons for this was electoral considerations. The core elements of the original Christian–Liberal reform agenda were electorally risky if not outright unpopular, as could be said about a liberalization of dismissal protection and the per capita premium in health care funding. Given that economic problems were decreasing substantially over time, as unemployment and the budget deficit went down, the government did not see a need to pursue these risky reforms. Time simply was not ripe for far-reaching economic and social policy reforms in Germany after 2009.

These electoral considerations seem to have paid off for the Christian Democrats in the 2013 election. There were hardly any policies or proposals left which the opposition could have criticized as socially unfair. This made it particularly difficult for the SPD, the Greens and the Left Party to attack the government, which was one reason for these parties' disappointing election results. The FDP, in contrast, seems to have paid a very high price for the Christian–Liberal coalition's reform avoidance in economic and social policy. Given the Liberals' limited success in pushing through market-liberal economic policy reforms, the party's supporters have evidently switched to other parties or stayed at home during the polls. As a result, in 2013, only four years after winning the best result at a federal election in its entire history, the FDP lost representation in the Bundestag for the first time since the founding of the Federal Republic.

References

Bandau, Frank, and Dümig, Kathrin. 2015. 'Verwaltung des deutschen "Beschäftigungswunders" – Die Arbeitsmarktpolitik der schwarz-gelben Koalition 2009–2013'. In *Politik im Schatten der Krise. Eine Bilanz der Regierung Merkel 2009–2013*, edited by Reimut Zohlnhöfer and Thomas Saalfeld, 373–96. Wiesbaden: Springer VS.

Bandelow, Nils C., and Schade, Mathieu. 2009. 'Konsens im Dissens? Konflikte in der Gesundheitsreform der Großen Koalition'. In *Gesundheitsreform 2007. Nach der Reform ist vor der Reform*, edited by Wolfgang Schroeder and Robert Paquet, 58–76. Wiesbaden: Springer VS.

Bundesministerium der Finanzen (BMF). 2013. Monatsbericht Februar 2013, Berlin.

CDU/CSU/FDP. 2009. *Wachstum. Bildung. Zusammenhalt. Koalitionsvertrag zwischen CDU, CSU und FDP*. 17. Legislaturperiode, Berlin.

Dümig, Kathrin. 2010. 'Ruhe nach und vor dem Sturm: Die Arbeitsmarkt- und Beschäftigungspolitik der Großen Koalition'. In *Die zweite Große Koalition.*

Eine Bilanz der Regierung Merkel, 2005–2009, edited by Christoph Egle and Reimut Zohlnhöfer, 279–301. Wiesbaden: Springer VS.

Egle, Christoph, and Reimut Zohlnhöfer (eds). 2010. *Die zweite Große Koalition. Eine Bilanz der Regierung Merkel, 2005–2009.* Wiesbaden: Verlag für Sozialwissenschaften.

Enderlein, Henrik. 2010. 'Finanzkrise und große Koalition: Eine Bewertung des Krisenmanagements der Bundesregierung'. In *Die zweite Große Koalition. Eine Bilanz der Regierung Merkel, 2005–2009*, edited by Christoph Egle and Reimut Zohlnhöfer, 234–53. Wiesbaden: Springer VS.

Faz.net. 2013. 'Schwarz-gelbe Restposten: Was vom Regieren übrig blieb'. Available from: http://www.faz.net/-gqg-7gxux (accessed 27 August 2013).

Gerlinger, Thomas. 2014. 'Rapider Politikwechsel in der Arzneimittelpreisregulierung – das Arzneimittelmarktneuordnungsgesetz der konservativ-liberalen Bundesregierung'. In *Rapide Politikwechsel in der Bundesrepublik. Theoretischer Rahmen und empirische Befunde*, edited by Friedbert W. Rüb, 127-152. Baden-Baden: Nomos.

Grasl, Maximilian, and König, Markus. 2010. 'Von außen getrieben. Die Finanzpolitik der Großen Koalition 2005–2009'. In *Die zweite Große Koalition. Eine Bilanz der Regierung Merkel, 2005–2009*, edited by Christoph Egle and Reimut Zohlnhöfer, 205–33. Wiesbaden: Springer VS.

Hartmann, Anja. 2010. 'Die Gesundheitsreform der Großen Koalition: Kleinster gemeinsamer Nenner oder offenes Hintertürchen?' In *Die zweite Große Koalition. Eine Bilanz der Regierung Merkel, 2005–2009*, edited by Christoph Egle and Reimut Zohlnhöfer, 327–49. Wiesbaden: Springer VS.

Hulverscheidt, Claus. 2013. 'Der Merkel-Missstand'. *Süddeutsche Zeitung*, April 20.

Jones, Brian D., and Baumgartner, Frank R. 2012. 'From there to here: punctuated equilibrium to the general punctuation thesis to a theory of government information processing'. *Policy Studies Journal*, vol. 40: 1–19.

Moog, Stefan and Raffelhüschen, Bernd. 2011. 'Ehrbarer Staat? Eine Zwischenbilanz schwarz-gelber Regierungspolitik'. *Zeitschrift für Staats- und Europawissenschaft*, vol. 9: 244–61.

OECD. 2012. *OECD Economic Surveys. Germany*. Paris: OECD.

OECD. 2013. *Recruiting Immigrant Workers. Germany*. Paris: OECD.

Pressel, Holger. 2012. *Der Gesundheitsfonds. Entstehung – Einführung – Weiterentwicklungen – Folgen*. Wiesbaden: Springer VS.

Reisenbichler, Alexander, and Morgan, Kimberly J. 2012. 'From "sick man" to "miracle": explaining the robustness of the German labor market during and after the financial crisis 2008–09'. *Politics and Society*, vol. 40: 549–79.

Saalfeld, Thomas. 2010a. 'Regierungsbildung 2009: Merkel II und ein höchst unvollständiger Koalitionsvertrag'. *Zeitschrift für Parlamentsfragen*, vol. 41, n. 1: 181–206.

Saalfeld, Thomas. 2010b. 'Coalition governance under Chancellor Merkel's grand coalition. A comparison of the cabinets Merkel I and Merkel II'. *German Politics and Society*, vol. 28, n. 3: 82–102.

Schmid, Josef. 2008. 'Die CDU nach 2005: Von Wahl zu Wahl – und doch kein Wandel?' In *Die Parteien nach der Bundestagswahl*, edited by Oskar Niedermayer, 67–150. Wiesbaden: Springer VS.

Schroeder, Wolfgang. 2010. 'Große Koalition und Sozialpartnerschaft: Von der Konfrontation über die Normalisierung hin zur wechselseitigen Stützung in der Weltwirtschaftskrise'. In *Die zweite Große Koalition. Eine Bilanz der Regierung Merkel, 2005–2009*, edited by Christoph Egle and Reimut Zohlnhöfer, 180–201. Wiesbaden: Springer VS.

Sturm, Roland. 2012. 'Eine Renaissance der Kanzlerdemokratie? Die Zwischenbilanz der Politik der christlich–liberalen Koalition'. In *'Superwahljahr' 2011 und die Folgen*, edited by Eckhard Jesse and Roland Sturm, 257–82. Baden-Baden: Nomos.

Von der Leyen, Ursula. 2012. 'Vorwort'. In *Kündigungsschutz. Alles was Sie wissen sollten*. Berlin: Bundesministerium für Arbeit und Soziales.

Vorländer, Hans. 2008. 'Partei der Paradoxien. Die FDP nach der Bundestagswahl 2005'. In *Die Parteien nach der Bundestagswahl*, edited by Oskar Niedermayer, 135–50. Wiesbaden: Springer VS.

Zohlnhöfer, Reimut. 2007. 'Zwischen Kooperation und Verweigerung: Die Entwicklung des Parteienwettbewerbs 2002–2005'. In *Ende des rot-grünen Projektes. Eine Bilanz der Regierung Schröder 2002–2005*, edited by Christoph Egle and Reimut Zohlnhöfer, 124–50. Wiesbaden: VS Verlag.

Zohlnhöfer, Reimut. 2010. 'New possibilities or permanent gridlock? The policies and politics of the grand coalition'. In *Germany after the Grand Coalition. Governance and Politics in a Turbulent Environment*, edited by Silvia Bolgherini and Florian Grotz, 15–30. New York: Palgrave Macmillan.

Zohlnhöfer, Reimut. 2011. 'Between a rock and a hard place: the German response to the economic crisis'. *German Politics*, vol. 20: 227–42.

Zohlnhöfer, Reimut. 2014. 'Eine zu spät gekommene Koalition? Die Bilanz der wirtschafts- und sozialpolitischen Reformtätigkeit der zweiten Regierung Merkel'. In *Bilanz der Bundestagswahl 2013 – Voraussetzungen, Ergebnisse, Folgen*, edited by Eckhard Jesse and Roland Sturm, 477-93. Baden-Baden: Nomos.

Zolleis, Udo, and Bartz, Julia. 2010. 'Die CDU in der Großen Koalition – Unbestimmt erfolgreich'. In *Die zweite Große Koalition. Eine Bilanz der Regierung Merkel, 2005–2009*, edited by Christoph Egle and Reimut Zohlnhöfer, 51–68. Wiesbaden: Springer VS.

Chapter 2

A New German Question?
Germany and European Integration
in Historical Perspective

Gabriele D'Ottavio

Introduction

> For most of the postwar period, the Federal Republic had a symbiotic relationship
> with Europe: the interests of the two were aligned. But this synergy depended
> on the peculiar situation in which West Germany found itself during the Cold
> War. In other words, European 'normality' was based to a large extent on West
> German 'abnormality'. Now that the reunified Germany is becoming more
> 'normal', it is undermining European 'normality' (Guérot and Leonard 2011, 4).

It is precisely due to the widespread belief that a historical caesura in Germany's
relationship with European integration is taking place or might take place that
disquieting, but historically and politically implausible, scenarios have started
circulating in some sectors of European public opinion. Like those envisaging
a de facto 'Germanisation' of Europe via the imposition of its economic and
monetary policy, or, vice versa, Germany severing its European ties.[1] In reality,
things are much more complex than a representation, based on the idea of a
supposed clear-cut distinction between Germany's past and present attitudes
towards European integration, might make us believe. Analysts tend to agree that
Germany's relationship to Europe is going through a period of intense change.
But what these changes really imply in terms of continuities and discontinuities is
still controversial. Even before the outbreak of the euro crisis a 'pragmatization'
of German European policy was detected (Schmalz 2001, 62–8). According to
another analysis, which today is also shared quite widely, a supposed process of
'de-Europeanisation', with special reference to some key areas, is taking place
(Hellmann 2006). Other scholars emphasize that Germany's commitment to
European integration has become more and more 'contingent' (Harnisch and

---

1   Even some leading German intellectuals, such as Ulrich Beck, Jürgen Habermas
and Wolfgang Streeck, with their critiques of Angela Merkel's European policy, have
contributed to the circulating of some of these very unlikely scenarios (Beck 2012;
Habermas 2012; Streeck 2013).

Schieder 2006) and subject to domestic pressure (Harnisch 2009) on the one hand, while on the other hand it seems no longer securely anchored in public opinion (Paterson 2010).

Against this backdrop, this chapter aims to provide a narrative which allows us to fully capture the historical dimension of the two main issues that are at the cutting edge of the more recent debate on Germany's relationship to Europe: first, Germany's increasing actorness in European affairs – but also the limits of Germany's leadership role (Chapter 3 infra; Bulmer and Paterson 2013) – and, secondly, the supposed erosion of Germany's traditional 'European vocation' (Paterson 2010). This chapter argues that the Federal Republic's relationship to European integration in the past was less 'abnormal' than other studies have suggested (Müller-Roschach 1980; König and Schulz 2004; Müller-Brandeck-Bocquet and Schukraft 2009). West Germany had started pursuing its national interests long before unification, even if it did so within specific boundaries imposed by its past and the Cold War, and even if these interests were framed as predominantly *pro-communautaire* and consensus-oriented. Already in the negotiations culminating in the signing of the Treaties of Rome in 1957, the Federal Republic was able to upload its preferences at European level. However, even at that time German people were not very passionate about the European Community (EC). Their attitude was basically permissive, rather than actively supportive of European integration. This is an important difference that has often been obscured by much exaggerated pro-integrationist rhetoric. In the 1960s, the Federal Republic gained further capacity to act in European and international affairs. Ironically, this was made possible by France, the historical arch-enemy of Germany, the progressive hardening of Gaullist France's intransigent stand allowing West Germany to play a pivotal role in both transatlantic relations and those between the member states of the EC. From the 1970s onwards, West Germany played an even more active and self-reliant role, also as a consequence of its increasing economic power. It is during this period that West Germany's new profile as a 'civilian power' (Harnisch and Maull 2001) became fully visible. And it was at that time that West Germany started to be perceived as 'économie dominante' (Kreile 1978). In the aftermath of the fall of the Berlin Wall, there were many evoking the concerns that a newly unified Germany could fall into temptation and attempt to adopt a new 'special way' (*Sonderweg*). Such concerns were soon dispelled when Germany contributed decisively to the birth of the European Union. At the same time, it was precisely in the creation of the Economic and Monetary Union that Germany showed herself to be better equipped than the other member states, and perhaps even more skilled at asserting her position over those of the other countries. The past 20 years have raised a number of questions that remain open. After German reunification, the birth of the euro-area, the 2004 enlargement and the growing asymmetry between core countries and those on the periphery, it has become evident that the domestic and external preconditions of the previous German European policy have changed dramatically.

This chapter does not aim to offer an exhaustive overview of Germany's European policy over the last 60 years. Rather, the purpose is to gain from a historical perspective a better understanding of what is increasingly being outlined as the 'new German question' (Guérot and Leonard 2011; Rödder 2012; Garton Ash 2013).

The Treaties of Rome: International Constraints and National Interests

Right from the beginning, European integration has been closely linked to attempts by Western powers to incorporate West Germany within the boundaries of a collective security system, enabling the strengthening of its resources in the struggle against international communism and the prevention of a possible German threat, within the framework of 'double containment' (Hanrieder 1995). The development of the first European Communities – the European Community of Steel and Coal (ECSC) and the unsuccessful European Community of Defence (EDC) – showed how the drive for European integration was fostered by times of great international tension. However, when these tensions seemed to fade away, new reasons for division and competition arose among European countries. It is precisely at this stage that the Federal Republic's role in European integration became more active. After the failure of the EDC treaty and with Germany retrieving its sovereignty with the signing of the Paris Treaty in 1954, the West German political elite started to become increasingly convinced that European integration was no longer a historical necessity mostly imposed from above, but also a project – both political and economic – which could be shaped and developed according to specific needs (D'Ottavio 2012). In this way, we can also understand the request by the German government, later accepted, to be allowed to sign a German-language version of the Treaties of Rome (1957), establishing the European Economic Community (EEC) and the European Atomic Energy Community (EAEC).

In this context, the debate within the German government that emerged during the negotiations around the methods and forms of European integration is quite significant (Küsters 1990). The debate revealed the presence of an important divergence inside the party in government, the CDU/CSU, concerning the motivations and aims of Germany's European policy. More precisely, Adenauer's minister of economy, Ludwig Erhard, countered the institutional functionalism inspired by Monnet and supported by the then secretary of state, Walter Hallstein, with the formula of 'functional integration'. In other words, the building of a common market, based on a customs union and supranational institutions, was countered by the minister of economy with the project of a less binding free trade area enlarged to the signatory countries of the General Agreement on Trade and Tariffs (GATT) and the member states of the Organisation for European Economic Cooperation (OEEC). The latter represented, in his opinion, the only economically viable solution and the most respectful of German national interests (Neebe 2004). It is known that, on the day the German parliament first discussed the Treaties of

Rome, Erhard called the whole project 'nonsense from a macroeconomic point of view'.[2] Erhard's objection to the *kleineuropäisch* approach was by no means unfounded. As a matter of fact, at the time, 75 per cent of West Germany's exports went to countries outside the future common market (Patel 2011, 778).

The controversy which further developed around the economic arguments against those of 'high politics' illustrated an important confrontation between ministries concerning the repartition of European policy competences, which was to endure. Driven by events perceived as epoch-making, like the Suez and Hungary crises (1956), and in view of a rapid closing of negotiations, Chancellor Adenauer dictated his government's policy by using his agenda-setting powers (*Richtlinienkompetenz*) and his will to compromise with France, compared to the intransigence shown by some of his ministers. Eventually the German delegation succeeded – albeit not without having made important financial concessions on the atomic energy dossier and the association of overseas territories – in getting the result Bonn most aspired to: the setting up of a common market to be developed in stages, via the progressive liberalization of the movement of goods, capital and people (Segers 2008).

With the passing of time, the common market turned out to be the main cause of modernization, growth and development for the economies of EEC countries, and Germany's in particular, due to its strong and export-oriented industry. However, the political effects of the Treaties of Rome were even more significant. Via the creation of an original institutional setup, a context of ongoing negotiations between member states and a series of political and economic obligations were established, which made de facto irreversible the Federal Republic's anchoring to Europe. The fact that the German delegation managed to secure an important formal commitment from the signatory countries that they would not recognize the division of Germany as permanent should not be underestimated. Firstly, the common external tariff was not to be applied to trade relations between the Federal Republic and the Democratic Republic; secondly, in the additional protocol of 28 February 1957 the five European partners agreed to add a clause allowing for the revision of the treaties in case of a future reunification of the two German states. This result also contributed to facilitating the support for the Treaties of Rome of the German Social Democratic Party (SPD), which up to then had clearly refused to accept rapid and unconditional participation in Western multilateral organizations, as they feared that a full integration policy would further aggravate the division of the two countries (Ramuschkat 2003).

At the Origins of Germany's 'European Vocation': Divergences and Permissive Consensus

The analysis of the shift, which saw the SPD abandoning its initial sceptical attitude in favour of a more pragmatic attitude towards European integration in the

---

2   *Neue Zürcher Zeitung*, 21 March 1957.

mid-1950s, enables us to better understand the historical tenets on which the idea of the 'European vocation' of Federal Germany at the time of the Cold War is still based today. The change within the SPD's attitude towards European integration became explicit only after the vote in favour of the ratification of the Treaties of Rome in July 1957 (D'Ottavio 2007). As a matter of fact, it was the first time that a European initiative, supported by Adenauer's government, received the approval of the main opposition party. Until that time, the German Social Democratic Party had rejected all the main integrationist steps, voting against the establishment of three important bodies of European cooperation, namely the Council of Europe, the European Coal and Steel Community and the European Defence Community.

Both external and domestic factors were important in shaping the SPD's shift from opposition to support for European integration. On the one hand, with the Federal Republic becoming a member of NATO as a consequence of the Treaties of Paris in 1954–5, the issue of defence was separated from European integration, so that, from that time onwards, the backing by the SPD of a project for a united Europe based on economic integration became much easier. Furthermore, the context of a favourable resolution of the Saar question, after the defeat of the referendum of October 1955, removed a second important issue which until then had made it difficult for the SPD to support the integration process. On the other hand, different internal factors contributed to the changes in the SPD's European policy, including the pressure of trade unions, which already in 1950 had decided to support the Schuman Plan, and the growing influence in the party of figures like Willi Birkelbach, Fritz Erler, Karl Mommer and Herbert Wehner. Thanks to their experience in the Parliamentary Assembly of the ECSC and the Advisory Assembly of the Council of Europe, these politicians had acquired relevant negotiating skills on issues of European politics and, more importantly, an increased awareness of how widespread was the association between economic wealth and European integration in the publics of the six founding countries (Paterson 1974).

But if we want to stretch this interpretation, we may suggest that the domestic aspects were perhaps more important than the external aspects, if not the outright determinant of the SPD's shift in position. In particular, the general election set for September 1957 certainly played an important role. In this regard, Fritz Erler's statement during the meeting of the party's executive committee of 30 May 1957 is revealing:

> We must keep on stating our criticism, also in the case of us voting in favour. However, we cannot afford that in the election the SPD is accused of voting 'no' once again, or of not knowing what to do. Abstention is almost a 'yes'. This is why we must say a clear 'yes'.[3]

---

3   Archiv der sozialen Demokratie (AdsD), Protokolle 1957: *Meeting of the party's executive committee*, 30 May 1957.

Against this backdrop, the SPD's change in its attitude towards European integration may be interpreted in close connection with the phenomenon of de-ideologization of the party, leading to the turning point of Bad Godesberg in 1959 and the SPD becoming a 'catch-all-party', according to the well-known definition by Otto Kirchheimer. From the mid-1950s in the Federal Republic, European integration increasingly acquired the value of a source of legitimation that a responsible political force with governing ambitions could not forego.

However, the SPD's acceptance of the European project was not the moment from which European policy de facto stopped representing a ground of political division between the two main political forces of the country (Paterson 1974, x). As a matter of fact, the SPD voted in favour of the ratification not only because, as Karl Mommer said in 1963, it did not contain 'any trace of a crushing victory of the majority',[4] but also because it offered the party a big opportunity to counter the charge of being anti-European, without forcing it to openly challenge the guidelines of its foreign policy and its *Deutschlandpolitik*. One of the main differences between the attitudes of the CDU and SPD towards the Treaties of Rome was that, while Adenauer continued to consider Europe (and the creation of a common market) as a containment tool, Ollenhauer stressed its détente potential. As they were a framework agreement, the Treaties of Rome left ample room for interpretation with regard to future directions for Europe.

We have here, in other words, what seems to be a paradox. When European integration ceased to represent a political-ideological cleavage within the German political system, the two main political parties – the CDU and, from that time onward, the SPD – started to consider European integration ideologically, as something that had always to be supported, regardless of where the integration process was or was not going, regardless of its specific contents and meanings, and independent of the two parties' diverging strategic goals and perspectives. This was also possible because the German people's increasing consensus on European integration was by no means deep-seated. In 1958, only about one quarter of the population knew that the Treaties of Rome had already been concluded, while 73 per cent thought that German unification was more urgent than European integration (Noelle and Neumann 1957, 342). As pointed out by Kiran Patel, 'The Europe that the EEC stood for was the project of a small elite, while most Germans continued to live in the mental container of the nation state' (Patel 2011, 779).

The Reconciliation with France: History's Twists and Turns

The fact that the Federal Republic's playing a more relevant role in European and international affairs was made possible thanks to Germany's historical enemy, France, appears to be one of those twists and turns that history, in its perfidy, likes

---

4   *Neue Gesellschaft*, 10, 3 (May–June), 1963, p. 192.

to amuse itself with. The famous Élysée Treaty, which, in January 1963, marked the 'Franco–German reconciliation', was particularly eventful. In the long run, probably the Federal Republic was to benefit most from an agreement that, at the time, seemed to have produced more harm than benefits, in view of the fact that it brought about a conflict of priority between its two main partners – the United States and France – which the German political class had tried to escape from, to no avail (Lappenküper 2001). Despite the efforts made by the government in Bonn to reassure the United States and the other European partners, the decision to sign a treaty with France just one week after General de Gaulle had vetoed Britain's accession to the EEC was received with great annoyance and dismay, especially in Washington and London (Granieri 2003).

For the first time since 1949, West Germany's reliability and loyalty were questioned by the two allies that, up to that point, had most staunchly supported its return to a more expansive role in the international arena. On the other hand, from then on, the way the Federal Republic was perceived internationally changed. All of a sudden, West Germany was no longer seen as a 'problem' in international relations just because it found itself along the demarcation line between East and West, or because it represented the most important stake in the East–West competition, but also because of the geopolitical consequences of the choices that its political class, now seemingly divided between the 'Atlanticists' and the 'Gaullists' (Geiger 2008), would or could make. Similar considerations may also be made with reference to the preamble that the Bundestag voted in May 1963 as preliminary to the ratification of the Élysée Treaty, de facto reincorporating the meaning of the bilateral entente within the more comprehensive framework of its Atlantic obligations. If, on the one hand, the preamble marked the boundary which Adenauer could not cross with his country – even if he had wanted to – given the strategic dependence of the Federal Republic on the United States, on the other hand it represented the launch pad from which West Germany took up a central role in both transatlantic relations and the relations between the member states of the EEC.

By distancing themselves from Paris, the 'Atlanticist' leaders, represented by Chancellor Ludwig Erhard and minister of foreign affairs Gerhard Schröder, also became the interpreters of a new awareness of West Germany's newly acquired importance in the international arena. Within the framework of Europe's integration policy, this awareness was explicitly translated into the April 1963 proposal by the minister of foreign affairs, Schröder, to apply the principle of 'synchronisation'.[5] The idea envisaged parallel working panels that would provide member states with an updated comprehensive vision of individual issues, in order to facilitate the reaching of compromise-based solutions via mutual compensation in specific sectors. Introduced as a tool to bring the EEC out of its crisis, the idea of 'synchronisation' was also the expression of a much deeper change taking place at the level of relations between member states (Ludlow 2007). From a situation where the mechanism

---

5   Council of Ministers Archive (CMA), R/295/63 Council minutes, 1–2 April 1963.

of mediating between the differing interests of individual member states did not necessarily imply equal compensations, a shift was taking place to a position that demanded it explicitly. In the past, according to Schröder's analysis, not everyone had benefited equally from the European agreements reached. In particular, the system of '*préalables*' had ended up by penalizing those, like the Germans, who had made great concessions without receiving in exchange the benefits promised in other sectors of the economy. The example of agriculture, mentioned by Schröder, was a clear expression of the minister's attempt to state Germany's new negotiating stance in the Community, which was undoubtedly less compliant than in the past with respect to demands from de Gaulle's France, and more focused on Germany's economic interests. At an early stage, 'synchronisation' actually succeeded in bringing the EC out of the decision-making standstill which had occurred after de Gaulle's veto on Britain's accession. However, this was achieved at the expense of an inevitable shift from long-term to short-term priorities. In particular, from 1963, the new priorities of Germany's European policy were focused on accelerating the process of market liberalization within the scope of the Kennedy Round and supporting wheat prices in favour of its farmers, in addition to attempts to revamp negotiations for the enlargement of the EC to include Great Britain (Patel 2009).

Gaullist France's stubborn intransigence in the context of the 'empty-chair crisis' eventually enabled the Federal Republic to gain credit with smaller countries and supranational institutions of the EC as the upholder of the Treaties of Rome, although Germany did not always seem equal to the leadership role that, around the mid-1960s, the composite anti-Gaullist front seemed willing to confer on it (Bajon 2012). The second unsuccessful attempt to convince de Gaulle to enlarge the EC to incorporate Great Britain is a good example of Bonn's limited capacity to play a real leadership role in Europe at the time (Türk 2006).

The 1970s: West Germany as 'Civilian Power'

The supposed incompatibility between *Deutschlandpolitik* and *Europapolitik* was solved for good at the time of the East–West détente, when the Federal Republic's room for manoeuvre looked somewhat different than in the first two postwar decades. From the end of the 1960s onwards, West Germany's role in Europe became more independent and increasingly assertive. At the same time, it was during this period that West Germany's identity as 'civilian power' became fully visible. According to Harnisch and Maull, the civilian power role concept includes at least three essential norms:

> 1. The willingness and ability to civilise international relations as a promoter or initiator of international action; 2. The willingness to transfer sovereignty or autonomy to supranational institutions as a promoter of collective security and opponent of unilateral action; 3. The eagerness to realise a civilised international

order, even if this implies foregoing short-term national interests (power or plenty) (Harnisch and Maull 2001, 4).

In this regard the following German initiatives merit consideration: the new *Ostpolitik* whereby the Social Democrat-led government pursued a policy of normalizing relations with Eastern European countries, which went beyond the hitherto dominating strategy of *Westintegration* and *containment* (Creuzberger 2009). Again around the mid-1970s, West Germany carved for itself a central role in the processes of stabilization and democratization of Southern European countries recently emerged from their dictatorships – namely Greece, Spain and Portugal – thus replacing the United States' temporarily tarnished leadership in that region of the Western front (Varsori 2009). At the same time, Bonn actively contributed to the setting up of some innovative tools for the strengthening of European political, economic and monetary cooperation, to improve the efficiency of decision-making processes and to bypass the problem of the democratic deficit. In particular, the following were established: the European Political Cooperation (EPC), a foreign policy coordination mechanism (1972), and new rules for the fluctuation of member states' currencies, first with the monetary snake (1972) and later the European Monetary System (1978), accompanied by innovative mechanisms of intervention and monetary credit (Möckli 2009; Wilkens 2010). The practice of holding summit meetings of heads of state and government (1974) was established as well, together with the introduction of the direct election of the European Parliament, held for the first time in 1979.

Germany's increasing self-confidence in European and international affairs was also a consequence of some important domestic performances. More precisely, in those years, the young but evidently mature German democracy succeeded in meeting the challenges that youth protest at first and terrorism later had launched against the governability of the political system, and distinguished itself for its peculiar development model (*Modell Deutschland*), based on a mix of highly skilled workers and high wages, which was capable of building consensus in its merging of economic growth with welfare policies, and in its merging of efficiency with the idea of social justice. Again in the 1970s, the Federal Republic stood out in Europe for a better management of the economic crisis in comparison with all the other member states, thus establishing and presenting itself as a reference model of macroeconomic stability, inclusive social policy and a sustained growth of industrial production (Markovits 1982).

The 'civilian power' role concept does not exclude the pursuit of a 'national interest' as the main bearings for decision-makers. However, it reshapes it within a framework in which the actor is no longer an isolated and self-sufficient nation state, but instead a well-integrated country that is part of a system of articulated and multilateral federated structures. It is against this backdrop that Germany's willingness to take in consideration the early plans for closer economic and monetary cooperation may be understood, as well as the government's determination to see its preferences prevail in the debate between 'monetarists' and 'economists'

(Mourlon-Druol 2012). In this regard, Chancellor Helmut Schmidt's statement of September 1974 in Paris, concerning possible progress towards a real economic and monetary union, appears quite significant:

> … the time has not yet come to return to the pursuit of economic and monetary union: Extreme disequilibria in current balances of payments might cause the Community to drift further apart rather than grow closer together. … Under these circumstances, the only way to success is to continue an European stability programme with a view to harmonizing national economic policies'.[6]

As a matter of fact, according to the German position, a prerequisite for the birth of the Monetary Union was reaching a sufficient level of convergence between member states in economic and monetary policies. Thanks also to the better economic performance shown during the management of the economic crisis in the 1970s, in the event Germany's position was judged to be the most secure. And it was at that time that West Germany started to be perceived – be it right or wrong – as '*économie dominante*' (Kreile 1978), which, however, was not reflected in its representation in the more political domains, especially on security and defence issues. Although there were tentative forays into foreign and security issues, the EC primarily remained an economic creature, with the member states, including Helmut Schmidt's Germany, opting more and more for an intergovernmental Europe in place of a supranational form of integration.

This may also help to explain why, as before, a large majority of Germans accepted integration, though remaining permissive rather than actively supportive of the process. When, in 1973, the European Communities started polling all member states about public support and opposition, 59 per cent of German citizens positively assessed the national membership, while only 6 per cent thought that their country's membership in the EC was a bad thing (Vanke 2010, 673). However, when, in 1979, the first direct election of the European Parliament was held, voter turnout in Germany only reached 66 per cent, whereas Bundestag elections attracted 89 per cent in 1980 (Patel 2011, 785). But even more significant is the fact that, in both national and European elections, Europe remained a 'non-issue' in the campaigns of the pro-integrationist established German parties.

The Maastricht Treaty and its Interpretations

In the aftermath of the fall of the Berlin Wall, there were many evoking concerns that a newly unified Germany could fall into temptation and attempt to adopt a new 'special way' (*Sonderweg*), by freeing itself from the European and Atlantic obligations that were contracted in the second postwar period, or even giving

---

6   Historical Archives of the European Union (HAEU), Fond Emile Noël, EN 599: *Chancellor Helmut Schmidt in Paris*, 14 September 1974.

in to new hegemonic drives. Statespeople like Margaret Thatcher, François Mitterrand and Giulio Andreotti, from rather different cultural backgrounds and political orientations, warned that a united and powerful Germany could lose its interest in European integration or even become a threat to its neighbours. Such concerns were soon to be dispelled, when Germany contributed decisively to the birth of the European Union by showing during the Maastricht negotiations more openness than the other European countries with regard to the waiving of national prerogatives deemed necessary to make progress in the integration process. At the same time, it was precisely in the creation of the Economic and Monetary Union (EMU) that Germany showed itself to be better equipped than the other member states, and perhaps even more skilled in uploading its preferences to European level (Bulmer, Jeffery and Paterson 2000). In this period, after the fall of the Wall, the German government undoubtedly came under strong pressure and, in some circumstances, had to bow down to requests by other member states. However, it is likewise evident that, eventually, the Federal Republic succeeded in making its point, thus exporting the two main features of its model of Central Bank – political independence and anti-inflationary position – and especially forcing less virtuous member states to undergo a strict budget discipline through the setting of rigorous criteria of economic and financial convergence, in view of the final stage of establishing the Monetary Union (Dyson and Featherstone 1999, 370–451). At most, it may be assumed that the German delegation was quite skilful in convincing its European partners that the birth of the EMU and the subsequent adoption of the euro were something that was squeezed out of it, precisely in order to strengthen its negotiating position, which also exploited the strong domestic reserves from the Treasury and the powerful Bundesbank. In the early 1990s, also, other international events of great importance – the breaking out of the first Gulf War, the collapse of the communist regimes in Eastern Europe, the forthcoming disintegration of Yugoslavia and the Soviet Union – weighed on the Germans' willingness to bring about, with the Maastricht Treaty, an entity that could aspire to becoming a more authoritative and incisive actor on the international stage.

In the last 20 years, however, this historical reality has often been exploited by Western Europe's political elites. In particular, in countries like France and Italy, the ruling classes have long profited from the assumption of a presumed 'geopolitical exchange' involving German reunification and the Monetary Union, in view of the fact that it enabled them to present themselves to their publics as those who succeeded in averting the danger of a possible revival of the German threat, through the 'Europeanization of the Mark'. In Great Britain, instead, in order to legitimize as well the British government's decision to opt out of the EMU, the opposite interpretation was preferred, which saw the birth of the euro-area as the tool by which the Germans had de facto initiated the Germanization of Europe. These two interpretations have also been taken up by some scholars who could not resist the temptation of seeing in the Germans' negotiating attitude a confirmation of the Federal Republic's condition of a limited-sovereignty country or Germany's stronger assertiveness in defending its specific interests. In this regard, the thesis supported by Carsten Hefeker (1997) and taken up by Andrew Moravcsik (1998) is emblematic, in its assumption that the choice of the German government to share the goal of the EMU was mostly due to economic reasons linked to pressure exercised by interest groups – the so-called 'interest group explanation'. Of course, some of these views of the Treaty of Maastricht present interesting key interpretations, but some are also clearly off the mark (Heisenberg 2005).

These positions also enable us to better understand the ambivalent representation of the way Germans have been relating to the treaty establishing the EMU and the single currency in the past 20 years, according to which they are at times pictured as the makers of the euro, or instead as the victims of blackmailing, ending precisely with the sacrifice of the Mark. This ambivalent representation of the Germans has engendered one commonplace that was further strengthened just after the outbreak of the euro crisis: namely, that there was a supposed majority of Germans in favour of a possible return to the national currency. The fact that this commonplace has found confirmation in some recent studies carried out by accredited research institutes, and has been refuted by other such studies, is of some interest. More precisely, according to the results of a survey conducted in 2010 by the Allensbach Institute, an influential public opinion polling centre based in Germany, an overwhelming majority of Germans did not trust the euro anymore. However, these findings have been questioned by another analysis, which concluded that:

> … the dramatic fall in trust in the euro, as depicted by the Allensbach Institute, will most likely concern trust in money in general, but does not necessarily mean a loss of German support for the euro as the centrepiece of European integration – the (Economic) and European Monetary Union. Secondly, although there is undoubtedly a significant fall in trust in the euro, … alternative interpretations of the data show that the decline in trust in the euro is not so dramatic. Thirdly, … German citizens seem to blame the governance structure behind the euro (*the ECB*), but not the EMU and the euro itself (Gros and Roth 2011, 10).

In view of such conflicting findings, we may ask whether the image of the Germans' relationship with the euro conveyed by these views would lend itself to political exploitation, as it did 20 years ago. What is certain is that these contradictions and the uncertainty conveyed by them may be of help in explaining why European public opinion may fall into the temptation to take unconvincing scenarios seriously, like those envisaging the 'Germanization' of Europe or, on the contrary, the German engine severing its European ties.

Conclusion: A New German Question?

There are two big historical issues closely linked together, which Germany's most recent European policy and the different ways of representing it have contributed to bringing to the surface. The first, as old as Germany itself, refers to the specific nature of German leadership in Europe, while the second refers to the increasingly shaky relationship between the 'Europe of the elites' and the 'Europe of its citizens'. In particular, starting from the 1970s and more clearly from the 1990s, Germany seemed increasingly aware of its role in the international arena but still reluctant to translate the new acquisition of power into European leadership. Additionally, this contradiction was matched by the growing ambiguity of the EC, now European Union, that on the one hand wished for, and at the same time also feared, Germany's increasing actorness. The birth of the European Monetary System in 1978 and the later establishment of the EMU showed that it was in the collective European interest that Germany carry out the role of leading country at the economic and monetary level. Besides, the main international crises of the post-1989 period (the Gulf, former Yugoslavia, Iraq, Afghanistan) have also shown the limits, difficulties and contradictions of Germany as a 'civilian power' in exercising its leadership role also at the political level (Maull 2006). Thus, the most recent international crises, from Libya to Mali to Syria, have again highlighted the objective and subjective difficulties hindering Germans from exercising a true political leadership, especially on security and military issues (Chapter 4 infra). But it was mostly the 2008 financial and economic crisis that clearly showed the problems of the specific nature of German supremacy in Europe. At least for the time being, Germany seems to have succeeded in handling the crisis better than other European countries. In this regard, its strong manufacturing sector has helped, due to continuing demand from the BRICS countries and other developing economies. More generally, Germany has shown itself to have an adequate idea – at least for the purpose of defending German interests – of how to govern problems linked to the growing integration of capital markets, to have a stable political and institutional system, and a pragmatic ruling class capable of promoting even very brave reforms (Bonatti and Fracasso 2013). However, the German ruling class does not seem to be able to convince other European countries to adopt their recipe. Historically and politically, Germany's emphasis on fiscal prudence is easy to explain. The hyperinflation of 1923 and the currency reform of 1948 are very real memories that many middle-class and upper-class families in Germany have to the present day (Chapter 3 infra). These traumatic experiences produced an unwavering commitment to sound money and a political system with several institutional 'guardians' – for example, the Central Bank, the Constitutional Court, the Bundesrat – that constrain the federal government's room for manoeuvre (Katzenstein 1997; Dyson and Goetz 2003). However, outside of Germany there is less and less understanding of the German perspective. The very recent economic and financial crisis has in fact contributed to bringing forth a growing impatience among less 'virtuous' countries with regard to the rigour of Angela Merkel's Germany, an impatience further aggravated by the belief that the German recipe is bringing great benefits to Berlin, but also much harm to the countries on the periphery of Europe. The European election results on 25 May 2014 showed this very clearly. It is rather relevant that such impatience with the German government's policies of rigour has been vented recently by the United States as well. In particular, according to what the Department of the Treasury said in its six-monthly report on international policies for the economy and exchange rates, by its maintaining an exaggerated surplus in the balance of payments with respect to the existing demand, Germany would penalize growth and employment worldwide.[7] Germany, then, is the only country with the right credentials to aspire to Europe's leadership, although still lacking the most important ingredient to exercise it: legitimacy. Its *Weltanschauung* based on the idea of stability and rigour (which in the case of less virtuous countries is transformed into austerity) is in fact not very convincing for European public opinion, which in the last twenty years has felt, perhaps subconsciously, deprived of the rather more captivating 'American way of life' which for the entire Cold War period had contributed to legitimizing US supremacy in Europe.

The second big problem, which is part and parcel of what is increasingly being outlined as the 'new German question', is indissolubly linked to the issue of Germany's unexpressed or incomplete leadership potential. It concerns the short-circuit which with the passing of time has developed between the 'elite views' and the 'mass views'. On the one hand, national public opinions, having realized the growing influence of the European Union on their daily lives, are demanding increased attention for their specific interests from their representatives. On the other hand, decision-makers, in order to respond to their demands, have ended up adopting ambivalent, at times manifestly contradictory, behaviours and, as we have seen with the different interpretations of the Maastricht Treaty, by conveying warped representations which may also engender destabilizing effects. The current short-circuit is the result of and, at the same time, a powerful catalyst for a more general phenomenon of renationalization of European politics. In the case of Germany this phenomenon has found its explicit expression not only in the more assertive role played by Angela Merkel's government, but also in the growing demands for an increased defence of their prerogatives in issues pertaining to the European Union by the other political-institutional players participating in the German decision-making process, like the Bundestag, the Länder or the Bundesbank. These demands have been accompanied by some relevant actions by law-makers. In this context, a very important role has been played by the Federal Constitutional Court which, starting from the decision on the Lisbon Treaty on 30 June 2009, stood in the defence of an interpretation of the democratic principle which recognized the pre-eminence of the national constitution, thus questioning again the previous German jurisprudence on the relation between national and European judges. More in general, in Germany the

---

7   US Department of the Treasury-Office of International Affairs, *Report to Congress on International Economic and Exchange Rate Policies*, 30 October 2013.

domestic debate on European issues has become more heated than in the past – especially in the matter of decisions made by the German government about the allocation of a package of extraordinary aid to Greece or, more recently, by the European Central Bank to support the sovereign bonds of the countries in crisis – and has brought to the surface German Eurosceptic public opinion, which in September 2013 and May 2014 supported the Alternative für Deutschland (Chapter 9 infra).

To conclude, it is clear that Germany's relationship to European integration is going through a new phase. However, it seems premature to talk about a historical caesura, getting to the point of questioning Germany's traditional 'European vocation'. Even in the past, Germany's European policy did undergo significant changes giving rise to anti-German fears, later shown to be unfounded. Undoubtedly, Germany's attitude in the last years has revealed a novel assertiveness and an increasing 'domestication' of its EU policy. However, it is highly unlikely that this supposed 'new course' might lead to the relinquishment of the tenets of the Federal Republic's foreign and European policy. Germany, in fact, is still not solely the country that by virtue of its historical responsibilities cannot afford to nurture neo-nationalistic hegemonic drives, but also one which continues to draw great benefits from its participation in the European construction and in particular in the common market and the euro-area. Nor should the supposed erosion of the prevailing pro-European consensus among German public opinion be overstated. Even in the past, the pro-European consensus was not much more deep-seated than it seems to be now. As a matter of fact, German people have never been passionate about the Europe the EC/European Union stood for. Moreover, and as documented above, even some recent findings on the trust in the euro among Germans appear contradictory, if not even misleading in places. Against the widespread belief that German citizens have turned against the centrepiece of the process of deeper European integration, the euro, a recent analysis, for example, has shown that, since its introduction in January 1999, a majority of German citizens has always supported the euro and the Monetary Union, and the percentage of those hankering for a return to the Deutschmark continues to decline (Gros and Roth 2011).

It is true that, until February 2013, one of the main differences with other member states was that Germany had not witnessed a relevant euro-critic political formation. However, if compared with the bigger hold that Euroscepticism is gaining in other national contexts – for example, in France or in the United Kingdom – the anti-euro AfD should (so far) not raise too much concern. Whether the new grand coalition led by Angela Merkel will be called upon to reconsider its European policy will probably depend more on external factors than on domestic ones.

References

Bajon, Philip. 2012. *Europapolitik 'am Abgrund'. Die Krise des 'leeren Stuhles' 1965–1966*. Stuttgart: Franz Steiner.

Beck, Ulrich. 2012. *Das deutsche Europa. Neue Machtlandschaften im Zeichen der Krise*. Berlin: Suhrkamp.

Bonatti, Luigi, and Fracasso, Andrea. 2013. 'The German model and the European crisis'. *Journal of Common Market Studies*, vol. 51, n. 6: 1023–39.

Bulmer, Simon, and Paterson, William E. 2013. 'Germany as the EU's reluctant hegemon? Of economic strength and political constraints'. *Journal of European Public Policy*, vol. 20, n. 10: 1387–405.

Bulmer, Simon; Jeffery, Charles; and Paterson, William E. 2000. *Germany's European Diplomacy: Shaping the Regional Milieu*. New York: St Martin's Press.

Creuzberger, Stefan. 2009. *Westintegration und Neue Ostpolitik. Die Außenpolitik der Bonner Republik*. Berlin: bre.bra Verlag.

D'Ottavio, Gabriele. 2007. 'The Treaties of Rome. Continuity and discontinuity in SPD's European policy.' *Journal of European Integration History*, vol. 13, n. 2: 103–14.

D'Ottavio, Gabriele. 2012. *L'Europa dei tedeschi. La Repubblica federale di Germania e l'integrazione europea, 1949–1966*. Bologna: Il Mulino.

Dyson, Kenneth, and Featherstone, Kenneth. 1999. *The Road to Maastricht. Negotiating Economic and Monetary Union*. Oxford: Oxford University Press.

Dyson, Kenneth, and Goetz, Klaus (eds). 2003. *Germany, Europe and the Politics of Constraint*. Oxford: Oxford University Press.

Garton Ash, Timothy. 2013. 'The New German question'. *New York Review of Books*, 15 August.

Geiger, Till. 2008. *Atlantiker gegen Gaullisten. Aussenpolitischer Konflikt und Innerparteilicher Machtkampf in der CDU/CSU, 1958–1969*. München: Oldenbourg.

Granieri, Ronald J. 2003. *The Ambivalent Alliance. Konrad Adenauer, the CDU/CSU and the West, 1949–1966*. New York: Berghahn.

Gros, Daniel, and Roth, Felix. 2011. 'Do Germans support the euro?'. CEPS Working Document no. 359 (December).

Guérot, Ulrike, and Leonard, Mark. 2011. 'The New German question: how Europe can get the Germany it needs'. European Council of Foreign Affairs Policy Brief, 30 (April).

Habermas, Jürgen. 2012. *The Crisis of the European Union: A Response*. Cambridge: Cambridge University Press.

Hanrieder, Wolfram F. 1995. *Deutschland, Amerika, Europa*. Paderborn: Schöningh.

Harnisch, Sebastian. 2009. '"The politics of domestication": a new paradigm in German foreign policy'. *German Politics*, vol. 18, n. 4: 455–68.

Harnisch, Sebastian, and Maull, Hanns W. 2001. *Germany as Civilian Power? The Foreign Policy of the Berlin Republic.* Manchester: Manchester University Press.

Harnisch, Sebastian, and Schieder, Siegfried. 2006. 'Germany's New European policy'. In *Germany's Uncertain Power: Foreign Policy of the Federal Republic*, edited by Hanns Maull, 95–108. Basingstoke: Palgrave Macmillan.

Hefeker, Carsten. 1997. *Interest Groups and Monetary Integration: The Political Economy of Exchange Regime Choice.* Boulder: Westview.

Heisenberg, Dorothee. 2005. 'Taking a second look at Germany's motivation to establish economic and monetary union: a critique of "economic interests" claims'. *German Politics*, vol. 14, n. 1: 95–109.

Hellmann, Günther. 2006. *Germany's EU Policy on Asylum and Defence: De-Europeanisation by Default.* Basingstoke: Palgrave Macmillan.

Katzenstein, Peter. 1997. *Tamed Power. Germany in Europe.* Ithaca: Cornell University Press.

König, Mareike, and Schulz, Matthias (eds). 2004. *Die Bundesrepublik Deutschland und die europäische Einigung 1949–2000. Politische Akteure, gesellschaftliche Kräfte und internationale Erfahrungen.* Wiesbaden-Stuttgart: Franz Steiner Verlag.

Kreile, Michael. 1978. 'Die Bundesrepublik Deutschland – économie dominante – in Westeuropa'. *Aus Politik und Zeitgeschichte*, vol. 26: 3–26.

Küsters, Hanns Jürgen. 1990. 'Der Streit um Kompetenzen und Konzeptionen deutscher Europapolitik. Der Streit um Kompetenzen und Konzeptionen deutscher Europapolitik'. In *Vom Marshallplan zur EWG. Die Eingliederung der Bundesrepublik Deutschland in die westliche Welt*, edited by Ludolf Herbst, Werner Bührer and Hanno Sowade, 335–70. München: Oldenbourg.

Lappenküper, Ulrich. 2001. *Die deutsch-französischen Beziehungen 1949–1963. Von der 'Erbfeindschaft' zur 'Entente élémentaire'* (two volumes). München: Oldenbourg.

Ludlow, Pierce N. 2007. *The European Community and the Crises of the 1960s.* London: Routledge.

Markovits, A. S. 1982. *The Political Economy of West Germany: Modell Deutschland.* New York: Praeger.

Maull, Hanns. 2006. *Germany's Uncertain Power.* Basingstoke: Palgrave Macmillan.

Möckli, Daniel. 2009. *European Foreign Policy during the Cold War: Heath, Brandt, Pompidou and the Dream of Political Unity.* London: IB Tauris.

Moravcsik, Andrew. 1998. *The Choice for Europe: Social Purpose and State Power from Messina to Maastricht.* Ithaca: Cornell University Press.

Mourlon-Druol, Emmanuel. 2012. *A Europe Made of Money. The Emergence of the European Monetary System.* Ithaca: Cornell University Press.

Müller-Brandeck-Bocquet, Gisela, and Schukraft, Corina. 2009. *Deutsche Europapolitik: Von Adenauer bis Merkel.* Wiesbaden: Verlag für Sozialwissenschaften.

Müller-Roschach, Herbert. 1980. *Die deutsche Europapolitik 1949–1977. Eine politische Chronik. Europäische Schriften des Instituts für Europäische Politik.* Bonn: Europa Union.

Neebe, Reinhard. 2004. *Weichenstellung für die Globalisierung. Deutsche Weltmarktpolitik. Europa und Amerika in der Ära Ludwig Erhard.* Köln: Böhlau.

Noelle, Elisabeth, and Neumann, Erich P. (eds) 1965. *Jahrbuch der öffentlichen Meinung 1958–1964*, Allensbach/Bonn: Verlag für Demoskopie.

Patel, Kiran K. 2009. *Europäisierung wider Willen. Die Bundesrepublik Deutschland in der Agrarintegration der EWG 1955–1973.* München: Oldenbourg.

Patel, Kiran K. 2011. 'Germany and European integration since 1945'. In *The Oxford Handbook of Modern German History*, edited by Helmut Walser Smith, 774–94. Oxford: Oxford University Press.

Paterson, William E. 1974. *The Spd and European Integration.* Westmead: Saxon House.

Paterson, William E. 2010. 'Does Germany still have a European vocation?' *German Politics*, vol. 19, n. 1: 41–52.

Ramuschkat, Dietmar. 2003. *Die SPD und der europäische Einigungsprozeß. Kontinuität und Wandel in der sozialdemokratischen Europapolitik 1949–1955.* Niebüll: Videel.

Rödder, Andreas. 2012. *From Kaiser Wilhelm to Chancellor Merkel. The German Question on the European Stage.* Lecture at the London School of Economics and Political Science, 7 November. Available from: www.lse.ac.uk/newsAndMedia/videoAndAudio/channels/publicLecturesAndEvents/player.aspx?id=1636 (accessed 11 November 2014).

Schmalz, Uwe. 2001. 'Deutsche Europapolitik nach 1989–1990: Die Frage von Kontinuität und Wandel'. In *Eine neue deutsche Europapolitik? Rahmenbedingungen-Problemfelder-Optionen*, edited by Heinrich Schneider, Matthias Jopp and Uwe Schmalz, 15–68. Bonn: Europa Union.

Segers, Mathieu L. 2008. *Deutschlands Ringen mit der Relance. Die Europapolitik der BRD während der Beratungen und Verhandlungen über die Römischen Verträge.* Frankfurt: Peter Lang.

Streeck, Wolfgang. 2013. *Gekaufte Zeit. Die vertagte Krise des demokratischen Kapitalismus.* Berlin: Suhrkamp.

Türk, Henning. 2006. *Die Europapolitik der Großen Koalition.* München: Oldenbourg.

Vanke, Jeffery. 2010. *Europeanism and European Union. Interest, Emotions, and Systemic Integration in the Early European Economic Community.* Bethesda: Academia Press.

Varsori, Antonio. 2009. 'Crisis and stabilization in Southern Europe during the 1970s'. *Journal of European Integration History*, vol. 15, n. 1: 5–14.

Wilkens, Andreas. 2010. *Wir sind auf dem richtigen Weg. Willy Brandt und die europäische Einigung.* Bonn: Diez.

Chapter 3

Germany, the Euro Crisis, and Risk Management: Europe's Reluctant and Vulnerable Hegemonic Power

Kenneth Dyson

Introduction

This chapter paints a portrait of a semi-hegemonic power in Europe, beset by policy dilemmas in how to manage existentially threatening crises within the euro-area. Germany is at once indispensable to the credibility of negotiated agreements on European economic governance reforms, whilst reluctant to be seen as coercing other Member States and fearing isolation within Europe. With respect to euro-area crisis management it lacks the capacity to bail-out other than a limited number of small euro-area Member States without inflicting both self-harm and collective harm, including huge costs to German taxpayers and loss of global competitiveness. Not least, consequent on the combination of European monetary union with the European single market, Germany is acutely vulnerable to contagion through its increased trade and above all financial links to other Member States. Its negotiators face the dilemma of what short- and long-term costs they are prepared to accept in abridging the no-bail-out principle – and justify before the German public – in order to avert the unravelling of the euro-area and the central project in European integration.

The paradoxes and dilemmas facing German policy in the euro-area expose its Federal Chancellor, Federal Finance Minister, Federal Foreign Minister, and president of the Bundesbank to charges of hesitation and weak leadership in euro-area crisis management. They can be represented as lacking ambition and boldness and as imperilling the extraordinary peace and prosperity that European integration has gifted to Europeans, and above all Germany, since 1945 (Glienicker Gruppe 2013; Schmidt and Fischer 2013). Support for European integration has been portrayed as written into the genetic code of postwar German politics, giving it a central position in German 'reason of state' (Dyson and Goetz 2003). This interdependence of vital national with European interests found material expression in a German trade surplus with the euro-area of 54.6 billion euro in 2012. Over 40 per cent of total German exports went to the other Member States of the euro-area, far eclipsing exports to China or the United States.

The Stakes in German Risk Management

The high stakes in German risk management were not lost on Federal Chancellor Angela Merkel. As early as May 2010, she used her speech in Aachen to claim that 'if the euro fails, Europe fails' (Merkel 2010). She returned to this theme. In her Bundestag speech of 26 October 2011, she sought to justify an enhancement of the capacity of the European Financial Stability Facility (EFSF) in the face of critics within the ranks of her Chancellor majority (Merkel 2011b). She did so by stressing both the historical responsibility of Germany for Europe and the role of the EU at the core of German 'reason of state'. 'No one should think that a further half century of peace and prosperity is assured. It isn't. And that's why I say if the euro fails, Europe will fail and that must not happen'. Merkel went on to stress the inseparability of German and European interests: 'What is good for Europe is good for Germany, half a century of peace and prosperity in Germany and Europe testify to that'.

Merkel's earlier Bundestag speech of 7 September 2011 echoed the rationale offered by former Federal Chancellor Helmut Kohl for Economic and Monetary Union (EMU) in 1991: 'History tells us: states that have a common currency do not go to war with each other. For this reason the euro is much, much more than just a currency. The euro is the guarantee of a united Europe: if the euro fails, Europe fails' (Merkel 2011a, 14470). According to Merkel, the central task of the legislative period 2009–13 was to ensure that both Germany and Europe came out of the crisis stronger than they entered the crisis.

The evolving euro-area crises of the Merkel Chancellorship, above all in her second period of office (2009–13), posed the gravest threat in the history of European integration. It soon became clear to her that the management of these complex crises would be the test of her Chancellorship, defining its character and her legacy. The high stakes in risk management led to an increasingly lonely form of Chancellor leadership. Merkel came to rely on a highly discrete system of a few trusted expert associates, as well as the unrivalled ministerial experience, network-building skills and political authority of her Federal Finance Minister, Wolfgang Schäuble.

The vulnerabilities to which Germany was exposed, not least through the transfer of liability and potential losses, posed new domestic political risks. The costs of euro-area crisis management threatened to exceed the willingness, and indeed the capacity, of Germany to bear losses. Hence, Chancellor Merkel pursued two priorities: to safeguard the interests of German taxpayers and to safeguard both the competitiveness of German companies and German creditworthiness in the financial markets. Neglecting these priorities would expose her to high domestic political risks, not least on the political right.

The complex processes of managing euro-area crises, and the process of designing new institutional arrangements for banking, fiscal and economic policy union, had the potential to provoke a new, divisive debate about the nature of the German state, about Europe, and about the relationship between Germany and Europe. In the 2013 federal elections the new anti-euro *Alternative für Deutschland* (AfD) sought to activate such a debate. It failed to break through into the Bundestag. Nevertheless, a vote of 4.7 per cent for a party only six months old testified to the potential for German public opinion to be mobilized behind a domestic challenge to the elite consensus of support for ever closer European union. The performance of the AfD, and its potential in view of the European Parliament elections of May 2014, sent a warning signal to German negotiators, inducing caution in the new grand coalition.

This chapter examines German attitudes to euro-area crisis management in an historical perspective. It argues that there are elements of both historical normality and distinctiveness in these attitudes. It casts doubt on the notion that German attitudes to economic crisis management have radically changed either since German unification or with generational change. In stressing German vulnerability, it underlines the historical lesson about the transience of creditor-state power. Germany may need to take out insurance against a post-creditor-state status, just as Britain may need to insure itself against a structurally imbalanced economy that is over-dependent on a highly volatile sector, finance.

German Euro-Area Crisis Management: Historical Patterns

German attitudes to euro-area crisis management can be seen as the expression of a recurrent historical pattern. Three episodes merit consideration: the onset of the Great Depression in 1931–3; the negotiations in 1941–4, leading to the Bretton Woods Agreement; and German attitudes within the European Payments Union (EPU) of the 1950s.

The Kindersley-Norman Plan of February 1931 has been neglected by historians of Keynesianism (Dyson 2010). This bold plan originated within a Bank of England that was under siege in the financial markets. The Bank faced the prospect of humiliating exit from the gold standard and a slippage of financial power from London to New York. The Kindersley-Norman Plan envisaged transforming the new Bank for International Settlements (BIS) into a huge supranational provider of credits to debtor states, notably Germany. The projected scale (some 1.3–2.5 trillion pounds at 2010 value) far outstripped the future International Monetary Fund (IMF) and the European Stability Mechanism (ESM) (Dyson and Quaglia 2010, 47–8). The plan was vetoed by the two great creditor states at that time: France and the United States. They had no intention of transferring their gold reserves to the BIS. In short, creditor-state power triumphed over the Bank's radicalism in pushing for a new regime for international policy coordination and liquidity creation. Notably, France stood in the way of bold supranational integration, against both Britain and Germany. These ideas were revived in HM Treasury in June 1932, but to no effect (Dyson and Quaglia 2010, 50–1). Keynes followed in 1933 with his proposals to the World Economic Conference for an international authority to issue gold-notes to the value of 5 trillion dollars. Roosevelt torpedoed the Conference with his argument that states must take responsibility for securing 'stability at home', again a classic creditor-state argument (Dyson and Quaglia 2010, 51–3). Keynes' later experience in 1941–4 in writing bold proposals for a new postwar international financial order suffered setback at the hands of the United States. On the liner transporting him back to the UK, he reflected on advocating to the British cabinet that it reject the IMF agreement.

This narrative of creditor-state power continued with the EPU in 1950–8. Initially the two main postwar European creditor states, Belgium and Switzerland, took a hardline, restrictive view on lines of credit. By 1954 a resurgent German economy – the beneficiary of a major debt restructuring in 1953 – was advocating a tightening of credit conditions. By 1957–8 France had become the main reference point of this toughened German attitude. President Charles De Gaulle was to opt for currency reform and domestic consolidation and liberalization as an alternative to a dependency relationship on Germany. Ludwig Erhard was to become the symbol of a highly restrictive and deeply suspicious approach to European monetary integration within German ordoliberalism (Dyson and Featherstone 1999).

In short, well before the European Monetary System (EMS), never mind monetary union, German attitudes had crystallized. From 1954 onwards there was continuity. Moreover, this continuity was wholly consistent with earlier French and US attitudes. They were the attitudes of a creditor state. Creditor states' interests lie in limiting their liabilities within any formalized system of international/European policy coordination and liquidity creation and management. These interests are justified by reference to a set of principles: avoidance of moral hazard, with states taking individual responsibility for stability and sustainable growth; no 'bail-out' rules; and, if bail-out is conceded, then only if creditor-state liability is matched by control, that is, ceding sovereign authority on the part of debtor states.

There is a further element of historical continuity. In any system of international or European coordination the historical pattern is that the number of debtor states exceeds that of creditor states (Dyson 2014). This numeric disadvantage has both negative and positive implications for creditor states like Germany. On the negative side, creditor states find themselves subjected to an external chorus of disapproval of their policies and underlying beliefs. The German government felt the full force of this counter-wind, and sense of isolation, at the G20 summit of December 2011 in Cannes. Debtor states marshal arguments that accuse creditor states of creating a deflationary bias in the international economy through advocacy of all-round fiscal austerity. Their export surpluses are seen as reflecting an excess of output over spending, not merely superior competitiveness. These arguments were deployed by the US Treasury against Germany in November 2013 and coaxed the European Commission into launching an in-depth investigation of German surpluses. Creditor states often find themselves politically isolated.

On the positive side, creditor states have powerful incentives to coordinate with each other. In any system of international or European policy coordination an informal creditor-state club emerges. One of the key attributes of euro-area crisis management was the evolution of such a club, focused around Germany, Finland and the Netherlands. In contrast, despite their superior numbers, debtor states have greater problems of collective action. Their interests lie in differentiating themselves from each other: 'Ireland is not Greece', 'Spain is not Italy', 'Poland is not Hungary', and so forth.

These characteristics of coalition behaviour stem from the arguing and the bargaining power that is possessed by creditor states. They have an aura of power associated with their structural attributes and with their policy performance. Creditor states have the capacity to frame debates about policy coordination and liquidity provision. They set agendas and others negotiate around their policy positions. Above all, they have bargaining power. No system of international policy coordination and liquidity provision has credibility unless creditor states participate. Hence they possess a latent power of threat of exit in any negotiations on creating new institutional arrangements. This was evident in the negotiation of EMU in the Maastricht Treaty (1988–91) and in the Stability and Growth Pact (SGP) negotiations (1995–7). Creditor-state power matters above all when that power is systemically significant, as with Germany both before and after the euro-area.

Three conclusions can be drawn. First, neither German unification nor generational change had much effect on this historical pattern in German attitudes. Secondly, should Germany's creditor-state status erode, German attitudes to the euro-area would be likely to undergo rapid change, perhaps not unlike the UK in 1931. This status is no historical given. It is vulnerable not just to euro-area contagion but also to domestic policy failures, for instance a continuing rapid decline in the share of investment in German GDP. Thirdly, if Germany's current attitudes to euro-crisis management can be characterized as 'arrogant' and 'bullying', then the same applies earlier to the United States, to France, and to pre-1914 Britain.

German Euro-Area Crisis Management: Historical Distinctiveness

Alongside historical patterns, German euro-area crisis management displays distinctiveness in three senses. First, it reflects Germany's particular ordoliberal mindset; its export-oriented model of economic growth based on high-quality consumer durables and capital goods and their global competitiveness; and the domestic institutional arrangements and interests that support them, notably the Bundesbank and negotiated corporate adjustment through social partnership (Dyson and Featherstone 1999; Bonatti and Fracasso 2013). Secondly, German euro-area crisis management is bound up with her historically conditioned attitudes towards the nature and the exercise of sovereign power in Europe. Germany has an ingrained bias to multilateralism in its diplomacy. This bias sits ill-at-ease with the ordoliberal mindset, with its principle-based approach to economic stability.

Both these characteristics of German euro-area crisis management rest on the creation of particular postwar historical memories. The persuasive power of German ordoliberalism rests on an ascendant domestic narrative of how German hyperinflation in 1923 contributed to the demise of political support for the Weimar Republic. The persuasive power of the narrative of German historic responsibility for peace and prosperity in Europe rests on the construction of historical memory of how German isolation in the centre of Europe led to geo-strategic insecurity, militarization, and catastrophic wars.

The third aspect of distinctiveness was that, after 1999, economic crisis management was taking place *within* a European monetary union. A sharp reduction in transaction costs had induced intensified trade and financial integration. Alongside domestic structural reforms and prolonged wage moderation, the effect had been an accumulation of German trade surpluses, capital exports and net financial assets. Germany was acutely vulnerable to euro-area deflation and to failures to repay loans.

These strands of historical distinctiveness gave a particular individual quality to the German approach to euro-area crisis management. They influenced its parameters of risk management. In particular, as we shall see, argumentative and bargaining power was less asymmetrically biased in German favour when reforming the institutional and policy arrangements of the euro-area than it had been when those arrangements were initially created (Dyson and Featherstone 1999; Heipertz and Verdun 2010; Dyson 2014).

First, a distinctive character is given to German argumentation and negotiating style by an ascendant postwar ordoliberalism. Its institutional epicentres are within German academic economics, with the Bundesbank as the guardian of orthodoxy. The distinctiveness of ordoliberalism as an economic theory is in its principles-based approach to economic stability. It is an edifice of rationally ordered, coherent thinking that gives a strongly didactic style to German argumentation. One reasons from constitutive and regulative principles about what is needed to safeguard a long-term stability orientation in monetary, fiscal and economic and social policies and achieve an efficient competition system (Dyson and Featherstone 1999). The Bundesbank remains the principal institutional repository of – and beneficiary from – the ascendancy of ordoliberal values. From the 1970s it succeeded in identifying itself with the notion of safeguarding German economic stability. Later, in the context of EMU, the Bundesbank redefined itself as the guarantor that German stability culture would be exported to the euro-area and safeguarded (Dyson 2014).

The ordoliberal type of argumentation provided great intellectual coherence to German negotiating positions. At the same time it contained various risks for German negotiating strategy. Its principle-based approach led readily to fundamentalism and the erection of strict 'red lines' in negotiations that constrained room for manoeuvre in crisis negotiations. A strongly didactic style threatened to impede agreement other than on terms that could prove humiliating to others and provoke resentment. It posed the question of whether ordoliberalism can provide a self-contained basis for making complex moral judgements. If one wishes to continue living together in a shared currency area, such judgements necessarily involve reciprocity and the mutual adjustment of interests. The 'solidarity of effort' that is required of debtor states must be balanced by the 'solidarity of mutual insurance' through banking, fiscal and macroeconomic policy union, as well as through operations undertaken by the European Central bank (ECB), such as the Outright Monetary Transactions (OMT) programme. A statesman-like risk management of euro-area crises faced the challenge of making this intellectual leap beyond fundamentalism and, crucially, carrying along public opinion in the process.

Secondly, the assertion of German ordoliberal principles exposes German negotiators to charges of hypocrisy. German negotiators could point to their own long period of wage moderation and structural reforms, especially to labour markets, as examples to others. In particular, the so-called Hartz labour market reforms and the Agenda 2010 reforms, launched by the Red–Green government of Gerhard Schröder in 2003, were presented as models. However, the Merkel governments were vulnerable to charges of a lack of ordoliberalism at home. Germany failed to push through major liberalization of its services sector, including utilities and the professions. Labour market and pension reforms were 'corrected'. Moreover, the rate of public and private investment continued to fall and had been since the 1990s, posing questions about Germany's long-term growth potential. The Merkel governments could be criticized for not practising what they preached, for displaying the procrastination in structural economic reforms against which they cautioned others.

Thirdly, ordoliberalism carried within itself an unresolved tension. The tension is between the notion that ordoliberalism is of universal validity, and within the grasp of all Member States, and the notion of its cultural specificity to Germany. In the first instance, it is a matter of testing whether other Member States are prepared to listen and act on the challenges of competitiveness and fiscal discipline. Crisis management and economic governance reforms were not seen as involving the creation of a 'German' Europe (Schäuble 2013). In the latter case, if ordoliberal principles are the product of a particular German historical experience, then their export to at least some other Member States is an illusion. This tension was brought to the surface as the euro-area crises intensified in 2011–12.

The second distinctive characteristic of German euro-area crisis management is the stress on embedding German power within a united Europe. As interpreted by the German foreign policy community, the lesson of history is that Germany must avoid isolation in Europe. This fear was at the heart of former Federal Chancellor Helmut Schmidt's open letter of rebuke in 1996 to the then president of the Bundesbank, Hans Tietmeyer. He accused Tietmeyer of lack of strategic acumen in his negotiations on the transition to the final stage of EMU (Schmidt 1996). Schmidt represented another distinctive strand in German argumentation and style: the sense of a historically conditioned German moral responsibility to promote peace and stability in Europe through its unification (Schmidt 2013).

In German euro-area crisis management the SPD and the Greens' leadership, which had never been as closely identified with ordoliberalism as the CDU/CSU and the FDP, aligned itself closely with this argument. Their initial support for debt mutualization in the form of Eurobonds, and later of European debt redemption, was framed in these terms (Bofinger et al.. 2011). Germany had to offer an economic policy framework that included a stronger 'growth impulse' to the European economy. This type of argument was more consistent with a neo-Keynesian attitude to euro-area crisis management.

German euro-area crisis management under Chancellor Merkel faced the demanding political challenge of reconciling these two distinctive attributes in defining German national interest. This challenge was by no means new. It reflected a particular German historical pattern. It can be traced back to the disputes about European integration between Chancellor Konrad Adenauer and Federal Economics Minister Ludwig Erhard in the 1950s and early 1960s. It surfaced in the mismatch between Chancellor Willy Brandt's support for a European Reserve Fund in 1969 and the proposals on EMU from his Economics and Finance Minister, Karl Schiller (Dyson and Quaglia 2010, 162–8, 198–201). However, the decisive change with the euro-area crisis management was the vastly higher stakes. In autumn 2012 Chancellor Merkel's backing for the ECB OMT programme against the opposition of the Bundesbank proved a decisive moment. This move contravened a basic strategic principle of German risk management on EMU: namely, to 'bind-in' the Bundesbank so that it could not emerge as an outside critic, inflicting political damage on the federal government. This principle acted to safeguard German ordoliberal values. Her assessment of the risks to Germany from the crisis engulfing Italy and Spain differed from that of the Bundesbank.

Already, in summer 2012, the political commitment of the German federal government to European banking union had opened up a divide within German ordoliberalism. This divide had been nascent since the emergence of the Greek crisis and the spread of the crisis to Italy and Spain in 2011. In particular, Hans-Werner Sinn (2012) had led the way in drawing public attention to the implicit risks for German taxpayers in the TARGET2 imbalance that had widened with the euro crisis. Banking union unleashed the 'war of the economic manifestos', which signalled a sharpening divide between fundamentalist ordoliberals, on the one hand, and a mix of realist ordoliberals and neo-Keynesians, on the other. It also gave rise to the foundation of the *Alternative für Deutschland*. This new party was led by an economics professor from Hamburg and celebrated itself as the party with the greatest concentration of economic expertise in Germany.

The third distinctive characteristic of German euro-area crisis management is its embedding within the dense institutional frameworks of the EU and the euro-area, as well as in the deep integration in banking and financial markets that had followed from freedom of capital movement, the single market in financial services and – not least – monetary union. Intense elite interaction within EU and euro-area institutional frameworks, along with the scale of cross-national capital flows and the depth of financial integration, distinguished the exercise of German hegemonic power from that of creditor-state predecessors like Britain, France and the United States. The exercise of this power is locked into these processes. It has a distinctive path-dependent character, suggesting that other historical models were of limited value in providing clear prescriptions for how to manage euro-area crises. For this reason Merkel's crisis management had a quality of pragmatic learning by doing, of avoiding entrapment in the belief that there was a 'magic bullet'. It rested on a detached attitude of suspicion towards experts who proffered simple answers.

German Asymmetric Negotiating Power

German euro-area crisis management is historically distinctive because it takes place within the framework of European monetary union. Germany is highly exposed to contagion through banking and financial markets, notably bond markets. In creating EMU, via the Maastricht Treaty and then the SGP, Germany acted as a reluctant hegemon, able to shape the terms and outcomes of negotiated agreements but fearful of the future costs of European commitments and of being characterized as seeking a 'German' Europe (Beck 2013; Schäuble 2013). Euro-area crisis management within a monetary union revealed Germany as an acutely vulnerable semi-hegemon. Crisis management created a difficult political tension in German policy preferences. On the one hand, German negotiating positions reflected exogenous policy preferences. They were rooted in domestic factors, notably a deep commitment to ordoliberal principles of economic stability. On the other hand, the negotiating process exposed German negotiators to endogenous preference formation under the influence of joint problem solving within euro-area institutional frameworks. It created a sense amongst fundamentalist ordoliberals that red lines were being crossed (Stark 2013). The asymmetry in negotiating power over outcomes diminished once it became clear to other negotiators that – unlike in 1988–97 – Germany lacked a credible exit strategy (Dyson 2014). It was easier to contemplate Germany exiting a negotiation about creating EMU than exiting, or putting in peril, the euro-area.

How could Germany restore negotiating power? By 2011 it had become clear that the main means of restoring Germany's asymmetric power in EMU negotiations was to take the lead in embracing and spelling out a strategy for moving towards European banking, fiscal, and political union. The creation of credible European institutional arrangements and policy instruments in these areas depended on active German commitment as both the main creditor state and the most systemically significant euro-area Member State. Germany had a credible exit strategy in negotiations on the fiscal compact treaty and on the three key components of European banking union: the Single Supervisory Mechanism, a Bank Resolution Mechanism, and a deposit guarantee scheme. This advantage was less evident in negotiations on reforms to existing institutional arrangements and policy instruments. At the December 2013 European Council meeting it became clear that Member States, disappointed about an outcome on a Bank Resolution Mechanism on German terms, were prepared to try to block German attempts to insert contractual arrangements in structural reform policies into EU law.

Continuity in German negotiating power could be safeguarded in other ways. Her negotiators could credibly stress the hurdle of domestic ratification difficulties (Putnam 1988). These difficulties included the tortuous debates in 2011 inside the FDP, leading to its membership ballot on the ESM in December 2011. Chancellor Merkel faced defections of CDU/CSU and FDP Bundestag members in the 11 crucial Bundestag votes on euro-area rescue programmes during the 2009–13 CDU/CSU/FDP coalition. They reached a peak in 2012, when 33 CDU/CSU/ FDP Bundestag members defected in the November vote on the second Greek rescue programme. Symbolically, the 'Chancellor majority' mattered a great deal. However, the scale of defections from within the Chancellor majority – and the fact that the SPD and Greens could be relied on to vote in favour, or at least abstain – reduced the external value of this bargaining resource. More significant, given the dual-majority structure of German politics, were potential ratification difficulties with the Bundesrat. From May 2010 Merkel could no longer rely on compliant Bundesrat majorities. In 2012 the SPD was able to tie ratification of the fiscal compact treaty and the ESM treaty in the Bundesrat to a new growth-oriented EU programme.

As in previous EMU negotiations, the federal government could stress the domestic ratification difficulties associated with the position of the Bundesbank as opinion-leader in Germany. It continued to place strong strategic emphasis on binding-in the Bundesbank in order to retain the support of German public opinion. German public opinion remained clearly opposed to debt mutualization through Eurobonds, strongly committed to fiscal consolidation, and supportive of public debt reduction. These positions were aligned with Bundesbank policies. Moreover, faced with highly technical and complex arguments, public opinion tended to rally behind long-trusted voices like the Bundesbank. Against this background, Merkel was quick to distance herself from the proposal for Eurobonds and from the proposal of the Council of Economic Advisers (*Sachverständigenrat*) for a European debt redemption scheme. The SPD leadership also muted its early endorsement of debt mutualization.

Most important of all, the federal government could stress the ratification hurdle posed by the Federal Constitutional Court. It could point to the prospect that specific rescue programmes – like that for Greece – and any treaty change – as with the ESM, the fiscal compact treaty, and, in future, the banking resolution mechanism – would trigger appeals to the Court. Moreover, as with the Lisbon Treaty ruling, the Federal Constitutional Court had a reputation for judicial activism. The Court's ruling of September 2011 on the Greek rescue programme and the EFSF and that of September 2012 on the ESM treaty and the fiscal compact treaty served to strengthen the role of the Bundestag in euro-area crisis management. In particular, the Court established the principle of prior approval by the Bundestag budget committee before guarantees were given under the

EFSF. It also ensured that the discretion of the federal government over use of the ESM was tightly circumscribed. The Court's constitutional concerns about the inseparable link between fiscal policy and democratic legitimacy narrowed the scope for German negotiations on European fiscal and banking union, at least without the hurdle of prior treaty change to create a European political union. Hence German negotiators narrowed their horizons to reforms that were feasible within the existing treaty.

Continuity in German negotiating power could be secured through other resources of influence. It could make creative use of the potential for issue-linkage. In October 2010 the Franco–German summit in Deauville involved a trade-off. Germany accepted a permanent collective financial assistance mechanism (the later ESM) in exchange for French concessions on strengthening sanctions under the SGP and for the principle of private-creditor bail-ins to rescue packages. In August 2011 the French-German *communiqué* linked French acceptance of a fiscal compact treaty to German ratification of the ESM treaty. This linkage was politically important in helping expedite Bundestag ratification of the ESM treaty. Also, the SPD Federal Finance Minister, Peer Steinbrück, had been the author of the German 'debt brake' which was uploaded in the fiscal compact treaty. Hence the SPD was inhibited from opposing this linkage.

Once Germany could no longer rely on a credible threat of exit, German negotiating power came to depend more on other bargaining resources. It could use the argumentative and persuasive power of German substantive economic policy expertise. German negotiators sought to ensure an early tabling of rationally constructed German negotiating positions. They provided the first and only contribution to the initial meeting of the task force to the European Council on 'strengthening economic governance in the EU', dated 20 May 2010, with two later contributions in July and September. Notably, this German contribution and the contributions from the other key creditor states – Austria, Finland and the Netherlands – preceded that of the European Commission on 17 June. In this way Germany was able to gain a negotiating advantage in shaping what became the 'Six-Pack' legislation. Already, in March 2010, just after the Greek crisis broke, Schäuble took the lead in proposing a European monetary fund, armed with tough sanctions including expulsion from the euro-area as a last resort. This proposal failed to make headway because the German federal government decided instead that the IMF should play a role in rescue programmes. The IMF could provide a less direct and better tested way of ensuring strict conditionality.

However, the success of this bargaining resource is contingent on the outcomes with which German economic policy expertise comes to be associated, especially in euro-area crisis states. If the policy outcomes were to prove highly dysfunctional in economic and in political terms, then this resource of negotiating power would lose credibility with others. It was especially vulnerable to rising levels of structural unemployment and 'lock-in' to economic stagnation or recession. This risk was above all apparent in southern Europe.

German negotiating power could also rely on two other bargaining resources. German negotiators could seek to ensure that they were better informed about the evolving policy positions of other actors, like the ECB, the European Commission, and other Member States. They could also accumulate and use their expertise in managing the process of negotiations. Negotiating power is strengthened when negotiators possess knowledge – gained from long experience and networks of contacts – about when best to bring forward proposals, and where. It benefits from knowledge of the appropriate institutional forums to use to maximize German influence. By 2011–12 Merkel and Schäuble had evolved cross-national networks that helped strengthen German capacity to exploit these sources of negotiating power.

Cross-national Networks: Delivering on Merkel's Distinctive Approach to Reform

The evolution of cross-national networks to exploit German negotiating capital became a key tool for maximizing German influence in euro-area crisis management and in euro-area institutional and policy reforms. Its evolution can be interpreted as a response to German perception of risks from a weakening in relative negotiating power. It was also a means of facilitating the Chancellor's quiet, business-like leadership in institution building and crisis management, her dislike for being rushed into decisions that had long-term and potentially negative implications.

Chancellor Merkel placed her key personal advisers in central positions at the heart of EU institutions. In May 2011, Jens Weidmann, her personal economic adviser since 2006, was appointed president of the Bundesbank. He ensured a strict ordoliberal voice in the Governing Council of the ECB, though one tempered by greater political sensitivity than his predecessor. In the following month, Uwe Corsepius, the head of her European division since 2006, became Secretary General of the Council of the EU. Then, in January 2012, Jörg Asmussen, the State Secretary in the Federal Finance Ministry responsible for fiscal, macroeconomic policy and European affairs since 2008, moved to the ECB directorate, responsible for EU and international relations. Though an SPD member, who in 2014 returned to take up office in an SPD federal ministry, he enjoyed Merkel's trust as a first-class deal maker. Asmussen, Corsepius, and Weidmann had been at the core of German euro-area crisis management under the previous grand coalition with the SPD and enjoyed Merkel's personal confidence.

Cross-national network building was facilitated by the presence of Klaus Regling as head of the EFSF/ESM; Werner Hoyer, as president of the European Investment Bank; and Horst Reichenbach, as head of the Greece Task Force of the European Commission. From February 2011, the pivotal figure was Nikolaus Meyer-Landrut, head of the Chancellor's European Division, previously deputy to Corsepius, and a career-long EU negotiator who had been involved with the

Amsterdam Treaty. Meyer-Landrut was a key architect of the newly activist German approach to banking, fiscal, macroeconomic and political union from summer 2011 (Kornelius 2013).

Corsepius occupied a special position in cross-national networking. As Secretary General of the Council of the EU, he was the acknowledged master of negotiating timetables of economic reform, especially the fiscal compact treaty and its linkage to the ESM treaty. In particular, Corsepius ensured the closest coordination between his boss, Hermann Van Rompuy, president of the European Council, and Merkel. Not least, he had been the source of ideas on the basis of which Merkel has evolved her new and, in German terms, distinctive views on the future of the EU. Corsepius can be seen as a vehicle for delivering on these views.

Merkel first spelt out her distinctive approach to EU reforms and to euro-crisis management at the College of Europe on 2 November 2010. She returned to this theme in an interview in *Der Spiegel* magazine on 3 June 2013. The Chancellor stressed a strategy of reform in 'small steps'. This strategy was based on her diagnosis of the crisis as a long-term challenge for which there was no single, simple policy cure and as centred in the failures of Member States to take ownership of their commitments within EMU. It was also seen as consistent with the unique nature of the EU so that there was no clear model for how to manage the crisis. The key to her thinking was the emphasis on finding a better way of making Member States take ownership of reforms than relying on the European Commission's surveillance and monitoring.

In her speech at the College of Europe, Merkel proposed the 'Union method' as opposed to the traditional 'Community method'. The speech took many by surprise, inside the CDU as well as in Brussels, including Schäuble. The Chancellor argued that integration and crisis management did not require more formal competences for the EU and a strengthening of the role of the European Commission. Instead, she sought a more powerful role for the European Council. Member States must take responsibility for their own areas of competence in a spirit of solidarity and mutual accountability, secured through a more active European Council. The move of Corsepius to the Council of the EU helped give momentum to this new approach. It meant a strengthening of the role of the Federal Chancellor and had the added advantage of compatibility with French views on European economic governance.

This new approach found expression in her newly found support for regular Euro Summits of heads of state and government in the euro-area. It took the form of German initiative to use the European Council as the venue for the new Euro Plus Pact, monitoring Member States' compliance with commitments on policies to promote competitiveness and growth. The European Commission feared marginalization with Merkel's new approach to crisis management. At the same time, Merkel's intervention did not amount to a simple choice in principle for the Union method. Rather it amounted to assessment on a case-by-case basis in every issue area. Much of the growth and competitiveness agenda, and of fiscal policies, seemed to fall under the Union method. However, European banking union was less easy to integrate into this new approach to economic reform. Even then, however, Merkel was keen to keep the European Commission away from banking union.

In her *Der Spiegel* interview, just three months before the federal elections, Merkel (2013) developed the thinking behind her earlier Bruges speech. The background was her irritation with the European Commission. She had rejected its Green Paper of 23 November 2011 for so-called Stability Bonds as both misconceived and untimely. Merkel now faced an imminent Commission proposal for a Single Resolution Mechanism, under its auspices as the second pillar of European banking union. In her view, the Lisbon Treaty provided a workable framework for euro-area crisis management and economic governance reforms. Both these Commission proposals required treaty change. However, according to Merkel, there was no need to revisit major treaty revision, with its attendant political risks. The challenge was to make the treaty work. Merkel stressed the lack of need to transfer powers to the EU. Notably, this position of Merkel departed from the CDU programme, with its commitment to European political union and the Community method, and she did not seek party endorsement. It was clear that she had no wish to spend her third term on comprehensive treaty revision. More concretely, she had made both Eurobonds and a single banking resolution mechanism dependent on treaty revision. Merkel had no wish to take Germany down either path. Her principal justification for this approach was fear that treaty revision would be used by Member States to evade responsibility for problems of their own making. Merkel repeated her insistence that it was essential to keep up external pressure on Member States to take responsibility for their own problems. She also lacked confidence in the European Commission, whose president, José Manuel Barroso, was an outsider of Merkel's cross-national networking. He did not occupy the position that Jacques Delors had enjoyed under Federal Chancellor Helmut Kohl.

Despite her reservations about the traditional Community method, by mid-2011 the gravity of the crisis, the clear threat of disaster to the EU as crisis spread to Italy and Spain, and the threat of growing German isolation made Merkel aware that a more comprehensive and proactive approach was required. Germany had to use its weight and bargaining resources to set the reform agenda. As conceived in the Chancellor's Office, the agenda had to focus on putting in place a new institutional framework with four pillars: financial stability, fiscal discipline, economic coordination to promote competitiveness and growth, and deeper political union. Fiscal union based on Member States' commitments to structural fiscal balance and banking union were two key elements on which Germany took initiative in 2011–12. The rationale was laid out in the Bundestag speech of 26 October 2011 and the European Parliament speech of 7 November 2012. Unlike in the Bruges speech and the later *Der Spiegel* interview, these speeches offered a more comprehensive historical legitimacy for her proposals.

An important factor in understanding the thinking behind the Bruges speech and the *Der Spiegel* interview was the successive rulings of the German Federal Constitutional Court, notably on the Lisbon Treaty and on the ESM. They underlined the democratic requirement that fiscal policy decisions must be rooted in parliamentary legitimacy. The effect was to strengthen the role of the Bundestag in what were seen as essentially intergovernmental arrangements for collective financial assistance. Any shift to a supranational ESM or the creation of a single banking resolution mechanism would require treaty change that would give new powers to the European Parliament. Merkel feared the political risks of treaty change in the context of painful economic crisis management. She looked to the European Council as the best means of securing a measure of democratic legitimacy for reforms.

What then of German negotiating power in the future? One of the most significant features of the German federal election campaign in 2013 was the dissonance between the top place that the euro-area crises had enjoyed in the work of the second Merkel government and its status as only the fiftieth or sixtieth most significant issue for the public. At the height of the campaign the two central crisis managers – Angela Merkel and Wolfgang Schäuble – were rated as the two most popular German politicians. In particular, Merkel emerged with enhanced reputation. Germany bucked the two key trends in EU politics. An incumbent leader was not only re-elected but also achieved a significantly improved majority over the major opposition party. Also, there had been no discernible shift towards right-wing national populism. This capacity to buck larger trends owed much to benign economic circumstances, with German output returned to pre-crisis levels unlike other Member States. It also coincided with the public's sense that the crisis was made, and had to be solved, outside Germany.

At the same time the ability of the newly founded AfD to come close to the 5 per cent hurdle for Bundestag representation sent a warning signal. It seemed unlikely that Germany could continue to put off a more fundamental debate about 'what kind of Germany, in what kind of Europe'. This debate was likely to come sooner rather than later if the euro-area rescue programmes failed to deliver a return to GDP growth, a fall in dangerously high unemployment levels, and sustainable public finances in states like Greece and Portugal. In such a context Germany would find itself increasingly isolated and increasingly vulnerable to potentially uncontrollable processes of euro-area unravelling. It would be subject to intensifying external pressures to assume more liabilities in crisis management and to reduce its current account surpluses by policies designed to strengthen domestic demand. External pressures – from the United States as well as from EU debtor states – would subject German policy to sharpening critique based on an alternative narrative of 'rebalancing'. It would suggest that Germany's own creditworthiness was at stake and that the price that Germany was paying for the euro was becoming too high.

Conclusion: Germany and the Decline of the Informal Creditor-state Club

The most vivid evidence of increasing German isolation was the relative decline of the informal creditor-state club at the heart of euro-area crisis management. Germany's leading role in organizing creditor-state coordination went back to the EPU in the 1950s (Dyson 2014). As we saw earlier, it derived from the high incentive of numeric disadvantage vis-à-vis debtor states. For practical purposes, during euro-area crisis management the informal creditor-state club was defined by triple-A-rated Member States. Initially activated by the Greek sovereign debt crisis, this group contained Austria, Finland, France, Luxembourg, and the Netherlands, as well as Germany. It accounted for 60.8 per cent of euro-area GDP and 58 per cent of the subscribed capital of the later ESM. However, by 2013 Austria and France had lost their triple-A rating. The informal creditor-state club was reduced from six to four Member States. It accounted for only 36.4 per cent of euro-area GDP and 35 per cent of the subscribed capital of the ESM. Consequently, the political cover that coordinating an informal creditor-state club provided for German negotiators was reduced. Moreover, domestic opposition to fiscal austerity made both Finland and the Netherlands less reliable club members.

References

Beck, Ulrich. 2013. *German Europe*. Cambridge: Polity.

Bofinger, Peter; Gabriel, Sigmar; Steinmeier, Frank-Walter; Özdemir, Cem; Roth, Claudia; Künast, Renate; and Trittin, Jürgen. 2011. 'Der Euro darf nicht an der Engstirnigkeit der deutschen Bundesregierung scheitern'. *Süddeutsche.de*, 8 December.

Bonatti, Luigi, and Fracasso, Andrea. 2013. 'The German model and the European crisis'. *Journal of Common Market Studies*, vol. 51, n. 6: 1023–39.

Dyson, Kenneth. 2010. 'Norman's lament: the Greek and euro area crisis in historical perspective'. *New Political Economy*, vol. 15, n. 4: 597–608.

Dyson, Kenneth. 2014. *States, Debt and Power: Saints and Sinners in European History and Integration*. Oxford: Oxford University Press.

Dyson, Kenneth, and Featherstone, Kevin. 1999. *The Road to Maastricht: Negotiating Economic and Monetary Union*. Oxford: Oxford University Press.

Dyson, Kenneth, and Goetz, Klaus (eds). 2003. *Germany, Europe and the Politics of Constraint*. Oxford: Oxford University Press.

Dyson, Kenneth, and Quaglia, Lucia. 2010. *European Economic Governance: Commentary and Documents, Volume 1 – History and Institutions*. Oxford: Oxford University Press.

Glienicker Gruppe. 2013. 'Mobil, Gerecht, Einig'. *Die Zeit*, vol. 43, 17 October: 30–1.

Heipertz, Martin, and Verdun, Amy. 2010. *Ruling Europe: The Politics of the Stability and Growth Pact*. Cambridge: Cambridge University Press.

Kornelius, Stefan. 2013. *Angela Merkel: Die Kanzlerin und ihre Welt*. Hamburg: Hoffmann und Campe.

Merkel, Angela. 2010. Speech given at the opening ceremony of the 61st academic year of the College of Europe in Bruges on 2 November. Available from: www.bruessel.diplo.de/contentblob/2959854/Daten/945677/ DD_RedeMerkelEuropakollegEN.pdf (accessed 16 March 2013).

Merkel, Angela. 2011a. Stenografischer Bericht. 17/123 Sitzung, Deutscher Bundestag, Berlin, 7 September.

Merkel, Angela. 2011b. Regierungserklärung zum Europäischen Rat und zum Eurogipfel. 17/135 Sitzung, Deutscher Bundestag, Berlin, 26 October.

Merkel, Angela. 2013. 'We are all in the same boat'. *Spiegel Online*, 3 June. Available from: http://www.spiegel.de/international/europe/spiegel-interview-with-angela-merkel-on-euro-crisis-and-arms-exports-a-903401.html (accessed 12 November 2014).

Putnam, Robert B. 1988. 'Diplomacy and domestic politics: the logic of two-level games'. *International Organization*, vol. 42, n. 3: 427–60.

Schäuble, Wolfgang. 2013. 'Wir wollen kein deutsches Europa'. Bundesministerium der Finanzen, 22 July.

Schmidt, Helmut. 1996. 'Die Bundesbank – Kein Staat im Staate'. *Die Zeit*, vol. 46, 8 November.

Schmidt, Helmut. 2013. *Mein Europa*. Hamburg: Hoffmann und Campe.

Schmidt, Helmut, and Fischer, Joschka. 2013. 'Europa braucht einen Putsch!' [Interview] *Die Zeit*, vol. 49, 28 November: 89.

Sinn, Hans-Werner. 2012. *Die Target-Falle: Gefahren für Unser Geld und Unsere Kinder*. München: Carl Hanser.

Stark, Jürgen. 2013. 'Es gibt keine rote Linie mehr'. *Handelsblatt Wirtschafts- und Finanzzeitung*, 26 July.

Chapter 4

Germany's Foreign Policy: Challenges and Opportunities after the Federal Election in 2013

Alister Miskimmon and Luuk Molthof

Introduction

Events since the German federal election of 2013 have brought back to the fore the centrality of Europe in German foreign and security policy. This centrality has two main strands. First, Europe still has the potential to be a region of instability, despite efforts since the end of the Cold War to stabilize the region in a dense web of interlocking institutions. Second, the EU remains centrally important for the reconciliation of differing approaches to international affairs by EU member states. The EU and its members' future influence rests on closer cooperation to chart a future strategy for the EU in a changing international context. The crisis in Ukraine has demonstrated that Germany continues to find balancing EU cooperation in foreign policy with national preferences tough. The grand coalition has found it challenging to balance bilateral interests with Russia with that of its commitments within the EU and NATO since the onset of the crisis in Ukraine. Complicating Germany's response to these challenges is a lack of clarity on Germany's foreign policy trajectory stemming from a reluctance to become more involved in international affairs, particularly in the area of security and defence policy.

Germany is faced with resolving the euro crisis, which it has made its top priority, rather than issues relating to foreign policy, under successive Merkel governments. Foreign relations have focused chiefly on maintaining Germany's economic advantage as a leading export power (Grant 2014; Kundnani 2011). Finding a resolution to the destabilization of Ukraine and pressing concerns in the Middle East and Africa have put German foreign policy under the spotlight. These are, however, not new dynamics in German foreign policy. German foreign policy has been heavily criticized for being inconsistent, preferring to retreat from difficult international crises instead of becoming entangled (Frankenberger and Maull 2011; Miskimmon 2012; Stiftung Wissenschaft und Politik [SWP] and German Marshall Fund of the United States [GMF] 2013). The CDU/CSU-FDP government of 2009–13 resisted new opportunities to deploy aggressive military force alongside its EU and NATO allies. Germany's abstention on the mission to enforce a no fly zone in Libya in 2011 and refusal to consider the deployment of force in Syria illustrated Merkel's reluctance to deploy coercive force. It will be difficult for Germany to maintain a minimalist role in security policy. Angela Merkel and the grand coalition will continue to come under pressure to play a more active role in international affairs from their closest allies. Calls from German President Joachim Gauck for Germany to take on more responsibility in international affairs to reflect Germany's increased influence within the EU are likely to go unheeded in favour of established German preferences for non-military strategies to resolve international disputes, if there is not a sustained German engagement with partners in the EU and NATO to forge a strategic vision for Europe's international role.

'Strategic Abstention', or an Emerging German Foreign and Security Policy?

Angela Merkel's election victory in 2013 was founded on her handling of the euro crisis. Foreign and security policy did not prove an important issue in the election. The government's cautious foreign policy, whilst frustrating Germany's close allies, received support at home. Foreign policy as an area of government focus during the 2009–13 period lost importance in the face of the centrality of the euro-zone crisis. Opportunities to become involved in crisis management operations in Libya and Syria were rejected in favour of a more cautious approach which limited Germany's international commitments and found favour with a majority of Germans favouring a civilian approach to international affairs. Criticism of Merkel and Westerwelle's foreign policy centred on their reluctance to take on the level of engagement in foreign policy mirrored in economic policy. The euro crisis dominated the agenda of the CDU/CSU–FDP government. Foreign and security policy was relegated to secondary policy, reflected in a continued preference in German society to play a less pronounced role in international affairs.

The cumulative impact of Germany's foreign policy under the CDU/CSU–FDP government was that cooperation within the EU and NATO on foreign and security policy was less prioritized in favour of expanding Germany's geopolitical reach to promote its economic interests and work towards building an international human rights-based international order. Looking beyond Europe for partnerships and economic opportunities was a sensible strategic calculation for the German government. The rise of the BRICS to challenge the economic and political dominance of the West, Washington's pivot to Asia, and a sense that, through EU and NATO enlargement, the problems of Europe were largely addressed or contained, were all factors that incentivized a recalibration of German foreign and security policy away from the focus on Europe which had dominated most of the 1990s and 2000s. However, as the crisis in Libya showed in 2011, alongside these developments a more self-confident Germany emerged during the first two terms of Merkel's time in office – one which did not feel compelled to agree to the demands of its partners in France, the UK and the USA to undertake military intervention to address international crises (Hellmann 2011). On the Libya issue, Germany openly opposed the contention of France and the UK that the West had a 'responsibility to protect' citizens in other countries and appeared to agree more with the arguments put forward by China and Russia on the limitations of intervention in the international order (Miskimmon 2012). Germany's main European focus was saving the euro-zone, rather than capacity building in NATO and in the CFSP and expanding Germany's international engagements.

The outcome of Merkel's foreign and security policy on the eve of her third term in office was an assessment that Germany was more confident to pursue its international interests, but less likely to agree with its closest European and transatlantic allies on the use of coercive force in international affairs, thus complicating cooperation within the EU and NATO and security and defence policy. For some, Europe had been demoted in importance without a clear sense of a strategy for German foreign and security policy emerging (Techau 2014). Jan Techau forcefully argued that Germany had taken up a policy of 'strategic abstention' (Techau 2013). Techau's criticism is that Merkel has lost sight of the centrality of Western integration to the detriment of both Germany and the EU and NATO collectively. Another leading German foreign policy commentator, Wolfgang Ischinger, argued, like Techau (2013; 2014), that German foreign policy elites are pursuing a strategy of privileging economic interests whilst trying to limit foreign entanglements. Short-term objectives driven by concerns about the euro crisis and Germany's economic position were displacing strategic considerations of the overall direction of German foreign and security policy (Ischinger 2013). German reluctance to play a more pronounced leadership role within NATO and the CFSP is further complicated by the USA's unwillingness to take the lead. As Bündnis '90/Die Grünen adviser Ann-Kristin Otto has argued,

> The U.S. is trying to lead from behind. Germany, meanwhile, has been pushed into a leadership role by the European debt crisis it still struggles with, and is unlikely to exert that leadership within NATO let alone in the military domain. Quite the contrary, recent decisions in German politics when it comes to military engagement seem to suggest: we take care of security monetarily, somebody else can do the military part. But leadership is no pick-and-choose game (Otto 2012).

This reluctance to take on a leadership role hampers both Germany and the multilateral forums it belongs to. Europeans have not sufficiently engaged in the sort of strategic discussions which would shape the direction of EU foreign and security policy and guide the development of resources and capabilities to achieve it. Whilst France and the UK have sporadically attempted to drive generating better European capabilities, Germany has consistently proved reluctant to play a more leading role, complicating the ability of the 'big three' in the EU to drive a collective response to the EU and NATO's challenges. Doug Stokes and Richard Whitman have reflected the frustration felt in some quarters with regard to Germany's reluctance to become more active in security and defence policy. They argue that 'Germany remains essentially strategically constipated in its unwillingness to assess the appropriate role and power it should play internationally. It remains irrelevant as a potential partner in jump-starting a European debate on European grand strategy' (Stokes and Whitman 2013, 1102).

This perceived lack of German leadership in foreign and security policy within the EU and NATO has come under significant scrutiny. Paradoxically, at a time of significant increase in German economic power through Germany's centrality in the euro-zone, we have not witnessed greater leadership in foreign and security policy (outside of a central role in trying to resolve the Ukraine crisis). Despite receiving buoyant tax revenues, Germany's defence budget has continued to hover unacceptably low compared with leading players in NATO. It was argued that if Germany, which had not experienced the same hardships as other euro-zone countries during the crisis, could not take on additional responsibility in foreign and security policy, serious questions could be asked over its commitment to building EU and NATO capabilities (SWP and GMF 2013).

In this context a debate emerged within Germany concerning what Germany's responsibility in the area of foreign and security policy should be. Driven initially by the Federal President Joachim Gauck, it has been taken on by the new German government as a means to drive discussion within Germany on Germany's emerging international role. At the 2014 Munich Security Conference, Gauck reinforced his understanding of what Germany's responsibility in foreign and security policy meant:

> More responsibility does not mean more throwing our weight around. Nor does it mean 'more going it alone'! On the contrary, by cooperating with other countries, particularly within the European Union, Germany gains influence. Germany would in fact benefit from even more cooperation. Perhaps this could even lead to the establishment of a common European defence (Gauck 2014).

Gauck's comments were mirrored by those of Foreign Minister Steinmeier and Defence Minister von der Leyen. In her conference speech von der Leyen argued that, '… to sit and wait is not an option. If we have means, if we have capabilities – we have the obligation and we have the responsibility to engage' (Von der Leyen 2014). Since the 2014 Munich Security Conference, the German Ministry of Foreign Affairs has launched a review of German foreign and security policy, coordinated by the Körber Foundation (http://www.Review2014.de). The review comes at a time when frustration has been building within and outside Germany over the future course of Germany foreign and security policy. On the day of the launch of the review an opinion poll carried out by TNS Infratest Policy Research for the Körber Foundation indicated that 60 per cent of Germans favoured a reduced international role (Braun 2014; Körber Foundation 2014). The difference in views between a policy elite which has indicated its willingness to consider taking on more responsibility in international affairs and the wider

German population hampers the emergence of a more proactive German foreign policy. The future success of any review of German foreign and security policy rests on Germany's sustained cooperation with its partners in the EU, NATO and the UN and an increased focus in domestic political debates on the centrality of Germany's international role and responsibilities to maintain support for government's policy objectives.

Current Challenges Facing the Grand Coalition

Germany, Russia and Ukraine

For President Gauck, Jan Techau and others, the solution to Germany's foreign policy predicament is closer cooperation with EU and NATO allies as a means to avert any sense of German unilateral intentions and as a means to drive renewed attempts to forge a stronger collective set of objectives in foreign and security policy within the transatlantic community. Events since the federal elections in 2013 have continued to test German foreign policy and its ability to cooperate with its closest allies. The 2014 crisis in Ukraine has put the foreign policy of the grand coalition under significant pressure. On the eve of the grand coalition assuming power it was considered that relations between Germany and Russia could prove to be an area of different accents between the Auswärtiges Amt and the Kanzleramt. Many of the reasons for this stem from SPD policy towards Russia since the Red–Green government 1998–2005. During Chancellor Schröder's two terms in office, German-Russian relations grew in importance (Chivvis and Rid 2009; Schröder 2014). Transatlantic differences over the Iraq war in 2002–3 further strengthened links between Berlin and Moscow, which were reinforced by financial agreements such as the Nord Stream natural gas pipeline project. Whilst Angela Merkel declared she would pursue a more balanced relationship with Washington and be more sceptical than Schröder towards Moscow, Russian-German relations have remained a priority for both states despite the instability in Ukraine. The most significant statement of a new basis for relations came from leading SPD politician Peter Struck who declared that Germany should pursue a policy of 'equal proximity' between Russia and the USA, implying that both bilaterals were of equal importance (Vinocur 2008). This accumulation of tensions between Berlin and Washington and concerns not to allow Moscow to become detached from pan-European politics has meant that engaging and stabilizing Russia is a major concern for Germany (Chivvis and Rid 2009). Closer ties are also seen as being helpful in addressing such issues as Iran's nuclear programme, the situation in Syria, and the Ukraine crisis. However, despite perhaps the best intentions, Szabo has argued that these actions – and a host of others – indicate that the USA and Germany are parting ways, despite the close ties that have bound them since 1945 (Szabo 2004).

After the Cold War, and in the tradition of Willy Brandt's Ostpolitik, the German leadership sought to engage post-Soviet Russia, hoping to integrate it in the new European order. Under Helmut Kohl, Germany was careful not to tread on Russia's toes, adopting a reserved position on the issue of former Soviet states entering NATO. The German leadership was a strong proponent of including Russia in formal meetings of the Group of Seven and World Trade Organization, and when Russia experienced economic recession in the 1990s, Germany was one of the Western nations to provide substantial financial assistance. As a result, the Kremlin came to view Germany as an important partner in the West, earning Germany significant goodwill from Russia (Rahr 2007, 138; Stelzenmüller 2009).

However, after the significant increase in energy prices helped Russia out of its dire economic situation, the Kremlin, under the leadership of Vladimir Putin, dropped its reserved position and started acting as a Great Power. Russia became more confident and less cooperative (Leonard and Popescu 2007, 7; Yoder 2013). Yet Germany, under the then Chancellor Gerhard Schröder, continued the rapprochement policy set out under Kohl as a means to engage Russia and limit the potential for Russian detachment in response to EU and NATO enlargement. The Schröder administration refrained from taking a critical stance on Russia's domestic politics, with Schröder famously calling Putin a 'flawless democrat' in 2004 (Stelzenmüller 2009; Yoder 2013). Under the 2005–9 grand coalition government, Germany's Russia policy was characterized by ambiguity, due to the coalition partners' different views on how to approach Russia. In particular, CDU Chancellor Angela Merkel and SPD Foreign Minister Frank-Walter Steinmeier clashed over the best policy towards Moscow. Whilst Merkel adopted a more critical, human rights-based approach, Steinmeier opted for a continuance of Schröder's policy of 'strategic partnership' with Russia (Stelzenmüller 2009; Meister 2012). The Ukraine crisis has challenged the new grand coalition government not to have Germany's Russia policy once more characterized by dualism between the Kanzleramt and the Auswärtiges Amt. Widely circulated images of Gerhard Schröder celebrating his 70th birthday with Vladimir Putin as the 2014 crisis in Ukraine unfolded brought past differences on how to engage with Russia to the surface at a deeply challenging time for German foreign policy (Spiegel Online 2014).

Despite her cooler attitude towards Russia, the Chancellor is critically aware of the importance of maintaining close relations with Moscow. Not only is Germany dependent on Russia for its energy needs, the bilateral relationship is seen as crucial for managing political stability in (Eastern) Europe (Joetze 2006; Stelzenmüller 2009; Thomas 2014). Even after Russian troops moved into Crimea in February 2014, Merkel was careful not to cut off Berlin's communications with Moscow as a means to help resolve the crisis. Merkel sought to reduce tensions and offer a non-military solution. In her speech to the Bundestag on 13 March 2014 Merkel argued,

We have to find ways to defuse this tense and dangerous situation. The conflict cannot be resolved by military means. I say to everyone who is worried and concerned: military action is not an option for us. Rather, this Government, along with our partners in the European Union and the United States, is pursuing a three-pronged political and economic approach (Merkel 2014).

Although Berlin was initially reluctant to impose strict economic sanctions – because of its reliance on Russian energy supplies – it subsequently played a leading role in shaping the use of further economic penalties as leverage in working towards a diplomatic solution to the crisis. The success of Germany's diplomacy will not only depend on economic leverage, however, but also on Berlin's ability to forge a common EU position and to facilitate the dialogue between Washington and Moscow (Evans 2014; Thomas 2014). Germany's preference to play an intermediary role between the West and Russia has come under significant strain (Chivvis and Rid 2009; *Economist* 2014; *Spiegel Online* 2014; Wagstyl 2014). The crisis in Ukraine will prove to be a test both for the strength of the strategic partnership between Germany and Russia and for the German government's capacity to project a more confident foreign policy within the constraints of its commitments within the EU and NATO.

The Ukraine crisis demonstrates Germany's continued unease in deploying coercive measures in international affairs (Seibel 2014). As Merkel's government declaration in the Bundestag in March 2014 demonstrated, Merkel wished to take a military response off the range of options Germany would consider. Germany was reluctant to consider any militarization of the West's response to the Ukraine crisis. Germany's response has been grounded on seeking to maintain communication with all parties through links with Moscow, discussions with NATO and the USA and within the EU, especially with the renewed focus of the Weimar Triangle of France, Germany and Poland as a means of assuaging Polish concerns about Russia's intentions in Eastern Europe. Multilateralism remains the bedrock of German foreign policy, despite the challenges it presents and expectations it places on German foreign policy makers in crisis management.

Germany and its Relations with Emerging Powers

As stated above, Germany is increasingly seen as displaying aspects of hegemonic leadership in Europe (Beck 2013; Crawford 2007; Paterson 2011). Whilst Europe has remained a focus for Germany's foreign policy since the crisis in Ukraine, Berlin still maintains a keen interest in expanding its global influence to represent its economic interests. However, transferring its regional influence to the global level is complicated as Berlin lacks many of the traditional trappings of emerging great powers such as a large military, nuclear weapons capability and a permanent seat on the United Nations Security Council – there is no political will within the government or in the wider population for a more interventionist security and defence policy. Germany remains influential, however, owing to its geo-economic reach (Kundnani 2011) and its ability to influence through non-military means (Maull 1992). In order to continue to influence, Germany will need to respond. The emerging powers of the BRICS – Brazil, Russia, India, China and South Africa – present a range of powerful new voices within the globalized world that serve both as important markets for German goods and potential economic competitors (Le Gloannec 2001).

Germany and China

Over the past decade, Germany and China have increasingly deepened their 'strategic relationship'. The nature of the relationship is, for now, primarily economic. Whereas the Chinese hope to learn from the technologically advanced German economy, the Germans view China as an important export market for their high-tech goods. Germany is China's most important trading partner in the EU whilst China, in turn, is Germany's most important economic partner in Asia (Heberer and Senz 2011, 674; Kundnani and Parello-Plesner 2012). However, Beijing sees Germany not only as an important economic partner but also as an important potential political partner. Now that Germany is increasingly perceived as Europe's 'reluctant hegemon' (Paterson 2011), the Chinese look to Berlin to influence EU decision-making (Kundnani and Parello-Plesner 2012; Scally 2012). According to Hans Kundnani and Jonas Parello-Plesner (2012, 7), China views Germany as the principal player in getting the kind of Europe it wants. From the potential EU recognition of China's market economy status and the potential lifting of the EU arms embargo against China, Beijing hopes that Berlin will argue China's case in Brussels.

Whilst the Chinese see in Germany an important strategic partner, Germany appears to treat the relationship, first and foremost, as an economic one (Scally 2012). However, this economic relationship brings with it important strategic and political challenges. First of all, the increasingly important trade relationship with China puts Germany's commitment to human rights significantly to the test. In 2007, Angela Merkel insisted that economic interests and human rights are 'one side of the same medal and should never stand in opposition to each other' (Dempsey and Bennhold 2007, par. 3). Yet in recent years, the Chancellor has adopted a quiet approach to human rights in China. In particular after she had received the Dalai Lama in her Kanzleramt in September 2007, an incident that put a huge strain on the relationship (BBC News 2007), Merkel significantly played down her (public) criticism of China's domestic politics (Heberer and Senz 2011; Deggerich, Neukirch, and Wagner 2012; Kornelius 2013; Kundnani and Parello-Plesner 2012). However, the German government contends that its policy towards China is not inconsistent with a foreign policy based on the protection of human rights. Indeed, its policy is based on the premise that trade is conducive to societal change (Kundnani 2013). The argument runs that economic development, through trade, will give rise to an expanding middle class which will eventually demand a say in political affairs. This modernization thesis, most commonly associated with the works of Seymour Martin Lipset, informs not only Germany's China policy, but also that of many other Western states. However, as a recent paper of the SWP and GMF (2013, 34) warns, '... it is equally conceivable that trade contributes primarily to stabilizing a regime, or even gives it new leverage over its own society'. Moreover, years of economic liberalization have so far failed to trigger significant political liberalization in China. The question therefore arises whether German elites truly believe in the modernization thesis or whether the thesis serves as a mere justification for continuing to trade with China – whilst adopting a quiet approach to human rights (Kundnani and Parello-Plesner 2012; Kundnani 2013).

Second, by focusing on the economic element of the relationship, the German leadership risks overlooking the strategic implications of China's rise (Kundnani and Parello-Plesner 2012, 8). The rise of powers such as China, Brazil and India poses an important challenge to Europe's influence in the world. In order for the European powers to maintain a say in global affairs, it is important that they act together, that they develop a strategic vision for an increasingly multipolar world, and that they formulate common strategies towards non-EU powers such as China (Howorth 2010). However, as mentioned above, Beijing is increasingly looking to Berlin, instead of Brussels, to influence EU decision-making, which may undermine the development of a true strategic partnership between the EU and China (Kundnani and Parello-Plesner 2012). If the new government is serious about finding a solution to the EU's waning influence in the world, therefore, it would do well to redirect Beijing to the EU institutions. This is central to arguments made by Techau that Germany's bilateral concerns focusing on German economic advantage have the potential to restrict the EU's ability to plan strategically for shifts in the international order resulting from China and the BRICS's rise (Techau 2014).

Not only is the deepening of trade relations between Germany and China of importance to Europe, it is also of significance to one of Germany's most important allies, the United States. Washington is increasingly concerned about the impact of China's rise on US global and regional influence, about its impact on stability in the Asia-Pacific region, and about its implications for the US-led liberal world order. The United States has responded to China's rise with a policy of both engagement and containment (Christensen 2006; Friedberg 2012). German technological transfers to China not only endanger Germany's own competitive advantage in the long run (Kundnani and Parello-Plesner 2012, 3), but also hamper the containment efforts of its ally. Although the German government does not aim to contain China's rise, as one of the main beneficiaries of the US-led liberal world order, it does stand to lose from a global order led by an autocratic China. Thus, it may be that, in the not too distant future, the German government will have to choose between pursuing its economic interests and preserving the current world order (SWP and GMF 2013).

Wider Issues Influencing German Foreign Policy: Germany and the Middle East

It has been argued that Germany's Middle East policy is relatively underdeveloped (Steinberg 2009). As the situation in Libya, Syria and the continued negotiations surrounding Iran's nuclear programme have demonstrated, Germany's position as a global actor is increasingly challenged by developments in the Middle East and North African region. Considering Germany's 'special relationship' with Israel (Kornelius 2013), the relatively good reputation it enjoys in the Middle East, and its involvement in the Iran nuclear talks, Germany is well placed to take on greater responsibilities in the region and to increase its visibility through cooperation with its EU partners.

Germany and the Israeli–Palestinian Conflict

Germany has a core interest in finding a solution to, or at least preventing a further escalation of, the Middle East conflict, in light of Germany's 'special relationship' with Israel (Perthes 2002). In her speech to the Knesset in 2008, Merkel emphasized the special relationship between Germany and Israel, stating that: 'Germany and Israel are and will always remain linked in a special way by the memory of the Shoah' (Merkel 2008, par. 9). Israel has been crucial in providing political rehabilitation to the postwar Germany. Germany, in its turn, has proven itself committed to safeguarding the security of the Jewish state (Feldman 1984; 1999; 2002; Berenskoetter 2012). Indeed, in her speech, Merkel stated that protecting Israel's security is part of Germany's *raison d'être*. However, Germany also believes in the Palestinian right of self-determination (Overhaus 2002, 6). Berlin is one of the main donors to the Palestinian Territories. In 2008, together with the Palestinian Authority, it launched 'Future for Palestine', a project aimed at improving infrastructure, education and governance in the Palestinian Territories, and in 2010 it established the German–Palestine Steering Committee, aimed at enhancing German–Palestinian cooperation (Auswärtiges Amt 2013; De Vita 2013).

As with many other Western states, including the United States, Germany is in favour of a two-state solution to the Israeli–Palestinian conflict. Not only does Germany have a normative commitment to the Palestinian right to self-determination, it also believes that the development of a Palestinian state is in the interests of Israel's security. However, the Netanyahu administration has so far shown little interest in a two-state solution, as indicated by its settlement policy. This has led to much disappointment among German elites (Overhaus 2002, 6; Berenskoetter 2012; Kulish 2012). Ultimately, however, Berlin's influence over Israel is limited, due to an ultimately unequal relationship between the two countries. As Felix Berenskoetter (2012, par. 6) suggests, the memory of the Shoah 'puts Germany in the bind to make good for past actions that can never be forgiven and, hence, to pay off a debt that can never be paid off'. According to Berenskoetter, this allows Israeli elites to take advantage of the German guilt whilst German elites are restrained from voicing criticism of Israel's policies. The outrage in 2012 over Günter Grass's Israel poem serves as a case in point (Harding and Sherwood 2012). That being said, Merkel's condemnation of Israel's settlement policy reveals that the Chancellor is both willing and able to assume a tougher stance on Israel. The German abstention in the UN vote on Palestine in 2012, meanwhile, reveals that German support of Israel's position can no longer be taken for granted (Sherwood 2011; Kulish 2012; De Vita 2013). With the public becoming increasingly critical of Israel (Berenskoetter 2012; Kulish 2012), the new grand coalition government may be inclined to adopt a more critical approach. The question is whether a tougher stance with Israel will benefit the peace process, or whether it will merely put a strain on the special relationship, further limiting German influence over Israel.

Pressing Issues for the Grand Coalition: Instability in Iraq and Syria and Resolving Iran's Nuclear Programme

The grand coalition will be immediately faced with a number of pressing issues. Germany's involvement in the EU '3+3 negotiations' with Tehran, alongside the USA, Russia and China, over the Iranian nuclear programme have put it at centre stage of global nonproliferation diplomacy (Hanau Santini 2010; Müller 2006; Harnisch 2007). Because of its interest in the security of Israel – and because of its nonproliferation interests more generally – Germany continues to view Iran's nuclear programme as a priority. A key trading partner of Iran, Germany has proven itself an important player in the EU-3+3 talks with Tehran. Berlin has been at the forefront of promoting the EU's policy of 'critical dialogue', a policy that so far has only had limited success (Lane 1995; Müller 2006; *Bergenäs* 2010; Crawford 2010; Nouripour 2011). Iran's nuclear programme was a major aspect of the Red–Green government's foreign policy agenda. Former Foreign Minister Joschka Fischer's concern to prevent Tehran acquiring nuclear weapons was very clear. In a newspaper comment shortly after leaving office, Fischer declared,

> The Iran crisis is moving fast in an alarming direction. There can no longer be any reasonable doubt that Iran's ambition is to obtain nuclear weapons capability. At the heart of the issue lies the Iranian regime's aspiration to become a hegemonic Islamic and regional power and thereby position itself at eye level with the world's most powerful nations. It is precisely this ambition that sets Iran apart from North Korea: Whereas North Korea seeks nuclear weapons capability to entrench its own isolation, Iran is aiming for regional dominance and more (Fischer 2006).

Despite their concern, Schröder and Fischer sought to limit moves towards using military force against Iran to coerce cooperation.

With the recent election of Prime Minister Hassan Rouhani, an opportunity has presented itself for the EU to demonstrate that a cooperative approach towards Iran is the most effective method for securing a nuclear deal. In contrast to his predecessor, Mahmoud Ahmadinejad, Rouhani uses appeasing language and has expressed a willingness to negotiate with the West over a nuclear agreement, most notably in his speech to the United Nations in September 2013 and through his skilful use of social media (*Economist*, 2013a). Iran has fundamentally changed the way it communicates with the West. Contrast former Prime Minister Ahmadinejad's UN speech in 2012 with that of his successor, Rouhani, in 2013. Rouhani's speech to the United Nations General Assembly (UNGA) of 13 September challenged the 'propagandistic and unfounded faith-phobic, Islamo-phobic, Shia-phobic and Iran-phobic discourses', which, he added, posed 'serious threats against world peace and human security … Iran poses absolutely no threat to the world or the region'. A central preoccupation of the Iranian government since Rouhani came to power has been to change the way Iran is talked about in international negotiations. This would allow Iran to re-emerge from the unproductive discourse of the last decade. Chancellor Merkel has continued to support the work of the EU-3+3 and the coordination of efforts by the EU's High Representative for Foreign Affairs and Security Policy. The interim agreement of 24 November 2013 signals a chance to address the fundamental questions concerning Iran's nuclear programme (*Wall Street Journal* 2013; European External Action Service [EEAS] 2013). Israel's prime minister, Benyamin Netanyahu, remains sceptical about Iran's intentions, stating that 'soothing words and token actions will enable it [Iran] to continue on its path to the bomb' (*Economist* 2013b) and this rhetoric has only increased in its critical tone in the aftermath of the 24 November 2013 framework agreement. Iran represents an issue of mutual interest between Washington and Berlin. The USA's cautious optimism about Iran's new course (*Economist* 2013b) has grown since November's agreement, despite considerable domestic criticism of the deal. Although there is certainly a real possibility that Iran is hoping to mislead the West with its moderate language, from the perspective of Washington and Berlin, engagement with Iran should be given a chance. Germany, in cooperation with France and the UK, will have to convince the other players of the benefits of engaging with Iran. The recent developments are a crucial opportunity for both Germany and the EU to increase their profile on the world stage and perhaps a rare example of member state cohesion supporting the work of the High Representative for Foreign Affairs and Security Policy.

The new government will perhaps be most concerned, however, with the developments in Syria and Iraq. After the reported gas attack in Syria in the summer of 2013, calls for a military intervention grew. Although the German government agreed that the use of chemical weapons should not be left unpunished, it ruled out any German involvement in a military strike (*Deutsche Welle* 2013). It appeared that, after Libya, Germany, once again, would stand on the sidelines. Due to the US–Russia deal on Syria's chemical weapons, signed in September 2013, the plan for an intervention lost its momentum. Yet the rise of ISIS in both Iraq and Syria renewed the calls for military action. Although Germany has contributed arms to the fight against ISIS, Berlin has ruled out any direct involvement. However, with many of its allies participating in the airstrikes initiated by the US, the German government is under growing strain to expand its commitment (Borck 2014). While any plans for a more direct contribution are likely to face resistance from the German public, the government is under pressure to make true on its pledge to assume more (military) responsibility in international affairs. The rise of ISIS thus presents the government with an important challenge. Relations with emerging powers and working towards a more stable Middle East require collective responses. The grand coalition's main challenge is to co-opt partners to influence and achieve international objectives (Rummel 1996). Germany's growing position of leadership implies, as Gauck and others have argued, that Germany should play a leadership role in forging agreements to address international challenges, and, if necessary, engage in difficult crisis management to overcome instability. Europe, as the crisis in Ukraine has demonstrated, still has the potential for instability. A common European and transatlantic response requires German engagement and the willingness to shoulder more of the burden. The agency of Gauck, Steinmeier and others to forge a narrative of German responsibility to shape policy discussions within Germany is necessary to overcome domestic reluctance with regard to an increased international role. This would provide a permissive consensus for German policy makers to think more strategically about the challenges facing them (Techau 2014).

Conclusion … More of the Same?

The grand coalition government will continue to be faced with pressures to take more responsibility in a changing world characterized by greater competition for influence. Germany's predicament is that the dominance of the euro-zone crisis in the minds of German politicians, coupled with the potential risks this exposes Germany to, has exacerbated an already existing trend towards greater caution in foreign and security policy among German elites. Nevertheless, influencing the transformation of the international liberal order in the face of the rise of China and other powerful new voices has been a priority area for German elites (Ikenberry 2009). Germany's foreign policy remains limited outside of the multilateral contexts in which it has invested so much energy since 1949, despite the incentives to exploit closer relations with China and Russia. Germany remains tied to NATO and the EU. Whilst the German government still strives for a permanent seat on the UN Security Council, there are no signs that this will become a reality in the near future. Germany will focus on stabilizing the euro-zone and, in the face of calls to undertake greater international responsibility for the maintenance of the liberal order, continue to avoid expanding the use of military force in its foreign and security policy.

The government's power-base within Germany is assured for its term in office. As a grand coalition government it enjoys an unbeatable majority in the Bundestag. The European Parliament elections of May 2014 have reinforced the positions of the CDU and SPD as the dominant parties in Germany. This should allow the government some space to discuss Germany's international role. The review conducted by the Auswärtiges Amt is one step in this direction. Closer cooperation within the EU to outline a comprehensive strategy for the EU's international role requires German leadership not only to overcome its domestic 'culture of restraint' but to demonstrate to its EU partners that Germany is willing to undertake the greater responsibility in international affairs that its power demands. Outlining a more responsible German role within the EU, NATO and the United Nations also has the advantage of maintaining Germany's multilateral trajectory, which has been central to its success since 1949.

References

Auswärtiges Amt. 2013. 'Aid for the Palestinian Territories'. Available from: http://www.auswaertiges-amt.de/EN/Aussenpolitik/RegionaleSchwerpunkte/ NaherMittlererOsten/IsraelPalaestinensischeGebiete/ZukunftPalaestina/ Uebersicht_node.html (accessed 7 November 2013).
BBC News. 2007. 'Merkel angers China on Dalai Lama'. 23 September. [Online]. Available from: http://news.bbc.co.uk/1/hi/world/europe/7008931.stm (accessed 7 November 2013).
Beck, U. 2013. *German Europe*. Cambridge: Polity.
Berenskoetter, F. 2012. 'Germany and Israel: is it friendship?' *International Affairs at LSE* [blog], 10 October. Available from: http://blogs.lse.ac.uk/ideas/2012/10/ germany-and-israel-is-it-friendship (accessed 6 November 2013).
Bergenäs, J. 2010. 'The European Union's evolving engagement with Iran: two steps forward, one step back'. *Nonproliferation Review*, vol. 17, n. 3: 491–512.
Borck, T. 2014. *The True Surprise: Germany's Contribution to the Fight Against ISIS*. Royal United Services Institute. Available from: https://www.rusi.org/ analysis/commentary/ref:C54326261DA356/#.VIWrv6LN6uI (accessed 8 December 2014).
Braun, S. 2014. 'Deutschland soll weniger einmischen'. *Süddeutsche Zeitung*, 20 May. Available from: http://www.sueddeutsche.de/politik/aussenpolitik-deutschland-soll-sich-weniger-einmischen-1.1969285 (accessed 11 November 2014).
Chivvis, C. S., and Rid, T. 2009. 'The roots of Germany's Russia policy'. *Survival: Global Politics and Strategy*, vol. 51, n. 2, 105–22, doi: 10.1080/00396330902860850.
Christensen, T. J. 2006. 'Fostering stability or creating a monster? The rise of China and US policy toward East Asia'. *International Security*, vol. 31, n. 1: 81–126.

Crawford, B. 2007. *Power and German Foreign Policy: Embedded Hegemony in Europe*. New York: Palgrave Macmillan.

Crawford, B. 2010. 'The normative power of a normal state: power and revolutionary vision in Germany's post-Wall foreign policy'. *German Politics and Society*, vol. 28, n. 2: 165–84.

De Vita, L. 2013. *What's Past is Prologue. Germany and Israel: Current State of Affairs of a Complex Relationship*. Annual Conference of the International Association for the Study of German Politics (IASGP), 14 May. London: IASGP.

Deggerich, M.; Neukirch, R.; and Wagner, W. 2012. 'Merkel in China: Berlin's cozy new relationship with Beijing'. *Spiegel Online*, 29 August. Available from: http://www.spiegel.de/international/germany/angela-merkel-trip-to-china-to-test-strength-of-growing-ties-a-852288.html (accessed 7 November 2013)

Dempsey, J., and Bennhold, K. 2007. 'Merkel defends German foreign policy focus on human rights'. *New York Times*, 28 November. Available from: http://www.nytimes.com/2007/11/28/world/europe/28iht-germany.4.8517757.html?_r=0 (accessed 6 November 2013).

Deutsche Welle. 2013. 'Germany won't participate in Syria strike'. 31 August. Available from: http://www.dw.de/germany-wont-participate-in-syria-strike/a-17057769 (accessed 6 November 2013).

Economist. 2013a. 'Talking to Iran: curb your enthusiasm'. 28 September, pp. 16–18.

Economist. 2013b. 'Iranian nuclear talks: jaw-jaw for now'. 28 September, p. 54.

Economist. 2014. 'Which war to mention: Germany's Russia policy'. 22 March. Available from: http://www.economist.com/node/21599410 (available 11 November 2014).

European External Action Service (EEAS). 2013. *Joint Plan of Action*. Geneva, 24 November. Available from: http://eeas.europa.eu/statements/docs/2013/131124_03_en.pdf (accessed 24 November 2013).

Evans, S. 2014. 'Ukraine crisis: Germany's Russian conundrum'. BBC News, 5 March. [Online]. Available from: http://www.bbc.com/news/world-europe-26440560 (accessed 10 November 2014).

Feldman, L. G. 1984. *The Special Relationship Between West Germany and Israel*. Boston: Allen and Unwin.

Feldman, L. G. 1999. 'The principle and practice of "reconciliation" in German foreign policy: relations with France, Israel, Poland and the Czech Republic'. *International Affairs*, vol. 75, n. 2: 333–56.

Feldman, L. G. 2002. 'Germany's policy toward Israel and the Israeli-Palestinian conflict: continuity and change'. *German Foreign Policy in Dialogue*, vol. 3, n. 7: 24–9.

Fischer, J. 2006. 'The case for bargaining with Iran'. *Washington Post*. [Online]. Available from: http://www.washingtonpost.com/wp-dyn/content/article/2006/05/28/AR2006052800978.html (accessed 24 November 2014).

Frankenberger, K.D., and Maull, H.W. 2011. 'Gimme a break: in foreign policy, Germany takes time out from a complex world'. *Deutsche-Aussenpolitik*.

de, *Foreign Policy in Focus*, 494. Available from: http://www.deutsche-aussenpolitik.de/digest/op-ed_inhalt_59.php (accessed 10 November 2013).

Friedberg, A. L. 2012. 'Bucking Beijing: an alternative US China policy'. *Foreign Affairs*, vol. 91, n. 5: 48–58.

Gauck, J. 2014. 'Germany's role in the world: reflections on responsibility, norms and alliances'. Speech by Federal President Joachim Gauck at the opening of the Munich Security Conference on 31 January 2014 in Munich. Available from: http://www.bundespraesident.de/SharedDocs/Downloads/DE/Reden/2014/01/140131-Muenchner-Sicherheitskonferenz-Englisch.pdf?__blob=publicationFile (accessed 24 November 2014).

Grant, C. 2014. 'What is wrong with German foreign policy?' Centre for European Reform. Available from: http://www.cer.org.uk/insights/what-wrong-german-foreign-policy (accessed 6 May 2014).

Hanau Santini, R. 2010. 'European Union discourses and practices on the Iranian nuclear programme'. *European Security*, vol. 19, n. 3: 467–89.

Harding, L., and Sherwood, H. 2012. 'Günter Grass's Israel poem provokes outrage'. *Guardian*, 5 April. Available from: http://www.theguardian.com/books/2012/apr/05/gunter-grass-israel-poem-iran (accessed 7 November 2013).

Harnisch, S. 2007. 'Minilateral cooperation and transatlantic coalition-building: the E3/EU-3 Iran initiative'. *European Security*, vol. 16, n. 1: 1–27.

Heberer, T., and Senz, A. 2011. 'Die deutsche Chinapolitik'. In *Deutsche Außenpolitik*, edited by T. Jäger, A. Höse and K. Oppermann, 673–92. Wiesbaden: VS Verlag.

Hellmann, G. 2011. 'Normatively disarmed, but self-confident'. *IP Journal*, 31 January. Available from: https://ip-journal.dgap.org/en/article/18435/print (accessed 11 November 2014).

Howorth, J. 2010. 'The EU as a global actor: grand strategy for a global grand bargain?' *JCMS: Journal of Common Market Studies*, vol. 48, n. 3: 455–74.

Ikenberry, G. J. 2009. 'Liberal internationalism 3.0: America and the dilemmas of liberal world order'. *Perspectives on Politics*, vol. 7, n. 01: 71–87.

Ischinger, W. 2013. 'German foreign policy lacks big ideas'. *Guardian*, 29 November. Available from: http://www.theguardian.com/business/2013/nov/29/german-foreign-policy-coalition-caution (accessed 11 November 2013).

Joetze, G. 2006. 'Pan-European stability: still a key task'. In *Germany's Uncertain Power: Foreign Policy of the Berlin Republic*, edited by Hanns Maull, 152–65. Basingstoke: Palgrave Macmillan.

Körber Foundation. 2014. *Involvement or Restraint?* Available from: http://www.koerber-stiftung.de/en/international-affairs/special-topics/survey-foreign-policy.html (accessed 11 November 2014).

Kornelius, S. 2013. *Angela Merkel: Die Kanzlerin und ihre Welt*. Hamburg: Hoffmann und Campe.

Kulish, N. 2012. 'Netanyahu chides Germany on UN vote: Berlin's Palestine policy and Israeli settlements cause tensions to rise'. *International Herald Tribune*, 6 December, p. 4.

Kundnani, H. 2011. 'Germany as a geo-economic power'. *Washington Quarterly* 34, n. 3: 31–45.

Kundnani, H. 2013. 'The Ostpolitik illusion'. *Internationale Politik*, 17 October. [Online]. Available from: https://ip-journal.dgap.org/en/ip-journal/topics/ostpolitik-illusion (accessed 6 November 2013).

Kundnani, H., and Parello-Plesner, J. 2012. *China and Germany: Why the Emerging Special Relationship Matters for Europe*. European Council on Foreign Relations. Available from: http://ecfr.eu/page/-/ECFR55_CHINA_GERMANY_BRIEF_AW.pdf (accessed 6 November 2013).

Lane, C. 1995. 'Germany's new Ostpolitik: changing Iran'. *Foreign Affairs*, vol. 74, n. 6: 77–89.

Le Gloannec, A. M. 2001. 'Germany's power and the weakening of states in a globalised world: deconstructing a paradox'. *German Politics*, vol. 10, n. 1: 117–34.

Leonard, M., and Popescu, N. 2007. *A Power Audit of EU-Russia Relations*. European Council on Foreign Relations. Available from: http://ecfr.eu/content/entry/eu_russia_relations (accessed 7 November 2013).

Maull, H. W. 1992. 'Zivilmacht Bundesrepublik Deutschland. Vierzehn Thesen für eine neue deutsche Außenpolitik'. *Europa-Archiv*, vol. 47, n. 10: 269–78.

Meister, S. 2012. 'Entfremdete Partner: Deutsch-russische Beziehungen nach Putins Rückkehr'. *Osteuropa*, vol. 6–8: 475–84.

Merkel, A. 2008. Speech by Federal Chancellor Angela Merkel to the Knesset in Jerusalem on 18 March. Available from: http://www.knesset.gov.il/description/eng/doc/speech_merkel_2008_eng.pdf (accessed 7 November 2013).

Merkel, A. 2014. 'Policy statement by Federal Chancellor Angela Merkel on the situation in Ukraine'. German Bundestag, 13 March 2014. Available from: http://www.auswaertiges-amt.de/EN/Infoservice/Presse/Meldungen/2014/140314-Merkel-Ukraine.html (accessed 24 November 2014).

Miskimmon, A. 2012. 'German foreign policy and the Libya crisis'. *German Politics*, vol. 21, n. 4: 392–410.

Müller, H. 2006. 'Germany and the proliferation of weapons of mass destruction'. In *Germany's Uncertain Power: Foreign Policy of the Berlin Republic*, edited by Hanns Maull, 49–65. Basingstoke: Palgrave Macmillan.

Nouripour, O. 2011. 'Plädoyer für eine eigenständige deutsche Iranpolitik'. *Zeitschrift für Außen-und Sicherheitspolitik*, vol. 4, n. 1: 9–18.

Otto, A-K. 2012. *Assessing Transatlantic Risks: The Erosion of Allied Solidarity*. American Institute for Contemporary German Studies. Available from: http://www.aicgs.org/publication/assessing-transatlantic-risks-the-erosion-of-allied-solidarity (accessed 11 November 2014).

Overhaus, M. 2002. 'A "new" German foreign policy in the Middle East?' *GermanForeign Policy in Dialogue*, vol. 3, n. 7: 5–7.

Paterson, W. E. 2011. 'The reluctant hegemon? Germany moves centre stage in the European Union'. *JCMS: Journal of Common Market Studies*, vol. 49, n. 1: 57–75.

Perthes, V. 2002. 'Germany and the Middle East conflict: what interests, if any?'
    German Foreign Policy in Dialogue, vol. 3, n. 7: 8–15.
Rahr, A. 2007. 'Germany and Russia: a special relationship'. *Washington
    Quarterly*, vol. 30, n. 2: 137–45.
Rummel, R. 1996. 'Germany's role in the CFSP: Normalität or Sonderweg'. In *The
    Actors in Europe's Foreign Policy*, edited by C. Hill, 40–67. London: Routledge.
Scally, D. 2012. 'Flirting with Beijing: while EU leaders struggle with the
    Eurozone crisis, China focuses its attention on Germany'. *Internationale
    Politik*, 30 August. [Online]. Available from: https://dgap.org/en/ip-journal/
    topics/flirting-beijing (accessed 6 November 2013).
Schröder, G. 2014. *Klare Worte: Im Gespräch mit Georg Meck über Mut, Macht
    und unsere Zukunft*. Freiburg im Breisgau: Herder.
Seibel, W. 2014. 'Berliner Versäumnisse'. *Frankfurter Allgemeine Zeitung*, 8
    March, p. 8.
Sherwood, H. 2011. 'Merkel rebukes Israeli PM Netanyahu for failing to advance
    peace'. *Guardian*, 25 February. Available from: http://www.theguardian.
    com/world/2011/feb/25/merkel-rebukes-netanyahu-peace-israel (accessed 12
    November 2013).
Spiegel Online. 2014. 'No special path for Germany in Ukraine crisis'. 5 May.
    Available from: http://www.spiegel.de/international/europe/spiegel-editorial-
    on-the-ukraine-crisis-a-967586-druck.html (accessed 11 November 2014).
Steinberg, G. (ed.). 2009. *German Middle East and North Africa Policy: Interests,
    Strategies, Options*. Berlin:SWP. Available from: http://www.swp-berlin.
    org/fileadmin/contents/products/research_papers/2009_RP09_sbg_ks.pdf
    (accessed 11 November 2014).
Stelzenmüller, C. 2009. 'Germany's Russia question: a new Ostpolitik for Europe'.
    Foreign Affairs, vol. 88, n. 2: 89–100.
Stiftung Wissenschaft und Politik (SWP) and German Marshall Fund of the
    United States (GMF). 2013. *New Power New Responsibility: Elements of
    a German Foreign and Security Policy for a Changing World*. Available
    from: http://www.swp-berlin.org/fileadmin/contents/products/projekt_
    papiere/GermanForeignSecurityPolicy_SWP_GMF_2013.pdf (accessed   6
    November 2013).
Stokes, D., and Whitman, R. G. 2013. 'Transatlantic triage? European and UK
    grand strategy after the US rebalance to Asia'. *International Affairs*, vol. 89,
    n. 5: 1087–107.
Szabo, S. 2004. *Parting Ways*. Washington, DC: Brookings.
Techau, J. 2013. 'Chancellor Merkel's double vision'. *New York Times*,
    19 September.
Techau, J. 2014. *Europe and the Western Alliance Come First!* Paper. Available
    from: http://www.review2014.de/en/external-view/show/article/europe-and-
    the-western-alliance-come-first.html (accessed 11 November 2014).
Thomas, L. 2014. 'As prime Russian trading partner, Germany appears crucial to
    ending crisis'. *New York Times*, 3 March. Available from: http://www.nytimes.

com/2014/03/04/business/international/as-prime-russian-trading-partner-germany-appears-crucial-to-ending-crisis.html (accessed 8 March 2014).

Vinocur, J. 2008. 'Imagining Germany in the middle of the road'. *New York Times*, 15 September. Available from: http://www.nytimes.com/2008/09/15/world/europe/15iht-politicus.1.16154604.html?pagewanted=all (accessed 12 November 2014).

Von der Leyen, U. 2014. Speech by the Federal Minister of Defense, Dr Ursula von der Leyen, on the occasion of the Munich Security Conference, 31 January 2014. Available from: https://www.securityconference.de/fileadmin/MSC_/2014/Reden/2014-01-31-Speech-MinDef_von_der_Leyen-MuSeCo.pdf (accessed 24 November 2014).

Wagstyl, S. 2014. 'Merkel seeks to navigate Germany's complex relations with Russia'. *Financial Times*, 1 May. Available from: http://www.ft.com/cms/s/0/b163e942-d07c-11e3-8b90-0144feabdc0.html#axzz32jNyqsUD (accessed 12 November 2014).

Wall Street Journal. 2013. 'Major powers reach deal with Iran to freeze nuclear programme'. 24 November. Available from: http://online.wsj.com/news/articles/SB10001424052702304791704579215593012329238 (accessed 24 November 2013).

Yoder, J. 2013. *Recent Debates in German Foreign Policy toward Russia*. Annual Conference of the International Association for the Study of German Politics (IASGP), 14 May. London: IASGP.

PART II
The 2013 Election

Chapter 5

Chancellor Merkel, the European Debt Crisis and the AfD: An Analysis of Voting Behaviour in the 2013 Federal Election

Matthias Mader and Harald Schoen

Introduction

On 22 September 2013, Germans elected the federal parliament for the first time since the start of the European debt crisis. This crisis and the austerity and liberalization policies which indebted states were forced to adopt destabilized the governments that implemented them, triggered, at least temporarily, a further deterioration of the living standards in the respective countries, and led to fierce protest by the affected populations, not only against these policies, but also against the German government and Chancellor Merkel. What is more, the European debt crisis also had repercussions on domestic politics in Germany that might have affected voters' decisions in the 2013 federal election. Despite differences on conditions for further financial aid, all parliamentary parties, except the Left Party, affirmed their support of the euro currency and the willingness to help highly indebted European countries (Kietz 2013). Accordingly, Chancellor Merkel could act as a representative who defended Germany's interests on the international scene – and whose popularity probably benefited from some kind of 'rally round the flag' effect. Moreover, the prevailing intra-parliamentary support for the policy of conditional support for indebted euro-zone countries resulted in a campaign in which the European debt crisis and Germany's role in it played a small role (Brost and Schieritz 2013).

Given the considerable number of voters who had mixed feelings about or opposed German financial support for euro-zone countries (see Table 5.1), this campaign focus, at first glance, might come as a surprise. Taking a closer look, it appears to be a consequence, rather than a contradiction. In February 2013, the party *Alternative für Deutschland* (AfD, 'Alternative for Germany') was founded to explicitly address the issue of the crisis and to offer a radical, euro-critic alternative to the German voters. The initiative to found this party came from economic liberals' discontent with the handling of the European debt crisis and the frequently forwarded framing of the policies as being 'without alternative' – hence the name, Alternative for Germany. Instead, this party suggested not to continue the relief efforts for the indebted European countries and to strive for the dissolution of the euro-area into smaller, economically more homogeneous parts. Furthermore, they suggested considering a comeback of national currencies, if economic needs be (Plickert 2013). Moreover, pundits and critics suspected that the party's anti-euro stance was combined with conservative views on social issues – for example, immigration, as well as some kind of anti-partyism (Bangel 2013; Geis 2013; Gensing 2013). Given a eurosceptic party aiming to capitalize on anti-euro sentiment in the electorate, mainstream pro-euro parties, relying on issue-ownership theory (Petrocik 1996), might have avoided highlighting this issue, because otherwise more voters might have learned about the existence and potential viability of the AfD. Instead, mainstream party campaigns focused on other topics. In particular, the Christian Democratic Party (CDU/CSU)[1] made considerable efforts to focus the campaign on its popular leader, Angela Merkel. In comparison, neither the SPD nor any one of the other established parties succeeded in putting one of their favoured issues on the agenda (Mader 2014).

Against this backdrop, the present chapter addresses two interconnected questions regarding vote choice in the 2013 federal election. First, we consider the effects of attitudes towards the European debt crisis on voting behaviour. Given the preceding campaign, we expect that the AfD could capitalize on euroscepticism as well as, on a more abstract level, on economic liberalism and conservative views in the social domain. Second, we analyse the extent to which candidate preference for Chancellor Merkel was the decisive factor in citizens' voting decisions. Given the candidate-centred campaign of the CDU/CSU, the question is whether Merkel's popularity transcended partisan and ideological divides and made her party eligible for larger parts of the German population. To address this question, we explore whether voters decided to vote for the CDU/CSU because they held Angela Merkel in high regard. If so, the second question is why citizens actually preferred Merkel as chancellor. If voters vary in their preference for Merkel depending on the policy predispositions they have internalized, it is hard to argue that Merkel does transcend partisan lines. Put differently, the claim that Merkel does not stand for clearly perceived policy principles would have to be modified.

The remainder of the chapter is organized as follows. In the following section, we outline a model of vote choice and propose several hypotheses. Afterwards, data, measures, and methods are described. We then confront the hypotheses with empirical evidence from regression analyses on how party identifications, policy-related predispositions, candidate orientations, and attitudes towards the European debt crisis affected individual vote choice in the 2013 election.[2] In the final section of the chapter, the key findings are summarized and implications are discussed.

---

1   Although the CDU and CSU are two independent parties, we treat them as one here.

2   An online appendix to this chapter which provides information on methodological details of the statistical analyses is available on the authors' homepages.

Theoretical Framework and Hypotheses

The analysis of the determinants of vote choice in the 2013 German federal election builds on the so-called Michigan approach of electoral research (Campbell et al. 1960). Basically, voting behaviour is most appropriately explained by voters' perceptions and evaluations of political objects. In an augmented model, candidate orientations and issue orientations, as short-term factors, and party attachments, values, and policy principles are the main forces that drive individual vote choice (Miller and Shanks 1996). While the latter can lend stability to voting behaviour, the former are suitable to account for change. Moreover, the impact of these determinants is variable, rather than constant. In particular, within a given political system, campaign communication is quite powerful in shaping the magnitude of the effects. A campaign focusing on a specific policy issue or candidates can increase the impact of issue attitudes and candidate orientations on vote choice. By the same token, a campaign fought strictly along partisan lines is likely to lead to quite strong direct effects of partisan identification on vote choice (Schoen 2004; 2007).

Given our research questions and the specific context of the 2013 German federal election, we rely on a three-stage model of voting behaviour. Vote choice serves as a dependent variable. As proximate determinants, we include candidate orientations and issue orientations. As more distal determinants, we employ political predispositions. In particular, our model comprises party identification and policy principles (Feldman 1988; Peffley and Hurwitz 1985). Both of these are treated as external to the specific election campaign being studied and therefore as potential determinants of candidate orientations and issue orientations (Campbell et al. 1960; Lodge and Taber 2000). This interrelationship implies that analyses of voting decisions which simultaneously include long-term and short-term factors as direct explanatory factors tend to underestimate the total magnitude of the effects of predispositions. As before, campaign communications and other contextual factors must be considered powerful determinants of the magnitude of these effects.

We include four policy-related predispositions which touch on issues central to German politics in recent years and especially to the 2013 election campaign. They are also consistent with more general findings on the ideological structure of citizens' belief systems (Arzheimer 2009; Jagodzinski and Kühnel 1994; Mair 2007). One supposedly important predisposition concerns the question of how much the state should get involved in economic affairs and refers to the socioeconomic dimension of political conflict (economic liberalism). A second important predisposition relates to the potential trade-off between economic and environmental concerns. Should the government actively try to protect the environment even if this has a negative effect on the economy? In Germany, this issue is closely entwined with the question of the nuclear power phase-out, the Green Party having been founded on this broader policy issue. A third overarching issue relevant in German politics in recent years concerns the adherence to traditional conceptions of morality (moral traditionalism). This predisposition touches on issues such as the role of religion in everyday life, gender roles, same-sex marriage, and abortion. It touches on the second dimension in two-dimensional conceptions of the policy space, the libertarian–authoritarian dimension. Finally, we consider a predisposition here that is concerned with ethnocentrism and, more specifically, the question of immigration.

Given the characteristics of the 2013 federal election campaign, we are in a position to form some expectations concerning the role of the short-term factors we are particularly interested in here, attitudes towards the European debt crisis and candidate preferences. Vote choice for the AfD should have been strongly influenced by the attitudes towards the European debt crisis, given the issue's prominence in the party's campaign. Voters who were critical of helping indebted European countries should have been more likely to vote for this party. In contrast, attitudes towards the crisis should have no, or only small, effects on the vote choice for the other parties. Citizens who preferred giving financial aid might have been somewhat more likely to vote for the CDU/CSU, the FDP, the SPD, the Greens, or the Left Party. All of these parties were in favour of such measures. At the same time, they did not campaign on the issue, which is why we expect the effects to be negligible. Positive evaluations of the respective candidates should have made it more likely for citizens to cast their vote for the respective parties. Given the CDU/CSU's candidate-centred campaign, candidate effects should have been especially strong in the case of Angela Merkel. If the pundits commenting on the campaign and the likely election outcomes were right, this Merkel effect should be widely prevalent in the German electorate. Specifically, voters without party loyalties should then be more likely to vote for the CDU/CSU.

The long-term factors can be expected to influence vote choice both directly and indirectly. As for the direct effects, the identification with a party should have substantially increased the probability of voting for this party. At the same time, the identification with one party might have decreased the probability of voting for another party, especially if it belonged to another party bloc. Taking into account general, rather than campaign-specific, party positions allows the formation of hypotheses about the direct effects of policy-related predispositions. The CDU/CSU is traditionally market-oriented, morally conservative, and rather sceptical about liberalizing immigration policies. Consequently, high scores on economic liberalism, moral traditionalism and ethnocentric views might have increased the likelihood of voting for this party. In light of the recent change in policy position regarding the nuclear energy phase-out, we refrain from formulating a hypothesis for the predisposition concerning the environment. The FDP is a strictly market-oriented party, for which environmental concern has only secondary significance. Although the sociopolitical profile has been less visible in the past, the FDP has retained the image of a rather liberal party in this dimension. Thus, economically liberal, environmentally unconcerned voters opposing morally traditional or intolerant policy positions should be more likely to cast their ballot for the FDP. The SPD and the Left Party are traditionally welfare-state-oriented. Opposition to economic liberalism might thus have made citizens more inclined to vote for the SPD and the Left Party. Given the liberal welfare and labour market reforms in the Schröder era, the SPD vote might not be affected as starkly as the Left Party vote. The Green Party has always been driven by environmental concerns. Consequently, citizens who share these concerns should have been more likely to vote for the party. Finally, the AfD has taken an economically liberal position and has been in favour of stricter immigration rules. Accordingly, economic liberalism and ethnocentric preferences might have been conducive to making citizens more likely to vote for the AfD.

Concerning the effects of party identification and policy-related predispositions on candidate preferences, we first anticipate that party identifiers were substantially more likely to have a preference for their party's candidate to be the future chancellor. Regarding policy-related preferences, we would suspect that voters holding predispositions in accordance with the traditional political values of a given party and its candidate should enhance the likelihood of supporting that party's candidate. Yet pundits have commented on both candidates as being somewhat atypical representatives of their parties, that is, Ms Merkel as less conservative in the social domain and Mr Steinbrück as economically more liberal than their parties. This might have made it difficult for voters to reconcile their perceptions regarding the party's and the candidate's values and thereby weakened the link. What's more, Chancellor Merkel has been characterized as a national mother figure (*Mutter der Nation*, or just *Mutti*) who stands beyond specific political content. In light of these circumstances, we refrain from formulating explicit hypotheses for the policy-related predispositions on candidate preferences and treat this part of the analysis as exploratory.

Data, Measures, Methods

The analysis utilizes data from a web survey of a random sample drawn from an online recruited panel, conducted as part of the German Longitudinal Election Study (GLES). 1012 German citizens eligible to vote completed the questionnaire. The survey was in the field from 6 to 21 September 2013. Given the fact that the online panel the sample was drawn from is not representative for the German population, the results of the empirical analysis can only cautiously be generalized. To attenuate the problem of non-representativeness, we use a representative weight that uses information from the 2012 micro census regarding gender, age, education, and regional origin.

The analysis of the determinants of vote choice is confined to voters of the four political parties that entered the German Bundestag (CDU/CSU, SPD, the Greens, and the Left Party) plus voters of the FDP and the AfD, which failed to leap over the 5 per cent-threshold by a small margin. Respondents who indicated a voting intention for another party, did not give an answer to the question on intended vote choice, or indicated that they did not intend to vote are excluded from the analysis.

To measure party identification, the standard indicator was used. Since only a few reported a party identification with the FDP, the Left Party or the AfD, these variables were not included in the following analysis.[3] Additionally, a dummy variable indicating voters with no party identification was included. This allows us to analyse whether some party garnered a disproportionately large share of votes from this growing part of the electorate. Three of the four policy-related predispositions we consider here were measured with two survey items, and one predisposition was measured with three items. Using a five-point Likert scale ranging from 1 (*strongly disagree*) to 5 (*strongly agree*), respondents were asked to indicate their level of agreement with nine statements. To aggregate the respective items to one predisposition measure we computed factor scores from a confirmatory factor analysis.[4] Given the large amount of variation in single-item measures that is due to short-term events, this procedure ensures a greater validity of the measures given the theoretical concepts.[5]

To capture candidate orientations, respondents were asked whether they preferred Angela Merkel, Peer Steinbrück, or neither as Chancellor of the Federal Republic. Two dummy variables were created identifying respondents with a preference for the CDU/CSU candidate and the SPD candidate. Finally, the issue positions concerning the European debt crisis were measured with an item that asked respondents to rate their disagreement with the statement that Germany should help other European countries which are in financial trouble during this time of the European debt crisis.[6] Respondents were able to grade their answer on a five-point Likert scale ranging from 1 (*strongly disagree*) to 5 (*strongly agree*).

As Table 5.1 shows, roughly one third of the survey respondents who have given a valid answer are affiliated with the CDU/CSU, and one third with the SPD. The last third consists of respondents identifying with the Greens, some other party, or exhibiting no long-term party loyalty. At the same time, roughly a majority of respondents prefer Angela Merkel as chancellor, while only a third has a preference for Peer Steinbrück. Provided candidate effects on vote choice, Ms Merkel's popularity might have gained the CDU/CSU some

---

3   See section 1 of the online appendix for the German question wording.

4   See section 2 of the online appendix for information on the exploratory and confirmatory factor analysis we conducted.

5   In addition to these variables capturing partisan and policy-related predispositions, we include a measure tapping into voters' general ideology. Although we run the risk of over-controlling for the predispositions' effects, we do this to avoid two potential sources of omitted-variable bias. One potential source is our inability to include variables measuring party identification for the Left Party and the AfD due to small-N problems. A second one stems from the conceptual overlap between ideological affiliation and policy-related predispositions. To gauge citizens' ideological position, the standard measure of self-placement on a left-right continuum was used.

6   In the following, we use the term 'opposition to financial aid' as a synonym for these attitudes.

additional votes. The short-term factors are clearly structured by long-term party affiliations. Virtually all CDU/CSU identifiers favour Ms Merkel (94 per cent) and most SPD partisans support Steinbrück (73 per cent). This difference in support probably stems from the fact that Steinbrück was controversial on the SPD's left wing for supporting the liberal welfare and labour market reforms of the Schröder chancellorship. While more Green identifiers support their natural coalition partner's candidate, Steinbrück, than the opponent's candidate, the unaffiliated segment of the respondents shows a stronger preference for Merkel. While only about four in ten respondents oppose giving financial aid to indebted European countries, it is noteworthy that opposition is considerably higher among respondents without party identification. As for the policy-related predispositions, the majority of the respondents show low support for economic liberalism.[7] A majority also rejects moral traditionalism. Finally, more respondents are ethnocentrically predisposed and environmentally concerned than not.

Table 5.1   Descriptive statistics of party-political explanatory factors

	All Respondents	**By Party Identification**			
		CDU/CSU	**SPD**	**Greens**	**No PI**
Party Identification					
PI CDU/CSU	33%				
PI SPD	29%				
PI Greens	11%				
No PI	17%				
Other	10%				
Candidate Preference					
Merkel (CDU)	51%	93%	16%	27%	46%
Steinbrück (SPD)	31%	3%	73%	41%	20%
Neither	18%	4%	12%	32%	33%
Issue Orientation					
Opposition to Financial Aid[a]	38%	38%	33%	26%	49%

Notes: Weighed data. Due to rounding, percentages may not add up to 100. [a] Reported are percentage of respondents indicating moderate or strong opposition to financial aid.

7   See Table A2.4 of the online appendix for detailed descriptive statistics on the policy-related predispositions.

In the following section, we present results from a series of regression models designed to confront the hypotheses formulated in the preceding section with empirical evidence. We first turn to the short-term determinants of voting behaviour, namely attitudes towards the European debt crisis and candidate orientations. Given the causal order assumed by the Michigan model, these are proximate concepts that have an (exclusively) direct impact on vote choice. To quantify these effects, results of a multinomial regression analysis are presented, in which vote choice is the dependent variable and both short- and long-term psychological factors are included as explanatory variables. Including the latter in this stage of the analysis is necessary because we would otherwise overestimate the impact of the former.

In a second step, we analyse whether long-term factors – namely, party identification and policy predispositions – drive both short-term factors and electoral choice. Given the causal order implied in our model, they can, as more distal concepts, influence vote choice in two ways. First, they can shape the proximate concepts which in turn exhibit an impact on voting behaviour. We analyse this mechanism empirically by regressing the short-term factors on the long-term factors. Second, they can have a direct effect. Citizens then decide to vote for a given party because they identify with this party or because it is most consistent with their policy predispositions. To gauge these direct effects, we present further evidence from the multinomial regression analysis in which vote choice is the dependent variable and both short-term and long-term determinants are included. Finally, to give an impression of the long-term factors' total effects, vote choice is regressed on the long-term factors exclusively.[8] While we discuss the findings in an untechnical fashion here, methodological details and all results, including regression tables, can be found in the online appendix.

Results

We first turn to the question of whether attitudes towards the European debt crisis had an impact on electoral choice. For the sample we analyse here, Figure 5.1 shows the predicted probabilities of vote choice for the AfD, the CDU/CSU, the SPD, and the Greens, conditional on opposition to financial aid and differentiated by partisan and candidate preferences.[9] As the slopes of the graphs in the second diagram of Figure 5.1 show, strong opposition to financial aid made a voting

---

8   For more details on this simple strategy of analysing mediation effects (and its drawbacks), see Baron and Kenny (1986) and Hayes (2009).

9   We have chosen the combinations of partisan and candidate preference we present depending on empirical significance. For instance, since the number of CDU/CSU identifiers who do not have a candidate preference for Ms Merkel is negligible (see Table 5.1), we do not present predicted probabilities for this group here. Voting decisions for the FDP and for the Left Party are completely unaffected by opposition to financial aid, which is why we do not present analogous graphs for these parties here.

decision for the AfD considerably more likely within the group of citizens without any party identification. In fact, given the virtually inexistent combination of support for granting financial aid to indebted European countries and AfD vote choice, opposition to this practice can be understood as a necessary condition for voting for this party. Thus, citizens that preferred either Merkel or Steinbrück for some other reason than their position on handling the European debt crisis were willing to support a party clearly in opposition to both the CDU/CSU and the SPD. In contrast, additional analyses suggest that this effect was much smaller, albeit still present, among citizens who also had a party identification with one of the established parties.[10]

Figure 5.1   Effects of attitudes towards the European debt crisis on vote choice for the CDU/CSU and the AfD (continued overleaf)

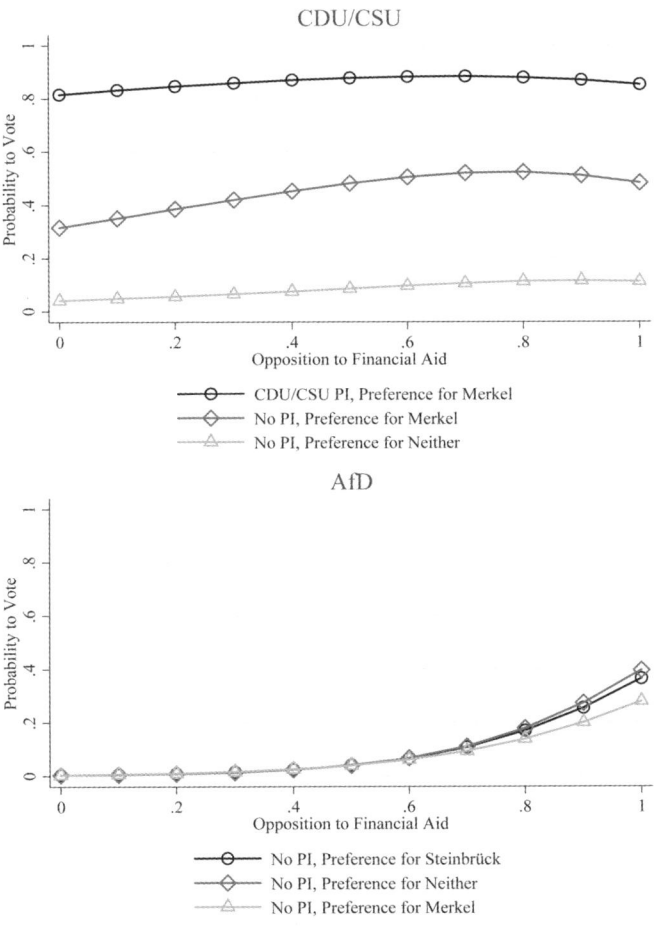

10   See Figure A3.1 of the online appendix.

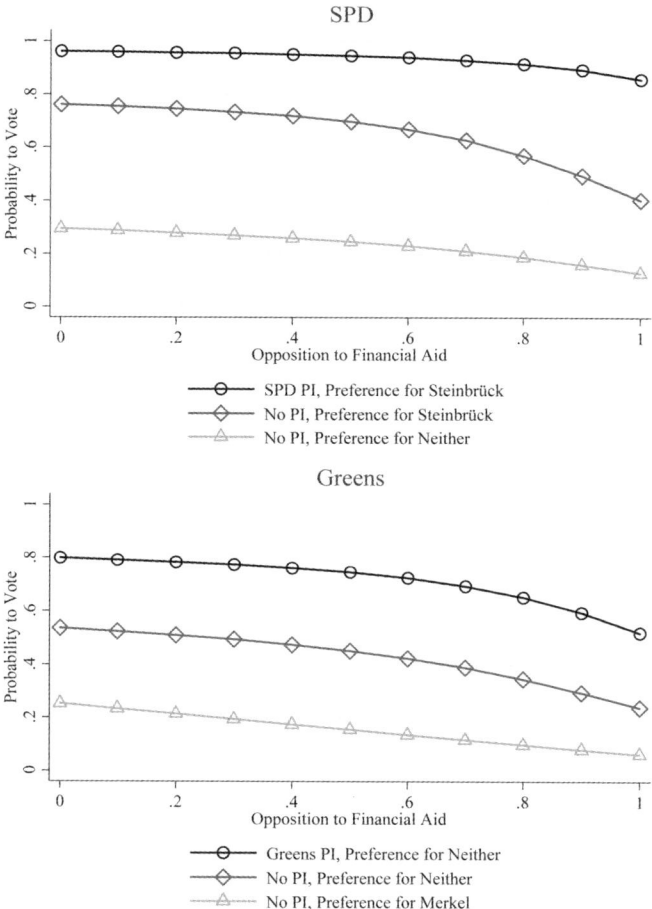

Notes: The graphs show predicted probabilities to vote for the respective party. They are derived from the multinomial regression model reported in Table A3.1 of the online appendix. Predictions are for citizens with average values for the policy predispositions and ideology.

As the other three diagrams show, opposition to financial aid only weakly, if at all, affected decisions to vote for the CDU/CSU, the SPD, and the Greens. There is some evidence that citizens without party identification but with a preference for Chancellor Merkel were somewhat more likely to cast a vote for the CDU/CSU at low and medium levels of opposition to financial aid (see first diagram of Figure 5.1). Similarly, it seems that in some subsections of the electorate strong opposition to financial support for indebted euro-zone countries tended to decrease the likelihood of casting votes for the SPD and the Green Party (see third and fourth diagram of Figure 5.1).

In sum, the evidence supports our hypothesis that only the vote choice for the AfD was influenced by attitudes towards the European debt crisis. This expectation was founded on the issue's menial role in all of the established parties' campaigns and the latter's agreement on this issue. If there is no real difference concerning an issue between parties perceived to be legitimately eligible, it is impossible to base one's decision on this criterion.

Table 5.2   Changes in probabilities of CDU/CSU and SPD vote choice

	CDU/CSU Vote Choice			SPD Vote Choice		
	PI CDU/CSU	PI SPD	No PI	PI CDU/CSU	PI SPD	No PI
Merkel	+36	+30	+41	-8	-20	-8
Steinbrück	-30	-5	-5	+39	+23	+44

Notes: Entries show changes in probabilities of voting for the CDU/CSU or SPD for voters with average values for the policy predispositions and opposition to financial aid. Results are calculated from the regression model reported in Table A3.1 of the online appendix. For example, the entry '+36' in the first row of the table indicates that voters who had a candidate preference for Merkel were 36 percentage points more likely to cast a CDU/CSU vote than a voter without a preference for either candidate.

We now turn to the second short-term factor, citizens' candidate preferences. The graphs in Figure 5.1 referring to the CDU/CSU and the SPD, respectively, show the considerable impact candidate orientations appear to have had on voting decisions for these parties. The difference between the probability of voting for a party for citizens without party identification decisively depends on whether they have a preference for that party's candidate (dark-grey line with diamond-shaped markers), or not (light-grey line with triangular markers). To give a more detailed impression of these patterns, Table 5.2 shows differences in the predicted probabilities depending on citizens' candidate preference.[11] Irrespective of party identification, voters were much more likely to vote for a party if they had a preference for that party's candidate. This effect seems to have been strongest for citizens who had no longstanding party affiliation. Our data analysis suggests that in this subgroup of the electorate the probability of voting for a candidate's party was more than 40 percentage points higher when citizens had a corresponding candidate preference than for citizens without a candidate preference. At the same time, a preference for one of the two party's candidates decreased the probability of voting for the opposing party. This effect appeared to be especially pronounced for party identifiers preferring the opposing party's candidate.

---

11   The absolute predicted probabilities were calculated for average levels of policy predispositions, ideology, and opposition to financial aid. See Table A3.2 of the online appendix for the estimates and the 95 per cent confidence intervals.

In the second step of the analysis, we consider the long-term factors underlying the short-term orientations. Figure 5.2 lends support to our expectations concerning the value-related underpinnings of the attitudes towards the European debt crisis. As the positive slopes of the graphs indicate, economic liberalism and ethnocentrism both appear to have increased citizens' opposition to granting financial aid to indebted euro-zone countries. While both predispositions' effects can be considered substantial, the evidence suggests ethnocentrism to have been more important in determining citizens' attitudes.[12] Moreover, net of predispositions, CDU/CSU identifications, but not others, appear to inhibit citizens from holding sceptical views about financial aid to indebted euro-zone countries.

Candidate preferences seem to have been shaped by party identification and policy predispositions as well. Not surprising is that an identification with the CDU/CSU raised the likelihood of preferring Merkel. Voters that identified with the CDU/CSU were 49 percentage points more likely than voters without any party identification to prefer Angela Merkel (94 per cent vs 45 per cent probability to support), while voters that identified with the SPD were 50 percentage points more likely to prefer Peer Steinbrück (72 per cent vs 32 per cent).[13]

More interesting are the results concerning the way policy-related predispositions affect candidate preferences. As an illustration, Figure 5.3 shows the likelihoods of the respective candidate preferences for citizens without party identification and different levels of policy predispositions. To begin with, support for economic liberalism was effective in decreasing the probability of preferring Mr Steinbrück. This finding fits nicely with the notion of Peer Steinbrück being a candidate of a party that endorses the welfare state, but is at odds with his image as an economically liberal politician. Moreover, liberal preferences in the socioeconomic domain and low levels of environmental concern somewhat increased the likelihood of holding a preference for Ms Merkel. These findings are in accordance with traditional images of CDU/CSU leaders. The (tentatively) negative relationships between a preference for Ms Merkel and high scores on moral traditionalism and ethnocentric views do not fit nicely with these traditional images. Taken together, these findings suggest that Ms Merkel's attempts to modernize her party by giving up long-held (conservative) positions has affected citizens' perceptions. In turn, it appears to have gained her some support from non-traditional CDU/CSU supporters.[14]

---

12   The regression coefficient of ethnocentrism equals .52 (p<.001), the coefficient of economic liberalism equals .22 (p=.006). Both variables were rescaled to 0–1. See Table A4.1 of the online appendix.

13   Changes in probabilities were calculated for voters with average values for the policy predispositions and opposition to financial aid from the regression model reported in Table A3.3 of the online appendix.

14   The (tentative) relationships reported in this paragraph hold, irrespective of whether party attachments are controlled for or not.

Figure 5.2   Effects of economic liberalism and ethnocentrism on attitudes towards the European debt crisis

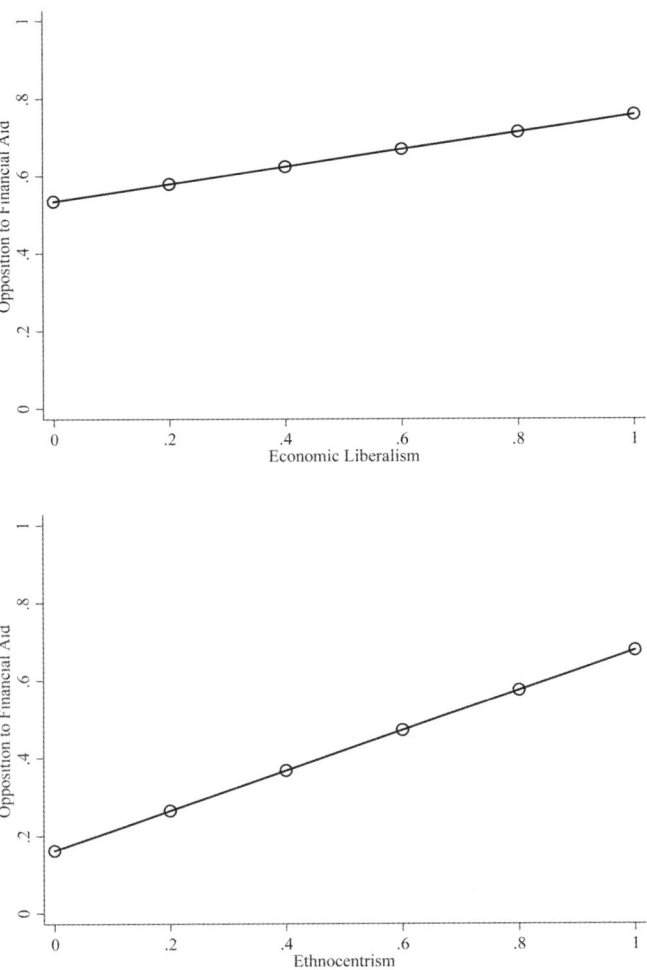

Note: The graphs show predicted values of opposition to financial aid. They are derived from the regression model reported in Table A4.1 of the online appendix. Predictions are for citizens with average values for the policy predispositions and ideology and with no party identification.

Figure 5.3   Effects of policy-related predispositions on candidate preference (continued on facing page)

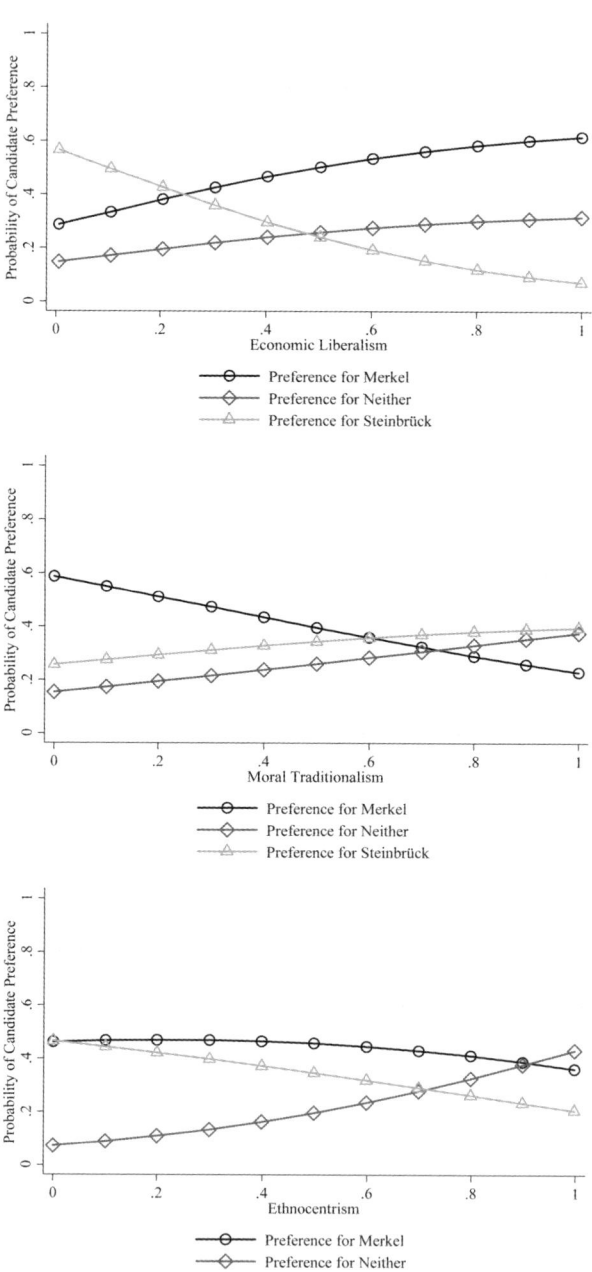

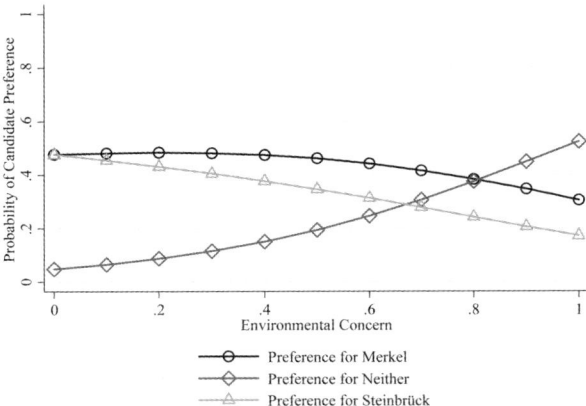

Notes:

Notes: The graphs show predicted probabilities to vote for the respective party. The graphs are derived from the regression model reported in Table A3.3 of the online appendix. Predictions are for citizens with average values for the other policy predispositions and ideology and with no party identification.

So far, we have demonstrated that candidate preference and issue orientations affected vote choice and were shaped by party attachments and policy-related predispositions. Put differently, the latter appear to have affected vote choice indirectly, via short-term orientations. To get a fuller picture of the role of party attachments and policy-related predispositions, we estimated models of vote choice in which these variables were the only predictors. This strategy permits us to gauge the total – the sum of direct and indirect – effects of the long-term factors.

The results can be interpreted as evidence for considerable total effects of the long-term factors. This is especially true for party identifications because they do not only shape candidate and issue orientations but also affect vote choice directly. In effect, they make a considerable (total) difference in vote choice. Similarly, policy-related predispositions had a considerable (total) impact on voting behaviour. As the results on voters without party attachments in Figure 5.4 illustrate, at least economic liberalism, ethnocentrism, and environmental concern appear to have had an influence on vote choice. Moral traditionalism, however, did not. Starting with environmental concern, as the forth diagram of Figure 5.4 shows, voters who are environmentally concerned are most likely to choose the Greens. This pattern is in accordance with traditional notions of party competences. The same holds for the finding that support for economic liberalism decreased the probability to cast votes for the SPD and, somewhat stronger, the Left Party, whereas it somewhat increased support for the CDU/ CSU and the FDP. It is remarkable, however, that economic liberalism did not affect vote choice for the AfD. By contrast, the AfD vote was strongly driven by general preferences concerning immigration that are rooted in some kind of ethnocentrism. Thus, while the AfD leadership attempted to present the party as being pragmatic and non-ideological regarding the European debt crisis, many of its voters appear to have cast their vote predominantly because of the denouncement of European solidarity implied in this policy position.

Figure 5.4   Effects of policy-related predispositions on vote choice (continued on facing page)

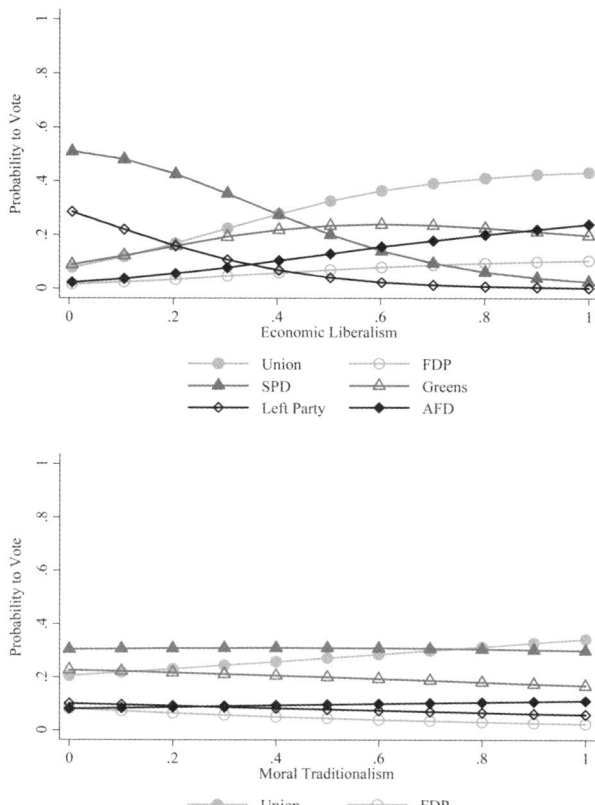

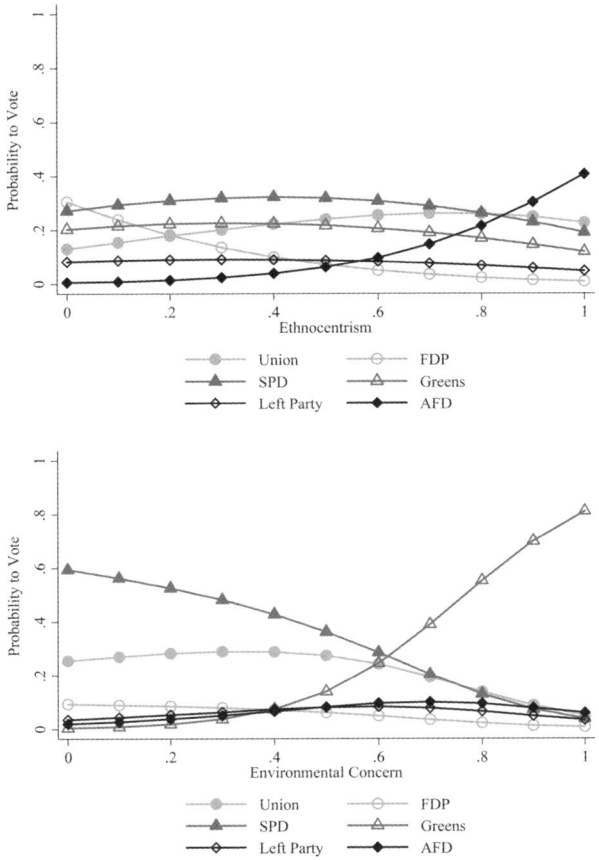

Note: The graphs show predicted probabilities to vote for the respective party. The graphs are derived from the regression model reported in Table A3.3 of the online appendix. Predictions are for citizens with average values for the other policy predispositions and ideology and with no party identification.

The findings concerning the explanatory factors of vote choice can, in conjunction with the distribution of these factors in the electorate, be used to draw some tentative conclusions regarding the driving forces of the aggregate electoral outcome. Most importantly, the greater popularity of Angela Merkel, not only among the respective party identifiers but also among the politically unaffiliated, was most likely a driving factor behind the strong electoral result of the CDU/CSU. In contrast, despite an apparent majority of voters critical of economic liberalism, the SPD, as the traditional welfare-oriented party, could not capitalize on this majority preference prevalent in the German public. The unpopular (especially among the unaffiliated voters) candidate, Steinbrück, appears to have been unable to draw votes away from the economically liberal segment of the electorate and to have failed to mobilize the socioeconomically left-leaning citizens to a sufficient degree. The relative success of the AfD, in contrast, can be attributed to the German citizens' critical stance on granting financial aid to indebted European counties. At the same time, longstanding loyalties towards one of the established parties and the majority's rejection of economic liberalism might be considered factors that have prevented an even greater electoral success of the AfD.

Conclusion

Building on an augmented version of the Ann Arbor model, this chapter discussed several determinants of individual voting decisions in the 2013 federal election in Germany. In particular, opposition to a continuation of German financial aid to EU member states affected by the debt crisis was the single most important explanatory factor of vote choice for the euro-critic AfD. Thus, despite the campaign tactics of parliamentary parties, in the 2013 federal election, attitudes towards European integration appear to have played a role in vote choice. By implication, European integration seems to have the potential to become an issue cleavage, as in other European countries (De Vries 2007; Schoen 2008). Taking a closer look at AfD voters and euro-criticism, the main driving forces appear to be socially conservative views rooted in latent ethnocentrism and exclusive solidarity, rather than economic liberalism.[15] This finding, which fits nicely with post-functionalist accounts of European integration (Hooghe and Marks 2009; Kriesi et al. 2008), suggests that there will be a considerable potential for euro-critic parties in Germany, particularly under the conditions of an ongoing European debt crisis.

Consequently, the future of the euro-critic AfD will be dependent on how the European debt crisis and its salience in German politics develops. If a constant or increasing share of the electorate opposes a continuation of German financial aid to EU member states affected by the debt crisis and the salience of the issue increases, the electoral results of the AfD in the upcoming elections might improve. Yet, whether these conditions will be met depends, inter alia, on the responses of other parties to the crisis as well as to the AfD. What is more, the AfD's programmatic mix of economic liberalism and social conservatism might prove viable and attract votes from various subsections of the electorate. Alternatively, it might lead to intra-party strains and endanger the party as unitary actor. Certainly, these implications point once more to the complex interplay of party behaviour and positions, political discourse about them, and voters' preferences and behaviour.

As for the vote decisions for the established parties, party identifications and candidate preferences were the most important determining factors. As far as we could account for them, party identifications appear to have had an equally substantive effect across all parties. This finding is interesting with regards to the

---

15   As noted above, these results are somewhat preliminary in that they are derived from a small empirical basis. Further research utilizing richer data is needed to reaffirm this finding.

SPD, as it was not clear before the election whether this party would be able to mobilize their supporters given the somewhat controversial candidate and because of the dominating opponent, Chancellor Merkel. The analysis of the candidate preferences revealed that, as far as the individual level is concerned, their effects were in large part comparable as well. At the same time, considering the fact that most voters preferred Angela Merkel to be the next chancellor, these equally sized effects on the individual level translate into many more CDU/CSU voters than SPD voters in the aggregate. Interestingly, the analysis points to the fact that this popular support for Merkel can only weakly be traced back to subparts of the population with distinct policy preferences in line with traditional guiding principles of Christian Democratic policies. What's more, Merkel appears to have clearly been the candidate of the economically liberal segments of the German populace. The opposite is true for the candidate of the SPD, Peer Steinbrück. The analysis did not lend evidence that Steinbrück attracted much support from beyond traditional supporters of his political camp, namely identifiers with the SPD or the Greens.

An important implication can be drawn from this analysis concerning the role of candidates for the electoral outcome. Although the SPD tried to raise several policy issues in their campaign, candidate preferences remained an influential determinant of voting. It appears that, against the popularity of Angela Merkel, it was impossible for the SPD to draw attention away from the candidates to the issues. The comparison of Ms Merkel and Peer Steinbrück remained the most commented on feature in the run-up to the election and an important determinant of individual vote choice. In this situation, it was probably a mistake by the SPD to nominate a candidate who did not really fit the policy profile advertised in the campaign. In contrast, it appears that (by now) voters have a reasonably clear picture of the policy principles Ms Merkel stands for and that she can capitalize on this image by gathering votes beyond those parts of the population loyal to the CDU/CSU anyway. Maybe the next election will show whether an SPD candidate who clearly stands for traditional Social Democratic values and who can authentically claim to be a candidate of the left is better suited to challenge Chancellor Merkel.

The reliability and generalizability of our results is subjected to restrictions stemming from the data source. First, the online survey we used was not drawn from a representative sample but from an online access panel. In these panels, the politically interested and better educated are typically overrepresented (Faas and Schoen 2006; Sanders et al. 2007). Second, it was conducted before the election actually took place, which is why we analysed intended and not actual voting behaviour here. Third, due to data limitations, we were not able to utilize completely appropriate measures in all instances or even to include relevant concepts, for example, anti-partyism. Finally, analyses of cross-sectional data are no tests of causality but yield only correlational evidence. Thus, it is not possible to foreclose that, for instance, attitudes towards the European debt crisis are influenced by candidate preference or vice versa. It is also possible that the policy-related principles that we assumed to be causally parallel to a party identification are in fact subordinate to it.

These limitations point to the need for further research on the underlying long-term psychological phenomena that drive short-term perceptions and behaviour. Most importantly, analyses of panel data would allow testing of central theoretical assumptions of electoral research. The *pre*dispositional character of, for example, policy-related predispositions might be confirmed in such an analysis, but it might also turn out that they are in fact influenced by campaign events and communications. This kind of research necessitates not only conducting panel surveys, but also employing reliable and valid measures of more general psychological constructs such as policy predispositions, social identities, or personality traits in these surveys.

References

Arzheimer, Kai. 2009. 'Ideologien'. In *Politische Soziologie: Ein Studienbuch*, edited by Viktoria Kaina and Andrea Römmele, 83–108. Wiesbaden: VS Verlag.

Bangel, Christian. 2013. 'Der Populisten-Spagat der AfD'. *Die Zeit*, 13 September.

Baron, Reuben M., and Kenny, David A. 1986. 'The moderator-mediator variable distinction in social psychological research: conceptual, strategic, and statistical considerations'. *Journal of Personality and Social Psychology*, vol. 51, n. 6: 1173–82.

Brost, Marc, and Schieritz, Mark. 2013. 'Die Rechnung, bitte!' *Die Zeit*, n. 33, 8 August.

Campbell, Angus; Converse, Philip E.; Miller, Warren E.; and Stokes, Donald E. 1960. *The American Voter*. Chicago: University of Chicago Press.

De Vries, Catherine E. 2007. 'Sleeping giant: fact or fairytale? How European integration affects national elections'. *European Union Politics*, vol. 8, n. 3: 363–85.

Faas, Thorsten, and Schoen, Harald. 2006. 'Putting a questionnaire on the web is not enough – a comparison of online and offline surveys conducted in the context of the German federal election 2002'. *Journal of Official Statistics*, vol. 22, n. 2: 177–90.

Feldman, Stanley. 1988. 'Structure and consistency in public opinion: the role of core beliefs and values'. *American Journal of Political Science*, vol. 32, n. 2: 416–40.

Geis, Matthias. 2013. 'Wie rechts ist die "Alternative für Deutschland"?' *Die Zeit*, n. 17, 18 April.

Gensing, Patrick. 2013. 'Populismus-Vorwurf gegen Anti-Euro-Partei'. *Tagesschau Online*, 14 April. Available from: http://www.tagesschau.de/inland/antieuro104.html (accessed 12 November 2014).

Hayes, Andrew F. 2009. 'Beyond Baron and Kenny: statistical mediation analysis in the new millenium'. *Communication Monographs*, vol. 76, n. 4: 408–20.

Hooghe, Liesbet, and Marks, Gary. 2009. 'A postfunctionalist theory of European integration: from permissive consensus to constraining dissensus'. *British Journal of Political Science*, vol. 39, n. 1: 1–23.

Jagodzinski, Wolfgang, and Kühnel, Steffen M. 1994. 'Bedeutungsinvarianz und Bedeutungswandel der politischen Richtungsbegriffe "links" und "rechts"'. In *Wahlen und politische Einstellungen im vereinigten Deutschland*, edited by Hans Rattinger and Oscar W. Gabriel, 317–67. Frankfurt: Peter Lang.

Kietz, Daniela. 2013. *Politisierung trotz Parteienkonsens: Bundestag, Bundesrat und die Euro-Krise*. Gütersloh: Bertelsmann Stiftung.

Kriesi, Hanspeter; Grande, Edgar; Lachat, Romain; Dolezal, Martin; Bornschier, Simon; and Frey, Timotheos. 2008. 'Globalization and its impact on national spaces of competition'. In *West European Politics in the Age of Globalization*, edited by Hanspeter Kriesi, Edgar Grande, Romain Lachat, Martin Dolezal, Simon Bornschier and Timotheos Frey, 1–22. Cambridge: Cambridge University Press.

Lodge, Milton, and Taber, Charles S. 2000. 'Three steps towards a theory of motivated political reasoning'. In *Elements of Reason: Cognition, Choice and the Bounds of Rationality*, edited by Arthur Lupia, Mathew D. McCubbins and Samuel L. Popkin, 214–63. Cambridge: Cambridge University Press.

Mader, Mattthias. 2014. Notes on recent elections: The German Federal election, September 2013. In *Electoral Studies*, vol. 34, n. 2: 353–356.

Mair, Peter. 2007. 'Left-Right orientations'. In *The Oxford Handbook of Political Behavior*, edited by Russell J. Dalton and Hans-Dieter Klingemann, 206–22. Oxford: Oxford University Press.

Miller, Warren E., and Shanks, J. Merrill. 1996. *The New American Voter*. Cambridge: Harvard University Press.

Peffley, Mark A., and Hurwitz, Jon. 1985. 'A hierarchical model of attitude constraint'. *American Journal of Political Science*, vol. 29, n. 4: 871–90.

Petrocik, John R. 1996. 'Issue ownership in presidential elections, with a 1980 case study'. *American Journal of Political Science*, vol. 40, n. 3: 825–50.

Plickert, Philip. 2013. 'Mehr als Euro-Kritik'. *Frankfurter Allgemeine Zeitung*, 15 April.

Sanders, David; Clarke, Harold D.; Stewart, Marianne C.; and Whiteley, Paul. 2007. 'Does mode matter for modeling political choice? Evidence from the 2005 British Election Study'. *Political Analysis*, vol. 15, n. 3: 257–85.

Schoen, Harald. 2004. 'Der Kanzler, zwei Sommerthemen und ein Foto-Finish. Priming-Effekte bei der Bundestagswahl 2002'. In *Die Bundestagswahl 2002. Analysen der Wahlergebnisse und des Wahlkampfes*, edited by Frank Brettschneider, Jan W. van Deth and Edeltraud Roller, 23–50. Wiesbaden: VS Verlag.

Schoen, Harald. 2007. 'Campaigns, candidate evaluations, and vote choice: evidence from German federal election campaigns, 1980–2002'. *Electoral Studies*, vol. 26, n. 2: 324–37.

Schoen, Harald. 2008. 'Turkey's bid for EU membership, contrasting views of public opinion, and vote choice. Evidence from the 2005 German federal election'. *Electoral Studies*, vol. 27, n. 2: 344–55.

Chapter 6

Party Manifestos in Representative Democracy: Strengthening the Electoral Connection?

Margret Hornsteiner

Introduction

The crisis of political parties has been a major theme in party literature since the 1970s. Many party scholars have been studying the weakening ties between parties and society and the challenges arising for (party) democracy in Germany, just as in many other West European countries (Chapter 9 infra).

On the one hand, these challenges are related to the external linkage of parties and their changing role in the electorate. The share of voters who identify with a particular political party is decreasing, levels of political trust are eroding (Dalton and Wattenberg 2000; Biehl 2013) and electoral turnout in German elections has fallen from about 90 per cent in the 1970s to 71.6 per cent in the 2013 election. Although specific circumstances of certain elections such as an uneventful, de-mobilizing campaign – for instance in 2009 and 2013 – can explain low turnout rates, Poguntke concludes that the overall erosion of turnout indicates a growing distance between the electorate and political parties (Poguntke 2012, 11–12). As a consequence of these changes, the electoral environment in which parties compete has become far more uncertain. The German election of 2013 clearly stands out in this respect. The index of volatility illustrates the rise of new parties such as the Alternative for Germany (AfD) and the Pirate Party as well as the demise of established parties such as the FDP since it summarizes the net changes of parties' aggregated electoral strength from one election to the next (Pedersen 1979). While aggregate volatility had remained relatively constant between the 1980s and the early 2000s (on average 7.2) it increased sharply in the 2009 election (12.6). In 2013, volatility reached its highest level in German postwar history (15.4). Hence, parties' strength in one election has become a less meaningful predictor of their strength in the following election. Poor leadership performance and unsuccessful government participation carry a much higher risk of severe electoral defeats. The German party system, therefore, seems to have lost much of the stability which used to be its defining characteristic (Smith 2003).

On the other hand, arguments about party decline are related to parties as organizations and their internal linkage. Party membership, in this respect, reflects the strongest connection between parties and society. Despite some regional and inter-party differences, party membership in Germany has been in marked decline, too, both in absolute terms and in relation to the size of the electorate (Van Biezen and Poguntke 2014; Saalfeld and Hornsteiner 2014). The two large parties, the CDU/CSU and SPD, are particularly affected by this downward trend. The declining strength of parties' membership organization has led many authors to raise questions about 'the end of the mass integration party' (Jun, Niedermayer and Wiesendahl 2009). New emerging organizational types such as the cartel party (Katz and Mair 1995) or the electoral professional party (Panebianco 1988) no longer rely on a large party membership as their main source of finance and campaigning. Instead, parties serve primarily as electoral vehicles for maximizing votes. Ideological differences become less important. In the case of German parties, Korte notes that 'it is becoming increasingly difficult to clearly distinguish between the policy of the Social Democrats and those of the Christian Democrats as both seek to appropriate for themselves what is referred to as the new centre' (Korte 2003, 112). Moreover, it is argued that grassroots members become marginalized in intra-party decision-making and are substituted by a strong party leadership and professional party managers. Findings from a recent survey among German party members support the decline of intra-party participation and involvement in policy development. As Spier shows, only a very small part of the membership of German parties participates actively in policy formulation (Spier 2011, 109).

From a party perspective on the German 2013 election, the signs of a weakening connection between parties and society seem clear. How does this party decline affect the functioning of representative democracy? Parties are, after all, the key intermediate actors and provide an active link between citizens and government institutions. According to Müller, it is the parties that make representative democracy and accountability work (Müller 2000). By formulating programmes, parties offer policy alternatives to the voters. Responsive parties, who transfer the citizens' interests in governmental action, are central to representative democracy and the concept of mandate theory. In contrast to the literature on party decline that suggests a weakening linkage between parties, society and the state, I will argue that German parties used their manifesto in the 2013 election to strengthen the electoral connection in representative democracy.

Representative Democracy and Mandate Theory

The underlying concept of modern representative democracy is the necessary correspondence of citizens' interests, party policy profiles and acts of government, as captured by mandate theory and the responsible party model (Downs 1957; Powell 2000; Däubler and Benoit 2013). In a synthesis of mandate theory literature, McDonald et al. find several conditions for a government mandate to emerge (McDonald et al. 2004, 4). The first criterion is party distinctiveness, that is, at least two parties have policy profiles distinct from one another. Secondly, voters become informed and recognize the policy profiles of each party. Thirdly, voters cast their ballots on the basis of the party policy profile they prefer to see implemented. Furthermore, the majority of votes having the same preference are then translated via the electoral system, designating the party to form a government. Finally, the party in government carries out its policies announced at the time of the election. Mandate theory, as a normative theory, provides a justification for representative democracy. As a descriptive theory, it provides an account of how democracy works and thus a framework for empirical testing.

The 2013 German election impressively renews questions about party decline and party change. By tracing recent developments in the German party system, it becomes evident that the environment of parties has become increasingly unstable. This chapter focuses on party manifestos, which are an integral part of party activity and have been described in terms of a 'life cycle' (Dolezal et al. 2012) since manifestos are present both in the pre- and post-electoral phase. Although manifestos constitute just one way of ensuring the necessary linkage between citizens and the state, they can be observed at various analytic levels of party politics: at the electoral level, at the organizational level, and at the governmental level. The manifesto perspective thus allows for testing three conditions of mandate theory outlined above. In addition, the intra-party dimension of manifestos sheds light on organizational aspects of party responsiveness with regard to manifesto formation. These four conditions are:

1. Party distinctiveness: do parties provide distinct policy profiles in their manifestos?
2. Voter information: how do voters perceive manifestos?
3. Manifesto formation: how are manifestos written?
4. Party policy commitment: to what extent are manifesto pledges fulfilled in government?

Before each of these dimensions is studied in detail, I shall provide a short introduction to the importance of manifestos in party politics and elections.

The Centrality of Party Manifestos

Like most of their European counterparts, Germany's median voter is a far more critical citizen than in the past (Dalton and Weldon 2005; Norris 1999). Not only do more of the voters use the ballot box to respond to the parties' performance in the past legislative period, many of them take an interest in the parties' manifesto pledges and make use of voting advice application. Election manifestos and pre-electoral assurances about the parties' future coalitional intentions have thus become ever more important signals that parties are sending out to the media and the electorate.

In the legalistic context of German parties, party programmes play a central role as the Party Law explicitly demands that parties 'specify their aims in political programmes' (see par. 6.4 below). The two main types of programme that can be identified in the German context are general, more long-term programmes (*Grundsatzprogramme*) and election programmes or manifestos (*Wahlprogramme*). Some authors regard governing programmes (*Regierungsprogramme*) as a third distinctive type (Kaack 1971), but this distinction has become increasingly blurred since both the CDU/CSU and the SPD refer to their recent manifestos as 'governing programmes'. As opposed to general programmes, manifestos are issued regularly before each election. In the German multi-level context of regional, general and European elections, parties issue several manifestos at relatively short intervals. In 2013, for example, the Greens issued five election manifestos in all: one for the national election, three for state elections in Lower Saxony, Hesse and Bavaria, as well as a manifesto draft for the European elections in 2014. In their account of German manifestos, Kercher and Brettschneider observe a certain 'programme inflation' among parties, publishing up to 12 versions of their manifestos: a long version, a short version, versions in foreign languages, as well as audio and video versions (Kercher and Brettschneider 2013, 269). The fact that parties make such great efforts when it comes to manifestos points to the importance parties attribute to these documents.

As detailed above, the manifesto perspective puts emphasis on four conditions of mandate theory: party distinctiveness, voter information, manifesto formation and pledge fulfilment. By analysing each of these dimensions, I will show that the German parties use their manifestos to strengthen the electoral connection.

Policy Distinctiveness: Party Positions on Key Dimensions of Political Space

During the last two decades, manifestos have become a widely acknowledged source of information in party literature. The influential work of the Comparative Manifesto Group (Budge et al. 2001; Klingemann et al. 2006) established a new subfield of manifesto research, which was accelerated by the development of new quantitative methods for analysing political text. In this body of literature, manifestos are regarded as the only representative and authoritative statements of party policies (Volkens 2002, 2). Hence, they constitute an ideal basis for inferring policy positions. Figures 6.1a and 6.1b are based on computer-assisted quantitative content analysis, using the Wordfish scaling model (Slapin and Proksch 2008) to derive estimates of the parties' policy positions from their manifestos between 1994 and 2013. The analysis includes the manifestos of CDU/CSU, SPD, FDP, Green and Left Party. For 2013, the Pirate Party was included, whereas the AfD's manifesto was too short to allow for reliable estimates. Parties' positions were estimated on the two most important policy dimensions that define German ideological space (Pappi 1984; Kriesi et al. 2006).

Figure 6.1a provides estimates over time about the parties' position on the dominant dimension of partisan conflict in German politics, macroeconomic and welfare policies. Low values indicate positions in favour of market liberalism;

high values indicate a position in favour of state intervention. In 2013, all major parties hold distinct policy positions on this dimension. The Left Party is clearly the most left-wing party in terms of economic and welfare policies whereas the FDP has consistently been the party with the strongest emphasis on economic liberalism. As the analysis of manifestos shows, the Pirate Party is the only party which has no distinct profile on economic issues. Its position is very close to the SPD because of great similarities, for example on the issue of minimal wages. The distance between the FDP and CDU/CSU is much lower in 2013 than between the CDU/CSU and SPD. Nonetheless, the poor result of the Liberals at the poll did not allow Angela Merkel to continue her preferred government coalition.

Over time, the most noticeable changes can be observed for the SPD. Between 1994 and 1998, the party moves towards a centrist position under Gerhard Schröder. His commitment to labour market and social policy reforms, the so called 'Agenda 2010', is clearly reflected in the data in Figure 6.1a. The party's 1998 manifesto shows a clear move towards the CDU/CSU's position in these policy areas. After its significant electoral losses of 2002 and 2005, the SPD's manifestos reveal a return to more traditional policies, a move which accelerated in 2005 after the Social Democrat Gerhard Schröder stepped down as chancellor. Subsequently the party suffered from a credibility gap with a more left-wing programme on the one hand and the party's centrist candidates for the chancellorship, Frank-Walter Steinmeier (in 2009) and Peer Steinbrück (in 2013), on the other, both having been key architects of the Schröder government.

Figure 6.1a also shows the dilemma of the Greens in economic policy. The party moved sharply to the centre in its 2002 manifesto and has since returned – equally sharply – to more pronounced left-wing positions. The latter development has led to criticism of the party leadership by the more conservative regional branches of the party, for example in the state of Baden-Württemberg. In 2013, the Greens' proposal for raising income taxes turned against them as these plans would have hit their own relatively wealthy supporters.

The Christian Democrats' gradual modernization under Angela Merkel's leadership after defeat in the Bundestag election of 2002 is reflected in Figure 6.1a, and even more strongly in Figure 6.1b, which covers the areas of home affairs and justice, including many issues relating to social liberalism such as legislation to tackle discrimination against women, immigrants, disabled or gay people. These changes from 2005 were moderate but are clearly reflected in the data in Figure 6.1b. Nevertheless, the CDU/CSU remains the most traditional party in the party system as far as home affairs, civil liberties and justice are concerned. The Pirate Party marks the most 'liberal' party on this dimension, emphasizing data security and privacy policies. It is also noteworthy that the SPD's move back to a more left-wing position in economic policies has been accompanied by a similar move towards more liberal positions in the areas of home affairs and justice, where its 2013 manifesto is much closer to the FDP's than to any other party.

Figure 6.1b also shows that the FDP's manifestos did respond to the party's growing struggle to distinguish itself from the Christian Democrats. In the

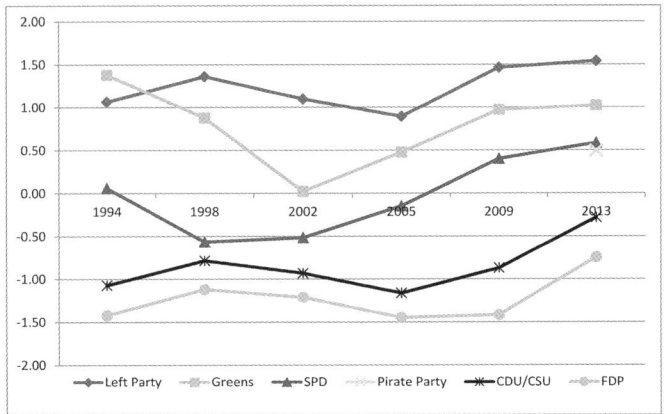

Figure 6.1a   Parties' Right-Left Positions in Macroeconomic and Welfare Policies, 1994–2013

Source: Author's own estimates based on the parties' election manifestos using the Wordfish method. Parties' positions are estimated on the basis of word frequencies on a single dimension. For a detailed description of the method see Slapin and Proksch (2008). Absolute values are not comparable across dimensions.

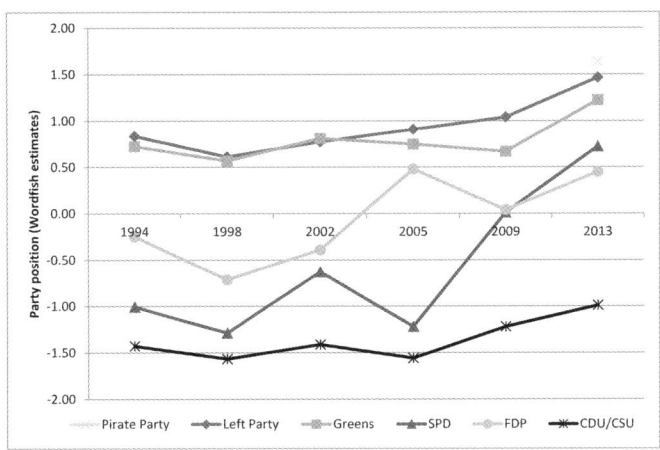

Figure 6.1b   Parties' Right-Left Positions in Home Affairs and Justice Policy, 1994–2013

Source: Author's own estimates based on the parties' election manifestos using the Wordfish method. Parties' positions are estimated on the basis of word frequencies on a single dimension. For a detailed description of the method see Slapin and Proksch (2008). Absolute values are not comparable across dimensions.

field of home affairs and justice, the party moved back to the liberal end of the spectrum between 1998 and 2005 and in its 2013 manifesto. Nevertheless, given the dominance of economic policy in the party's image, these changes were not reflected in voters' responses. The FDP's strong programmatic commitment to civil liberties was not recognized by the vast majority of voters, partly because the party did not have charismatic leaders associated with this dimension.

In sum, the Wordfish analysis of manifestos from 1994 to 2013 shows that parties do hold distinct policy positions on key dimensions of German policy space. Only the Pirate Party's position in economic and social policies differs in being almost identical to that of the SPD. This could be one explanation for the party's meagre election result in 2013. The development of the CDU/CSU shows a gradual modernization under the leadership of Angela Merkel, in which the party's position moves closer to the centre. However, in 2013, the CDU/CSU is still the most traditional party with regard to home affairs and justice.

Voter Information about Manifestos

Party manifestos play a prominent role in electoral campaigns. They serve as a means of communication and set forth a party's ideas and proposals for action in order to convince readers to vote for the party in the upcoming election. This view of manifestos as a signal to voters, directed at the external world of parties, has often been pronounced by definitions of party manifestos in contrast to other types of party programmes (Kaack 1971; Volkens 2002). As postulated by mandate theory, voters should recognize parties' policy profiles. This appears rather difficult in reality since voters hardly read party manifestos (Rölle 2002; Von Alemann 1995; Volkens 2002). According to the German election study (GLES), about 32 per cent of the respondents report having read a manifesto prior to the 2009 federal election, while 68 per cent admit to not having read one. However, these results should not be overstated since a certain risk of over-reporting due to social desirability has to be taken into consideration. In addition, as Maurer points out, the question of whether or not respondents have read a manifesto may be problematic in terms of validity. Using follow-up questions, he revealed a fundamental misunderstanding among many respondents, who had obviously mistaken the parties' flyers for their manifestos (Maurer 2008, 75). As a consequence, the question of manifesto readership was not included in the questionnaires of the 2013 German election studies. Hence, no reliable data on the readership of manifestos for the 2013 election were available, but there is no reason to expect any major change due to two reasons. Firstly, German party manifestos are lengthy documents and in 2013 all manifestos except for the AfD comprised about one hundred pages. Secondly, manifestos are written mainly by policy experts and use a highly technical language that is difficult to understand. Both factors provide only limited incentive to the average voter to read manifestos. How manifesto length and language apply to the 2013 manifestos will be explored in more detail.

Manifesto Length

One obvious reason why only a few voters actually read manifestos is their length. A general observation among party scholars is that manifestos have become significantly longer since the postwar years. For example, Dolezal et al. demonstrate that the average number of words in Austrian party manifestos increased markedly over the years, though not in a linear way (Dolezal et al. 2012, 882). Däubler and Benoit seek to explain variations of manifesto length in a cross-national comparison and find a general tendency towards an increase, too, but also considerable differences across countries as well as between parties (Däubler and Benoit 2013, 7). The authors conclude that manifesto length is determined especially by the parties' parliamentary status, party size and the available preparation time, that is, early elections have a negative effect on manifesto length (Däubler and Benoit 2013, 12–14).

With regard to the length of German party manifestos, it is quite safe to say that they have grown considerably over time. As opposed to the number of words, the mean number of quasi-sentences as coded by the Comparative Manifesto Project (Volkens et al. 2013) provides a more substantial indicator for manifesto length and issue coverage since a quasi-sentence is defined as 'an argument which is the verbal expression of one political idea or issue' (Volkens 2002). The data show that based on all party manifestos that were coded per election, manifestos were rather brief documents in the 1950s, containing on average less than 100 quasi-sentences. Their average length increased continually in the following decades, but remained comparatively short throughout the 1990s when manifestos contained on average between 400 and 500 quasi-sentences. Since the 2002 elections, there has been a sharp increase in manifesto length, resulting in an average of 1,105 quasi-sentences in 2005, 2,346 in 2009 and 2,545 in 2013. Hence, the 2013 election marks a clear peak with regard to manifesto length. Although the mean number of quasi-sentences is a good indicator for the overall length of manifestos over time, there are considerable inter-party differences which have to be taken into account. By and large, the Greens tend to produce the lengthiest manifestos, while the CDU/CSU and Left Party produce less extensive documents. However, in recent years, the manifestos of all major parties have increased significantly. In 2013, for example, the Greens' manifesto comprised by far the longest and most comprehensive manifesto with 5,427 quasi-sentences, followed by the SPD's (2,898), the FDP's (2,579), the CDU/CSU's (2,574) and the Left Party's programme (2,473). The manifestos of younger parties, namely the Pirates and the AfD, were much shorter, comprising 1,794 and 73 quasi-sentences, respectively. However, if length could explain voters' reluctance to read manifestos, it would fail to explain the same reluctance that political scientists had already found in the 1970s and 1980s (Rölle 2002).

Readability

A second explanation as to why voters might not read manifestos could be the language used in these documents. An index developed at the University of Hohenheim captures the 'readability' of political texts, in particular of party manifestos. It combines several linguistic formulas and parameters such as the use of nouns, the average length of sentences or the share of words containing more than six characters (Kercher and Brettschneider 2013, 276). The index ranges between zero (*hardly readable*) and 20 (*easily readable*) and has been applied to the party manifestos for the 2013 election (Brettschneider 2013). According to the 'Hohenheim Index of Readability', the election programme of the CDU/CSU was the easiest manifesto to read, though it reached a value of merely 9.9. All other manifestos were even more difficult to read and reached values of 8.4 (Greens), 7.7 (Left), and 7.3 (SPD, FDP). The programme of the Pirate Party notably uses many technical terms and foreign words, which led to a readability value of 5.8. Overall, these results indicate relatively low readability of manifestos. Moreover, Kercher and Brettschneider find that those parts of the manifesto which refer to complex policies, such as EU issues or the financial crisis, are characterized by highly technical and abstract language. Conversely, general parts such as the introduction or the conclusion use easier language (Kercher and Brettschneider 2013, 281 ff.). Parties are certainly aware of the difficulties and often provide a manifesto version in easy language on their websites. However, the only binding and authoritative document remains the long version.

In contrast to manifesto readership, party scholars tend to stress the key role of media in conveying the content of programmes. Recent findings from Austrian expert interviews conducted by Dolezal et al. support the view that journalists and media in general are in fact the main addressees of manifestos, disseminating parties' policy stances into the public sphere (Dolezal et al. 2012, 886–7). The analysis of German media reports shows that quality newspapers such as the *Frankfurter Allgemeine Zeitung* (*FAZ*) publish manifesto-related articles throughout the election year. For 2013, the number of *FAZ*-articles that are related to both the federal election and party manifestos was counted on a monthly basis. The results show that in 2013, the first peak of manifesto-related media coverage occurred in April, when the SPD and Greens launched their programmes. A second peak was reached in June, when the CDU/CSU published their programme. The same relationship between parties' manifesto processes and media coverage can be observed in 2009, albeit with a slightly different timing of party conferences. While manifestos were referred to in many articles prior to the election, attention gradually decreased during the immediate campaign period in July and August. This could point to a greater emphasis on candidates during this last phase of the electoral campaign. However, in September and October, coverage on party manifestos increased again. This 'late' attention peak was particularly high in the 2013 election compared to 2009. This could be explained by the post-electoral importance of manifestos and the difficult and protracted coalition negotiations that followed the election.

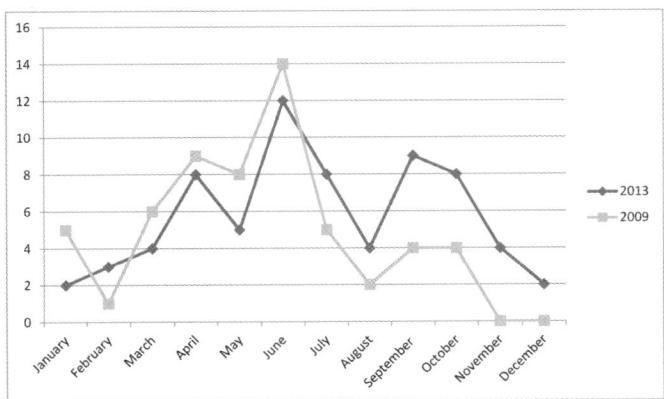

Figure 6.2   Manifesto-related media coverage

Source: Author's own analysis based on Frankfurter Allgemeine Archiv. Articles published in the Frankfurter Allgemeine Sonntagszeitung (FAS) and on the newspaper's website FAZ. net were not included.

While the content of party manifestos is primarily conveyed by the media, voting advice applications have become an increasingly popular tool for comparing parties' policy positions (Alvarez et al. 2014; Marshall and Schmidt 2010). The 'Wahl-O-Mat' has been applied to German federal, land, and European elections and was introduced in 2002 by the Federal Agency for Civic Education (*Bundeszentrale für Politische Bildung*, bpb).[1] The tool provides the user with 30 to 40 policy propositions, which have been derived from manifestos and revalidated by the parties themselves. Based on the users' agreement, disagreement or neutrality with these propositions and the weight users attach to certain propositions, the Wahl-O-Mat calculates the distance between the voter's and the parties' positions and displays the best match, that is, the party with the smallest distance. Empirical evidence of user numbers suggests that tools such as the Wahl-O-Mat have become very popular devices to perceive and compare parties' policy positions. According to official sources, the Wahl-O-Mat was used about 13.2 million times prior to the 2013 federal election (bpb 2013). This vast amount of users would represent 20 per cent of the whole electorate, but since these statistics are based on result-notifications they may include multiple users and users who are not eligible to vote. Nonetheless, the remarkable popularity of voting advice applications such as the Wahl-O-Mat stands out in comparison to previous elections in which the tool was used about 6.7 million (2009) and 5.2 million times (2005).

In sum, as far as voters' information about manifestos is concerned, it seems quite safe to say that only small parts of the electorate actually read manifestos. The manifestos of 2013 have been longer than ever and use highly technical

---

1   Similar tools exist in many other countries. For an overview see Heinrich Heine Universität n.d.

language, which is difficult to understand for the average voter. The content of manifestos is conveyed primarily by the media, which release manifesto-based reports throughout the election year. Coverage peaks when major parties publish their manifestos and when parties' policy positions become decisive in coalition negotiations, such as in 2013. In addition to media coverage, voters learn about parties' positions by increasingly using voting advice applications such as the Wahl-O-Mat. The second condition of mandate theory, voter information, can, therefore, be regarded as fulfilled. Although voters might not read manifestos directly, they may still be informed through different channels of communication such as media coverage and voting advice applications, which have become widely used tools, especially in the run-up to the 2013 election.

Manifesto Formation: The Intra-party Dimension

Since its inception, manifesto literature has focused largely on the generation of manifesto-based data on party positions and issue salience. In doing so, most authors follow (implicitly) the assumption that manifestos are the only representative and authoritative statements of party policies of the party as a whole (Budge et al. 2001; Volkens 2002). This common approach has always put strong emphasis on the external side of manifestos but disregarded their internal dimension. Manifestos do fulfil important intra-party functions: they integrate party members and provide a basis for cohesive party behaviour (Kaack 1971). The main addressees might, therefore, not be voters, but party members themselves. In a non-representative survey from the state of Baden-Württemberg, Kercher and Brettschneider (2013) asked party members of five German parties to evaluate different functions of manifestos. Their results, though limited, show that from an internal perspective, manifestos are a less viewed means of advertising and convincing voters. Party members regard their manifesto rather as a basis for party behaviour in the post-election phase, especially in coalition negotiations. Identification with the party and integration are also ranked among the most important functions, which further supports the argument that manifestos are also of internal importance (Kercher and Brettschneider 2013, 279).

As shown above, party manifestos have become comprehensive documents and parties devote great resources to their development. Prior to the 2013 election, all major parties (except for the Left Party) launched special campaigns, seeking proposals and broad participation in their manifesto-writing process, which differ from more general accounts of manifesto formation (Däubler and Benoit 2013). The FDP, for example, used a web-based platform ('Meine Freiheit') to put its manifesto draft up for public discussion. Registered users, which could be members as well as non-members, were allowed to suggest amendments, reformulations and cancellation of single words or whole paragraphs. Altogether, over 1,000 proposals were submitted via this platform, of which 700 proposals for amendment were discussed at the party conference, which finally adopted the manifesto.

The SPD chose a more traditional strategy to broaden participation and started a campaign called 'citizens' dialogue' (*Bürger-Dialog*), in which the party called for proposals on 'how to improve Germany'. Within six months of conferences and events, the party received over 40,000 proposals on postcards. The final 'citizens' convention' (*Bürger-Konvent*) resulted in 11 proposals that were directly included in the SPD manifesto. Although the manifesto was eventually adopted by a conference of party delegates, the strategy of increasing participation was not solely directed at party members. Instead, by giving non-members a say in the party's manifesto, the SPD, in a way, bypassed its own members and activists.

The CDU followed a more restricted process and opened its manifesto-writing process to members and non-members only in the early phase of manifesto writing. The campaign, called 'what lies at my heart', provided citizens with the opportunity to send in their ideas for the CDU manifesto via postcards. The party received more than 10,000 proposals, which were transformed into 45 theses. In the second phase, only party members were allowed to discuss, comment and evaluate those theses. However, the proposals did not have the same binding status as in the SPD and the party leadership ultimately took full control of the final manifesto.

Due to its origins and roots in social movements, intra-party democracy and participation have been of particular importance to the Green Party. Prior to the election of 2013, the Greens launched a series of membership ballots and formats for policy formation, the first being a membership ballot on the party's leading candidates for the federal election. In the process of manifesto writing, the party's executive committee discussed the draft directly with its members in the course of several programme forums, which were held throughout the country. At the party conference in April 2013, more than 2,600 proposals for amendment had to be dealt with. After the manifesto was adopted, the party started the next membership ballot on key projects and policy priorities, accompanied by an online debate and local events. Turnout was much lower than expected, as merely 26 per cent of the members cast a vote, compared with 62 per cent in the candidate membership ballot six months before. This time, party members could vote for 9 out of 59 key projects within three categories (energy turnaround, justice, modern society). The results only partly reflect the policy agenda of the leading candidates.

While the Greens and the FDP have a longer tradition of intra-participation in manifesto writing, the CDU and SPD introduced new formats prior to the 2013 national election. However, opportunities for participation varied crucially between parties with regard to inclusion of non-members, timing, and commitment. On the one hand, broadening participation in manifesto writing might be seen as a deliberate attempt to increase party responsiveness and provide a new linkage between voters, members and parties. In this sense, manifesto writing contributes to the emergence of a party mandate. On the other hand, these recent changes can be regarded as a strategic reaction to the success of the Pirate Party in several state elections – for example, Berlin, Northrhine-Westphalia, Schleswig-Holstein. Focusing on internet policy and transparency, the Pirate Party aspired to a new political style of intra-party participation, exercised through a web-based tool called 'liquid feedback'. Although the newcomer party was soon caught up in a conflict of its own participatory aspirations versus the realities and demands of professional politics (Niedermayer 2012, 58–60), the established parties adopted their political style as well as their core issue of internet policy.

With regard to intra-party participation, nearly all major parties introduced new ways of developing their 2013 manifesto. Most noticeably, the large parties, the SPD and the CDU, launched special campaigns in the early writing process although they had been rather reluctant to include grassroots participation before. The smaller parties, the FDP and the Greens, had some experience already in giving their members a say in their manifestos and allowed for grassroots participation throughout the whole process. The opening up of the large parties, which are strongest affected by membership decline, suggests that both parties learned from the successful mobilization of new competitors such as the Pirates. By involving members and supporters, both parties adapt to a growing demand for participatory opportunities and expand their network to a broader set of sympathizers (Gauja 2013, 123). The intra-party dimension reveals a strengthening connection, therefore, between parties and society. However, the final question remains: does party behaviour in government correspond with the policy profiles outlined before? How strongly are parties committed to their manifestos?

Pledge Fulfilment: Party Policy Commitment in Government

The last condition of mandate theory could be regarded as the most crucial one in establishing the necessary correspondence between citizens' interests and governmental action. This party mandate is most viable in majoritarian democracies, but also applies to multi-party governments. As Hofferbert and Klingemann (1990) have shown, there is a clear correspondence between party positions stated in their manifestos and government spending. While comparative studies on the fulfilment of election pledges is still rare, case studies have found remarkable evidence of pledge fulfilment, for instance in the UK (Royed 1996) and the Netherlands (Thomson 2001). Ferguson's analysis (2012) covers pledge fulfilment under the second red-green coalition (Schröder II, 2002–5) and the grand coalition (Merkel I, 2005–9). His results are displayed in Figure 6.3, which takes both full and partial fulfilment into account.

According to Ferguson, the SPD was able to fulfil 73 per cent of its pledges in the field of economic policy under the Schröder II government, whereas the Greens as its coalition partner fulfilled 67 per cent of its pledges. The opposition parties show much lower levels of pledge fulfilment. On average, they fulfilled 32 per cent of their pledges between 2002 and 2005. Under the grand coalition of Merkel I, the governing parties were able to fulfil only 57 (CDU/CSU) and 67 per cent (SPD) of their pledges. These findings suggest that greater policy distances between governing parties demand more substantial inter-party compromises, which reduce the level of pledge fulfilment.

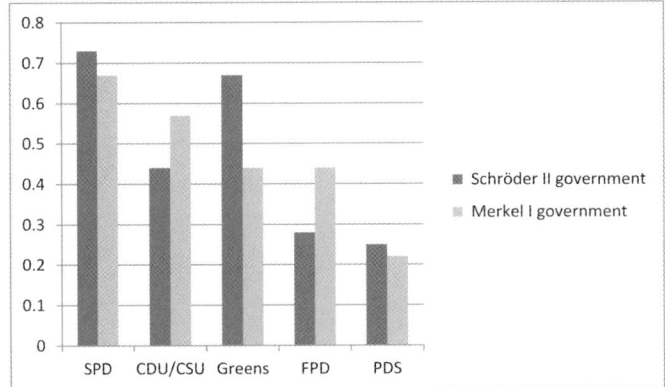

**Figure 6.3   Share of economic pledges fully/partly fulfilled under Schröder
II (2002–2005) and Merkel I (2005–2009)**

Source: Ferguson (2012, 114, 122).

Quite surprisingly, the opposition parties were able to fulfil even more pledges under the grand coalition than under the red-green coalition. The data provided by Ferguson does not allow for a more detailed analysis, but the high level of pledge fulfilment by opposition parties under Merkel I could be explained by congruent policies, that is, pledges that were shared by one of the governing parties.

These figures show that party behaviour corresponds to a great extent with the policy pledges laid out before the election. Although data on pledge fulfilment is still limited, there is clear empirical evidence that parties are committed to their manifestos and deliver on their promises. Eventually, these findings indicate that parties fulfil the last condition of mandate theory, although the level of pledge fulfilment varies between different coalition arrangements. The last grand coalition, especially, left the governing parties with fewer pledges fulfilled than under the red-green coalition, which was closer in policy terms.

Conclusion

Unmistakable signs of decline and increasing instability, which moves the German party system further away from what it used to be (Poguntke 2012), could be one interpretation of the 2013 election. This chapter has shown that German parties face serious challenges in a changing environment that is often referred to as the decline of party and the weakening of party linkages. However, while party membership decreases and volatility reaches historically high levels, parties remain the key actors in modern representative democracy and are still able to provide an active linkage between parties, citizens and the state. The 2013 German election supports the argument that parties are able to adapt and strengthen the connection between parties, members and voters through party manifestos.

Four conditions for the emergence of a necessary correspondence between party policy profiles, voters' preferences and governmental action in representative democracy have been derived from mandate theory literature. In light of the general election of 2013, they were put to an empirical test. With regard to party distinctiveness, it was shown that German parties still hold distinct positions on key dimensions of political space. On the socioeconomic dimension, which is defined by economic and welfare policies, parties take quite different positions between market liberalism and state intervention. In 2013, only the Pirate Party's position was almost the same as that of the SPD. On the social-liberalist dimension, which is defined by the policy fields of home affairs and justice, the CDU/CSU still stands out as the most traditional party. As far as the second condition (voters' perception of policy positions) is concerned, it has been shown that very few voters read manifestos. Two reasons contribute to the low readership among voters: the increasing length of manifestos and the language they use. Instead, parties' positions are conveyed by the media. In 2013, manifesto-related articles were published throughout the year. The extent of coverage increased when parties issued their programmes, as well as during the difficult coalition negotiations that followed in the post-electoral phase. Moreover, voting advice applications such as the Wahl-O-Mat have become very popular tools for comparing parties' policy positions. In 2013, the tool was used more than 13 million times – a frequency more than twice as high as in 2009. The second condition, voter information, can thus be regarded as fulfilled. The third condition, manifesto formation, focused on the intra-party process of manifesto writing. Both the SPD and CDU have introduced new formats and opportunities for party members and non-members to participate in the manifesto process, while the Greens and Liberals already had some experience in this respect. These recent changes can be seen as an attempt to increase parties' responsiveness, which strengthens the mandate relationship. However, this may not matter if parties are not committed to their manifestos. Using data on pledge fulfilment of two German governments (Schröder II and Merkel I), it was shown that parties are able to deliver on large parts of their manifestos. The fourth condition of mandate theory can, therefore, be regarded as fulfilled. As far as grand coalitions are concerned, they appear to reduce the capability of fulfilment, but further research is needed for a better understanding of the relationship between policy distance of coalition parties and pledge fulfilment. In contrast to the literature on party decline, which emphasizes the weakening of party linkages, this chapter has shown that parties, as well as voters, are finding new ways to strengthen the electoral connection.

References

Alvarez, R. Michael; Levin, Inés; Mair, Peter; and Trechsel, Alexander. 2014. 'Party preferences in the digital age: the impact of voting advice applications'. *Party Politics*, vol. 20, n. 2: 227–36.

Biehl, Heiko. 2013. 'Noch vertrauenswürdig?' In *Abkehr von den Parteien? Parteiendemokratie und Bürgerprotest*, edited by Oskar Niedermayer and Benjamin Höhne, 67–92. Wiesbaden: Springer VS.

Brettschneider, Frank. 2013. 'Verständlichkeit von Wahlprogrammen 2013'. *Die Welt*, 12 November. [Online]. Available from: http://www.welt.de/wirtschaft/article119351107/Wahlprogramme-der-Parteien-sind-unverstaendlich.html (accessed 11 November 2014).

Budge, Ian; Klingemann, Hans-Dieter; Volkens, Andrea; Bara, Judith; and Tanenbaum, Eric (eds). 2001. *Mapping Policy Preferences: Estimates for Parties, Electors, and Governments, 1945–1998*. Oxford: Oxford University Press.

Dalton, Russell J., and Wattenberg, Martin P. (eds). 2000. *Parties without Partisans: Political Change in Advanced Industrial Democracies*. Oxford: Oxford University Press.

Dalton, Russell J., and Weldon, Steven A. 2005. 'Public images of political parties: a necessary evil?' *West European Politics*, vol. 28, n. 5: 931–51.

Däubler, Thomas, and Benoit, Kenneth. 2013. *The Empirical Determinants of Manifesto Content*. Paper presented at the EPSA Annual Meeting, Barcelona, 10–22 June.

Dolezal, Martin; Ensser-Jedenastik, Laurenz; Müller, Wolfgang C.; and Winkler, Anna Katharina. 2012. 'The life-cycle of party manifestos: the Austrian case'. *West European Politics*, vol. 35, n. 4, 869–95.

Downs, Anthony. 1957. An Economic Theory of Democracy. New York: Harper & Row.

Ferguson, Mark J. 2012. *Pledge fulfilment in Germany: An examination of the Schröder II and Merkel I Governments*. PhD diss., University of Alabama.

Gauja, Anika. 2013. 'Policy development and intra-party democracy'. In *The Challenges of Intra-Party Democracy*, edited by William P. Cross and Richard S. Katz, 116–35. Oxford: Oxford University Press.

Heinrich Heine Universität Düsseldorf. *Wahl-O-Mat Research*. Available from: https://www.phil-fak.uni-duesseldorf.de/wahl-o-mat/en/facts-about-the-wahl-o-mat (accessed 12 November 2014).

Hofferbert, Richard I., and Klingemann, Hans-Dieter. 1990. 'The policy impact of party programmes and government declarations in the Federal Republic of Germany'. *European Journal of Political Research*, vol. 18: 277–304.

Jun, Uwe; Niedermayer, Oskar; and Wiesendahl, Elmar (eds). 2009. *Zukunft der Mitgliederpartei*. Opladen: Barbara Budrich.

Kaack, Heino. 1971. *Geschichte und Struktur des deutschen Parteiensystems*. Opladen: Westdeutscher Verlag.

Katz, Richard S., and Mair, Peter. 1995. 'Changing models of party organization and party democracy: the Emergence of the cartel party'. *Party Politics*, vol. 1, n. 1: 5–28.

Kercher, Jan, and Brettschneider, Frank. 2013. 'Wahlprogramme als Pflichtübung? Typen, Funktionen und Verständlichkeit der Bundestagswahlprogramme 1994–2009'. In *Wahlen und Wähler. Analysen aus Anlass der Bundestagswahl 2009*, edited by Bernhard Weßels, Harald Schoen and Oscar W. Gabriel, 269–90. Wiesbaden: Springer VS.

Klingemann, Hans-Dieter; Volkens, Andrea; Bara, Judith; Budge, Ian; and McDonald, Michael. 2006. *Mapping Policy Preferences II: Estimates for Parties, Electors, and Governments in Eastern Europe, European Union, and OECD 1990–2003*. Oxford: Oxford University Press.

Korte, Karl-Rudolf. 2003. 'The party system in Germany and party fragmentation in the European Union'. In *Political Parties and Party Systems*, edited by Ajay K. Mehra, D. D. Khanna and Gert W. Kueck, 100–28. New Delhi: Sage.

Kriesi, Hanspeter; Grande, Edgar; Lachat, Romain; Dolezal, Martin; Bornschier, Simon; and Frey, Timotheos. 2006. 'Globalization and the transformation of the national political space: six European countries compared'. *European Journal of Political Research*, vol. 45, n. 6: 921–56.

Marschall, Stefan, and Schmidt, Christian. 2010. 'The impact of voting indicators: the case of the German Wahl-O-Mat'. In *Voting Advice Applications in Europe. The State of the Art*, edited by Lorella Cedroni and Diego Garzia, 65–90. Neapel: Scriptaweb.

Maurer, Marcus. 2008. 'Wissensvermittlung im Wahlkampf – Ursache und Folgen politischen Wissenserwerbs im Bundestagswahlkampf 2005'. In *Integrative Modelle in der Rezeptions- und Wirkungsforschung. Dynamische und transaktionale Perspektiven*, edited by Carsten Wünsch, Werner Früh and Volker Gehrau, 65–80. München: Verlag Reinhard Fischer.

McDonald, Michael D.; Mendes, Silvia M.; and Budge Ian. 2004. 'What are elections for? Conferring the median mandate'. *British Journal of Political Science*, vol. 34: 1–26.

Müller, Wolfgang C. 2000. 'Political parties in parliamentary democracies. Making delegation and accountability work'. *European Journal of Political Research*, vol. 37, n. 3: 309–33.

Niedermayer, Oskar. 2012. *Die Piratenpartei*. Wiesbaden: Springer VS.

Norris, Pippa. 1999. Critical citizens. *Global Support for Democratic Governance*. Oxford: Oxford University Press.

Panebianco, Angelo. 1988. *Political Parties: Organization and Power*. Cambridge: Cambridge University Press.

Pappi, Franz U. 1984. 'The West German party system'. *West European Politics*, vol. 7, n. 4: 7–26.

Pedersen, Mogens N. 1979. 'The dynamics of European party systems: changing patterns of electoral volatility'. *European Journal of Political Research*, vol. 7, n. 1: 1–26.

Poguntke, Thomas. 2012. 'Towards a new party system: the vanishing hold of the catch-all parties in Germany'. *Party Politics* (doi: 10.1177/1354068812462925).

Powell, Bingham. 2000. *Elections as Instruments of Democracy: Majoritarian and Proportional Visions*. New Haven: Yale University Press.

Rölle, Daniel. 2002. 'Nichts genaues weiß man nicht!? Über die Perzeption von Wahlprogrammen in der Öffentlichkeit'. *Kölner Zeitschrift für Soziologie und Sozialpsychologie*, vol. 54, n. 2: 264–80.

Royed, Terry J. 1996. 'Testing the mandate model in Britain and the United States: evidence from the Reagan and Thatcher eras'. *British Journal of Political Science*, vol. 26: 45–80.

Saalfeld, Thomas, and Hornsteiner, Margret. 2014. 'Parties and the party system'. In *Developments in German Politics 4*, edited by Stephen Padgett, William E. Paterson and Reimut Zohlnöfer. Basingstoke: Palgrave Macmillan.

Slapin, Jonathan B., and Proksch, Sven-Oliver. 2008. 'A scaling model for estimating time-series party positions from texts'. *American Journal of Political Science*, vol. 52, n. 3: 705–22.

Smith, Gordon. 2003. 'The "new model" party system'. In *Developments in German Politics 3*, edited by Stephen Padgett, William E. Paterson and Gordon Smith, 82–100. Basingstoke: Palgrave Macmillan.

Spier, Tim. 2011. 'Wie aktiv sind die Mitglieder der Parteien'. In *Parteimitglieder in Deutschland*, edited by Tim Spier, Markus Klein, Ulrich von Alemann, Hanna Hoffmann and Annika Laux, 97–119. Wiesbaden: VS Verlag.

Thomson, Robert. 2001. 'The programme to policy linkage: the fulfilment of election pledges on socio-economic policy in the Netherlands, 1986–1998'. *European Journal of Political Research*, vol. 40, n. 2: 171–97.

Van Biezen, Ingrid, and Poguntke, Thomas. 2014. 'The decline of membership-based politics'. *Party Politics*, vol. 20, n. 2: 205–16.

Volkens, Andrea. 2002. *Manifesto Coding Instruction* (second revised edition). Berlin: Wissenschaftszentrum für Sozialforschung (WZB).

Volkens, Andrea; Lehmann, Pola; Merz, Nicolas; Regel, Sven; and Werner, Annika. 2013. *The Manifesto Data Collection. Manifesto Project (MRG/CMP/MARPOR)*. Version 2013b. Berlin: Wissenschaftszentrum Berlin für Sozialforschung (WZB).

Von Alemann, Ulrich. 1995. *Parteien*. Hamburg: Reinbeck.

Chapter 7

Programmatic Change in the Two Main Parties: CDU and SPD on Their Way to the Grand Coalition

Uwe Jun and Simon Jakobs

Introduction

The programmatic face of parties and its change have become an important focus in political science in recent years and constitute a well-developed field of party research (Merz and Regel 2013; Debus 2009). Party manifestos play a crucial role in party competition. They function as a means of self-understanding concerning values, beliefs, opinions and positions of party members and party sympathisers. In addition, party manifestos reflect the majority opinion of a party. To the outside they serve as an instrument for creating a profile and providing information to the electorate, giving the voters the possibility to inform themselves about the political aims and the parties' intentions to act. Finally, party manifestos serve as guidance for the parties' parliamentary groups on how to act and behave after the election. Therefore, party manifestos can partially serve as a guideline for the political positions taken by the party in parliament. Additionally, party manifestos influence coalition agreements to some extent, resulting in coalition agreements to be a kind of governing manifesto of the parties, which distinctively differs from the parties' platforms or their election manifestos.

Election manifestos, party platforms and government programmes in the form of coalition agreements can usually be seen as a compromise, for example between the horizontal and vertical groupings within the party or, in the case of a coalition already built, between the coalition parties. All these different programmes are reflecting society's lines of development, which influence parties and, at the same time, are causing certain social developments. The intra-party developments regarding the party objectives and the voter commitment and the restrictions of the party competition on the outside cross over and are interdependent (Eith 2010, 118).

While observing the inside of the major German parties, the CDU and the SPD, different factions with distinct interests, aims and programmatic ideas can be found. Especially concerning the programmatic aspect, disputes between modernizers and traditionalists, who want to focus on the party's traditional identity, come to the fore in the intra-party deliberation process. In order to distinguish traditionalists from modernizers, the latter prioritize electoral aspects, meaning that they are either willing to prioritize the pursuit of an electoral majority, or that they are willing to make concessions regarding the party manifesto in order to adjust to the restrictions imposed by governing. Both strategies of adaption were visible in the SPD when it was presided over by former chancellor Gerhard Schröder, and in the current CDU, led by present chancellor, Angela Merkel.

The following sections will analyse transition processes in the SPD and CDU, concentrating on the issue of modernization versus preservation of traditional identities. The main empirical foci of the analysis will be the party manifestos of the SPD and the CDU/CSU[1] published prior to the elections in 2013.

Moving to the Left: A Quantitative Analysis of the Election Manifestos of 2013

This section focuses on a quantitative analysis of the SPD and CDU/CSU party manifestos, aiming to measure the policy positions of the parties and rating the party manifestos as an essential data basis to extract those positions (Volkens and Klingemann 2002; Pappi and Shikano 2007, 118). To begin with, the quantitative analysis will locate party positions in a two-dimensional policy space before party manifestos are divided into different policy areas. In a further step, the five words used most frequently throughout the party manifestos will be identified and assigned to different policy areas. Afterwards, a qualitative content analysis of the manifestos will be conducted, extracting the central policy positions of the two main parties.

Table 7.1   Total amount of words counted in the party manifestos

	SPD	CDU/CSU	FDP	B'90/Die Grünen	Die Linke
Words	42,533	42,124	38,980	86,594	41,187
A4-pages	120	128	94	337	100

Note: As can be observed, the total amount of words counted in the party manifestos may vary in other publications (as in Bianchi et al. 2013, 4 or Zastrow 2013). Since counting mistakes in Microsoft Word when simply saving the pdf of a party manifesto as .doc can be noted, using the ABBYY FineReader and its OCR-function to scan the documents and then converting the party manifestos to UTF-8 and replacing all of the German umlauts with their grammatical equivalents seems to be more adequate.

---

1   As the party manifesto is mentioned as a joint policy statement of the CDU/CSU, both parties are mentioned in the context of the quantitative as well as the qualitative analysis of the party manifestos, whereas mentions of the CDU on its own refer exclusively to the CDU.

Comparing the total number of words in the party manifestos, the two main parties, the SPD and CDU/CSU, have an approximately equal number of words. The same applies to the party manifesto of Die Linke. The FDP manifesto contains the smallest number of words whereas the Green Party (B'90/Die Grünen) presents a rather extensive party manifesto, perhaps too long for the ordinary voter to read (Merz and Regel 2013, 224). The average number of words of all five party manifestos (50,283.6 words) might be a sign of the party manifestos' true function, since their unabridged versions probably do not serve to inform the ordinary voter, but rather reflect intra-party discussions with regard to the various party factions' viewpoints on current policies. As Kercher and Brettschneider (2013, 285) claim, the unabridged version of a party manifesto generally serves to create a self-concept, sort of a composition of the different policies of the party factions. However, the present analysis focuses on the unabridged versions of the SPD and CDU/CSU party manifestos as this is the only document type able to reflect the programmatic complexity and differentiated policies that are particularly suitable in assessing the future policy formulation and agenda setting of the governing parties.

Following the methodology applied in the study by Jun (2007), the present analysis aims to facilitate the comparison of the 2013 and 2005 party manifestos, which have been analysed in Jun's study mentioned above. Therefore, the positions of the two main parties are depicted in a two-dimensional space (see Figure 7.1). The x-axis marks the liberal market economy in contrast to state interventionism, whereas the y-axis represents a liberal and open society in contrast to a more authoritarian policy style, following the dividing lines of the present German party system explained by Niedermayer (2013, 125). To quantify the estimate of policy positions, different categories have been set up and all corresponding keywords have been counted, applying the same procedure as Jun (2007) and Grabow (2008). In the course of the evaluation each axial alignment was attributed the amount of context-relevant keywords which were further divided by the total amount of categories in order to attain the arithmetic mean. The arithmetic mean of the different axial directions was subtracted by another, resulting in the points marked on the x-axis and y-axis. It must be emphasized that all keywords used multiple times in the same context were counted as one, whereas the same keywords used in different contexts were counted two, three, … n-times. Keywords found in a historical, only descriptive, narrative context or in a context primarily aiming to isolate a competing party are not counted. This procedure proves to be highly beneficial with regard to the assessment of coalition preferences based on party manifestos, since it only focuses on the future policies of the party under consideration (Bytzek 2013, 233).

The analysis of the party manifestos of 2005 and 2013 reveals that the CDU/CSU does not strive for a liberal open society but for a more authoritarian policy style. The CDU/CSU is of late the only party formation left – amongst the established parties – that can be located in the conservative area as regards the socio-cultural dimension (Bianchi et al. 2013; Lehmann et al. 2013; Hildebrandt

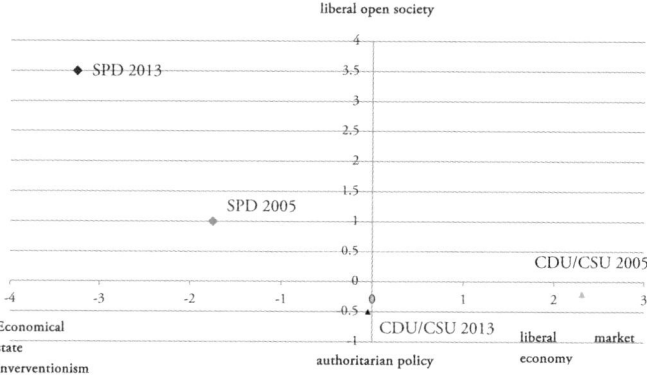

Figure 7.1   SPD and CDU/CSU in a two-dimensional policy space

and Weichold 2013). At the same time, the CDU/CSU has abandoned traditional attitudes in migration and family policies (Walter et al. 2011, 211 ff.), but has been able to put its distinctive Christian-conservative mark on some policy fields (Bösch 2013). Concerning the socio-economic position, the party is clearly moving to the left regarding the *x*-axis with a certain in-between policy style respecting state interventionism and free market economy. The SPD has moved to the left as well, preferring more state interventionism in the economic system as well as a liberal and open society. With regard to the results of the present analysis and the prospective qualitative analysis, it must be assumed that, in the future, the CDU/CSU will move further away from a liberal market economic policy towards a more welfare state-oriented policy, or a policy which provides further market regulations, a conclusion that seems adequate regarding the euro-zone crisis. In accordance with the majority of voters, the CDU prefers a more state-centric social and economic policy; at the expense of its traditional supporters, who prefer a free market economy, the party is heading significantly in the direction of social democratization. Furthermore, while the CDU/CSU has clearly moved to the left since 2005 (Zolleis and Schmid 2011, 46), it can also be argued that the SPD is trying to reclaim a 'back-to-the-roots' social democratic position in order to distinguish itself from the CDU/CSU and get back to the traditional welfare state policies which have been overshadowed in recent years by the 'Agenda'-policy (Jun 2013; Von Alemann and Spier 2011, 71) and Gerhard Schröder's catchphrase of 'demand and support'. Between 2003 and 2010, the party suffered from a defining conflict between modernizers and traditionalists (Jun 2010). Numerous intra-party compromises made this conflict come to an end and take a back seat. Party leader Sigmar Gabriel managed, partially at the expense of the consideration of the party's environments (Jun and Berzel 2014), to reintegrate the different party factions and scrape out the core identity of social democracy, namely social justice. In doing so, the party indeed relied on social justice, but avoided aligning with the policy of Die Linke. Still, the central positions of the modernizers predominate, such as the unaltered preservation of the 'Arbeitslosengeld II' as well as the retention of the 'Rente mit 67' (pension at the age of 67), although more exceptions have been allowed lately.

However, in isolation, this quantitative analysis is not able to offer a deeper insight into the party manifestos as it is certainly hiding their similarities as well as their differences. Thus, another fruitful way of analysing party manifestos is presented by Korte and Treibel (2009a; 2009b), Treibel (2010) and Bender et al. (2010). In their 'Duisburger-Wahl-Index' they suggest counting the five most frequently used political keywords in a party manifesto and contextualizing these in different policy fields. An advantage of this approach is that it can examine the stability of, and differences in, the use of certain political keywords utilized by a party and, in addition, compare them to those of a competing party. Furthermore, it is possible to compare these results to Korte and Treibel's analysis (2009a) of the party manifestos of 2009.

As a first step, the five most frequently used political keywords found in the two party manifestos, including all possible grammatical variations, both with a positive or pejorative connotation, were identified. Then, in order to capture the different policies in the manifestos, a coding scheme (GLES 2009) was applied maintaining the segmentation into different policy fields used by Korte and Treibel (2009a). The total amount of words counted for each policy was divided by the total amount of words of the party manifesto to ensure the comparability between the two parties. Afterwards, the five most frequently used words in the particular party manifesto were counted in the context of the particular policy, leading to the estimate of the share of frequently used political keywords of a party in the different policy fields.

Table 7.2   Most frequently used words in party manifestos (number of words used/total number of words)

SPD	CDU/CSU
Arbeit [work/labour] = 398 (0.94%)	Deutsch [German] = 319 (0.76%)
Sozial [social] = 294 (0.69 %)	Stark/Stärke [strong/strength] = 309 (0.73%)
Politik [policy/politics/political …] = 293 (0.69%)	Arbeit [work/labour] = 292 (0.69%)
Sicher [safe-] = 286 (0.67%)	Sicher [safe-] = 281 (0.67%)
Euro = 261 (0.61%)	Wirtschaft [economy] = 229 (0.54%)

Table 7.2 illustrates the predominance of the traditional social democratic term *Arbeit* in the party manifesto of the SPD with a total of 398 mentions. Noticeably lower, but still with a large count, is the traditional social democratic term *sozial* ('social'), which is in fact included in the name of the party, mentioned 294 times. The semantic field surrounding the term *Politik* is mentioned 293 times. *Sicher* is mentioned 286 times in the party manifesto, suggesting (economic) safety in the context of the euro-zone crisis. This leads to the word *Euro*, which ranks at the bottom of the five most frequently used words in the party manifesto, appearing a total of 261 times.

The manifesto of the CDU/CSU particularly emphasizes the semantic field surrounding the term 'German', reaching a total of 319 mentions in the party manifesto, followed by the semantic field *Stark/Stärke* with a total of 309. In conjunction, this value implies that the CDU/CSU is relying heavily on domestic strength, presumably suggesting that this strength has been achieved by the CDU/CSU itself as governing party. The terms *Arbeit* and *sicher*, following domestic strength in the third and fourth positions respectively, are perceived as confirming this assumption. Last, but far behind the preceding terms, is the term *Wirtschaft*, which is mentioned 229 times.

Altogether, the SPD seems to focus on traditional social democratic values, converting them into concrete policies, securing and generally contextualizing them into the European context, whereas the CDU/CSU is relying heavily on domestic strength, preserving jobs as well as emphasizing the role of the economy.

When comparing the present findings to Korte and Treibel (2009a, 6), the two most frequently used words in the manifesto of the CDU/CSU, *deutsch* and *Stark/Stärke*, were equally ranked in 2009, highlighting the 'suggestion of safety and homeland symbolism' (Walter et al. 2011, 209) already used in the past. The same applies to the 2013 manifesto. The subsequent ranks of the year 2009, *Entwicklung* [development], *Förderung* [support], and *Zukunft* [future] have now been replaced by *Arbeit, sicher* and *Wirtschaft*. In the case of the SPD, the order of the key terms used in their manifesto changed in parts: *Arbeit* and *sozial* were occupying the top ranks in 2009 as well, *sicher* ranked third, *Politik* fifth and *Wirtschaft* fourth, now being replaced by *Euro*. As the governing party, CDU/CSU does not change its main focus; neither does the SPD as an opposition party, except for minor changes.

It does not surprise that the CDU/CSU puts emphasis on security, because inner and foreign security, solid state finances and reliability constitute integrative and identity-building values for sympathizers of the party. The SPD, on the other hand, seems to stress security to offer useful guidance as a competent crisis manager in times of the euro-zone crisis and as a guarantor of the welfare state.

Table 7.3   Policies in party manifestos (total amount of words and percentage of each policy)

	SPD		CDU/CSU	
	Words	Relevance	Words	Relevance
Economic policy	5,369	12.6%	7,779	18.4%
Financial policy	2,634	6.2%	1,831	4.3%
Labour market policy/ welfare policy	**8,780**	**20.6%**	6,481	15.4%
Education policy	1,840	4.3%	2,711	6.4%
Health policy	1,989	4.7%	1,016	2.4%
Traffic policy	527	1.2%	1,799	4.3%
Environment policy	1,121	2.6%	2,034	4.8%
Energy policy	2,388	5.6%	1,419	3.4%
Family policy	302	0.7%	1,273	3.0%
Domestic policy	5,283	12.4%	**8,656**	**20.5%**
Foreign policy	2,533	6.0%	1,618	3.8%
European policy	3,289	7.7%	1,490	3.5%
Defence policy	817	1.9%	698	1.7%
Concept of democracy	2,724	6.4%	1,356	3.2%
Self-conception	1,538	3.6%	780	1.9%

Note: Missing values result from passages in the manifesto that could not be allocated to any specific policy.

The next step of the analysis is also based on Korte and Treibel's approach (2009a) calculating the total share of particular policies in the party manifestos as illustrated in Table 7.3. This procedure allows for the recognition of the policy focused on by the parties in their manifestos. Furthermore, it differentiates between the relevance of traditional and progressive policies mentioned in the manifestos.

As illustrated in Table 7.3 and Figure 7.2, the SPD highlights its traditional core policies, labour market policy and welfare policy, whereas the CDU/CSU primarily focuses on domestic policy. Following at a distance, economic policy ranks second in the manifesto of the SPD; the CDU/CSU by contrast focuses nearly as much on economic policy as on domestic policy, remarkably followed by a traditional social democratic sector, the labour market and welfare policy. As Table 7.3 and Figure 7.2 demonstrate, the top three policies of the CDU/CSU (domestic policy, economic policy, labour market and welfare policy) certainly dominate with a total of 54.3 per cent. The SPD as well as the CDU/CSU focuses on these three policies (but changes the order, beginning with labour market and welfare policy, followed by economic and domestic policy) with a total of 45.6 per cent and seems to be more varied in the manifesto as regards other policy fields. Compared to the results of Korte and Treibel (2009a, 5) stating that all German parties are primarily relying on domestic policy, the present analysis reveals that

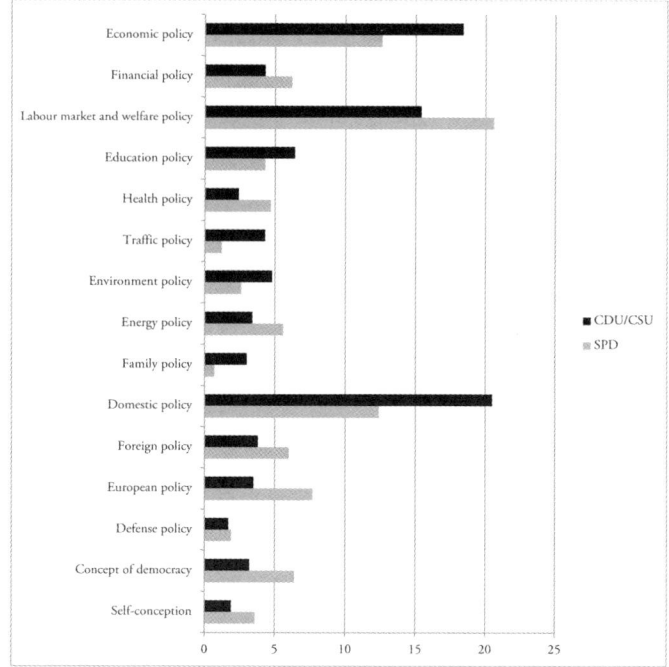

Figure 7.2   Policies in party manifestos (total amount of words and percentage of each policy area)

Note: missing values result from passages in the manifesto that could not be allocated to a certain policy.

with regard to the CDU/CSU no significant changes in its focus on domestic policy can be noted, but concerning the SPD a major shift to the labour market and welfare policy can be traced. This change might be indicating that the SPD is aiming for a return to a traditional social democratic concept of directing the economy to the benefit of the *Mittelklasse*. Another remarkable shift can be seen in the share of labour market and welfare policy of the CDU/CSU. Whereas this policy field made up only 5.8 per cent in the 2009 manifesto (Korte and Treibel 2009a, 5), the 2013 manifesto reveals a massive increase, supplying evidence that the CDU/CSU is strengthening its effort in occupying a more traditional social democratic policy stance than a few years ago.

The similarity of the three most important policy fields mentioned by the main German parties might imply a programmatic proximity which cannot be decoded by a purely quantitative manner, bearing in mind that the analysis of the party positions in the two-dimensional policy space clearly proves a programmatic distance. Other policies, such as the financial policy, education policy, health policy, traffic policy, environment policy, energy policy, family policy, foreign policy, European policy, the concept of democracy and the self-conception, are varying across the party manifestos but only within small intervals. Concerning defence policy a slight overlap can be observed which does not, however, play an essential role in both manifestos. Altogether, these other policies do not help in explaining the programmatic distance stated in the previous analysis.

Table 7.4   Most frequently used word of the 'Top-5' grouped for policy areas

Policies	SPD	CDU/CSU
Economic policy	Politik and Sicher (30; 0.56%)	Wirtschaft (117; 1.5%)
Financial policy	Politik (16; 0.61%)	Stark/Stärke (14; 0.76%)
Labour market policy/ welfare policy	Arbeit (248; 2.82%)	Arbeit (89; 1.37%)
Education policy	Sozial (11; 0.60%)	Deutsch/Stark/Stärke and Arbeit (18; 0.66%)
Health policy	Sicher (38; 1.91%)	Sicher (14; 1.38%)
Traffic policy	Sicher (4; 0.76%)	Deutsch (18; 1.00 %)
Environment policy	Politik (6; 0.53%)	Wirtschaft (18; 0.88%)
Energy policy	Sicher (20; 0.84%)	Sicher (13; 0.92%)
Family policy	Arbeit (4; 1.32%)	Arbeit (13; 1.02%)
Domestic policy	Politik (48; 0.91%)	Deutsch (92; 1.06%)
Foreign policy	Politik (46; 1.82%)	Stark/Stärke and Arbeit (19; 1.17%)
European policy	Euro (132: 4.01%)	Arbeit (19; 1.28%)
Defence policy	Politik (15; 1.84%)	Sicher (18; 2.58%)
Concept of democracy	Sozial (27; 0.99%)	Stark/Stärke (12; 0.88%)
Self-conception	Sozial (29; 1.89%)	Deutsch (13; 1.67%)

Note: See Table 7.2 on the policies mentioned in the party manifestos and their share in the total amount of words used to describe each particular policy.

More Profound Insights into the Manifestos: A Qualitative Analysis

In order to gain an in-depth insight into the manifestos, the main policy positions of the two German parties have been subject to a comparative content analysis. However, to facilitate the comparison between the CDU/CSU and SPD party manifestos in the long term, the policies presented in the manifestos according to the 15 policies listed above will be described first and then evaluated by appliance of the synopsis structure as presented in Jun (2007, 505). However, it must be emphasized that when conducting a content analysis in order to extract the policy positions listed below, the risk of negligence of reliability is still existent and cannot be completely dismissed (Bräuninger and Debus 2012, 39). Particularly, the use of computer programmes such as *Wordscores* (Laver et al. 2003) or *Wordfish* (Proksch and Slapin 2009) to decode party manifestos might increase reliability, but is at the same time endangering the validity and robustness of the results (Linhart and Shikano 2009, 302) for claiming that 'the language used by political parties expresses political ideology' (Proksch and Slapin 2009, 324). In addition, to extract policy positions with regard to specific subject areas by the appliance of *Wordfish*, specific passages in the manifestos have to be chosen manually, which endangers the reliability of the approach as well (Bräuninger and Debus 2012, 45). Furthermore, this methodology does not help to extract detailed policy positions with regard to the coalition negotiations. Moreover, the dataset provided by the Comparative Manifesto Project (Volkens et al. 2013) does not offer a satisfactory possibility to further investigate party preferences as a qualitative analysis. Hence, the authors have decided to use the 'human coder' – that is, to extract policy positions manually and non-automatically and finally compare them in the different party manifestos.

To begin with, concerning economic policy the SPD certainly aims at a regulation of the international financial markets and the appliance of a financial transaction tax on these markets (SPD 2013, 13). Furthermore, a 'sustainable and fair economy' (SPD 2013, 15) in the context of a so-called 'refounding of the social market economy' (SPD 2013, 66) should be provided, which moreover must be in accordance with a reduction of public debts, a high level of employment, a balanced current account, a more equitable income redistribution and ecological sustainability (SPD 2013, 14 ff.). In addition, the SPD wants to buttress the middle class and seeks to bolster consumer protection as well as market transparency. The CDU/CSU wants to strengthen the social market economy (CDU/CSU 2013, 4; 16) and is therefore relying on entrepreneurship and a strong middle class (CDU/CSU 2013, 7; 52 ff.; 18–19), which is the 'spine of our economy and one of the guarantors of our wealth' (CDU/CSU 2013, 18), at the same time referring to the importance of ecological and economical sustainability (CDU/CSU 2013, 30–1). Just like the SPD, the CDU/CSU demands regulation of the international financial markets as well as the application of a financial transaction tax (CDU/CSU 2013, 29–30).

In the sector of financial policy, the SPD demands an increase of taxes, 'not all taxes for everyone but some taxes for quite a few people' (SPD 2013, 12). In plain terms this implies the (re)introduction of a property tax which already existed in Germany in the era of Chancellor Kohl, an increase in the top rates of income taxation to 49 per cent and an increase in the so-called *Abgeltungssteuer* (SPD 2013, 67 ff.).[2] In addition, the SPD would abolish the special taxation for married couples, replacing it with individual taxation for each of the married partners (SPD 2013, 51). Contrarily, the CDU/CSU declines increasing taxes and clearly negates reintroducing a property tax (CDU/CSU 2013, 27). Concerning this matter, the

---

2   The German *Abgeltungssteuer* is a tax which applies to the capital yield of individuals, replacing the income tax on these revenues.

CDU/CSU refers to the high tax burden of the top 25 per cent of tax payers (CDU/CSU 2013, 26). With reference to the traditional values of the Christian Democrats such as 'marriage and family' (CDU/CSU 2013, 8), the CDU/CSU repudiates the idea of eliminating the special taxation for married couples. This is another example of the preservation of a traditional main focus of the CDU/CSU.

Labour market and social policy, a core policy field of the SPD, is dominated by the concept of full employment (SPD 2013, 17). Moreover, the SPD aims to overcome precarious working conditions and to introduce an overall minimum wage of 8.50 euro (SPD 2013, 19). In order to strengthen gender equality, the SPD claims to enact equal pay laws 'to terminate the structural wage discrimination of women' (SPD 2013, 20). Furthermore, a fixed gender quota of 40 per cent for the management and supervisory boards of publicly listed companies should be established (SPD 2013, 51). Concerning its social policy, the SPD plans to introduce a socially graded child benefit to support families, particularly those on low incomes (SPD 2013, 54). The provision for senior citizens should be enforced, too, by means of a minimum pension of 850 euro on the condition that 30 contribution years and 40 insurance years have been achieved as a minimum. To absorb the price increase in the housing markets, the SPD plans to provide social housing and to limit the increase in rental prices. Similarly to the SPD, the CDU/CSU is oriented towards a policy of full employment, but objects to the introduction of an overall minimum wage as well, negating a determination of wages by the government (CDU/CSU 2013, 7). The CDU/CSU prefers the maintaining of the principle of collective bargaining, only mentioning the obligation of bargaining in areas where collective agreements are not yet existent (CDU/CSU 2013, 7). It pledges a so-called *tarifliche Lohnuntergrenze* – agreed minimum wage level, not provided by the government but rather through negotiations between the employees and the employers – to avoid wage dumping.

The CDU/CSU does not push gender equality concerning equal payments as much as the SPD (CDU/CSU 2013, 62) and offers a so-called 'flexi-quota' (CDU/CSU 2013, 63), a quota system in which enterprises are able to set their own quota, and the specific moment in time they want to reach it. Concerning pension and retirement policy, the CDU/CSU is willing to strengthen the provision of private and company pensions, guaranteeing a minimum retirement pension of 850 euro provided that a private pension is already existent, as well as a minimum 40 years' compulsory contribution to the federal pension insurance system (CDU/CSU 2013, 73). Furthermore, the CDU/CSU plans to introduce the so-called *Mütterrente* (CDU/CSU 2013, 73), an increase in the retirement pension especially for parents, rewarding their efforts to raise children. Like the SPD the CDU/CSU is willing to intensify the provision of social housing and to limit the increase in rental prices (CDU/CSU 2013, 91–2).

Within the scope of education policy the SPD claims to provide parents with a legal entitlement to a place in a day care centre for their children, and furthermore to ensure equal starting opportunities in the education sector (SPD 2013, 43). In addition, the SPD plans to abolish the ban on cooperation in the federal education system, to massively increase public education expenditure (SPD 2013, 44–5) and, in addition, to expand and develop all-day classes (SPD 2013, 53). The CDU/CSU plans to implement obligatory language tests for children, 'who inadequately learn the German language at home from their parents' (CDU/CSU 2013, 32). In contrast to the SPD, the CDU/CSU emphasizes the maintaining of two different types of secondary school and clearly appreciates the preservation of the German *Gymnasium* – that is, the grammar school (CDU/CSU 2013, 32).

Examining health policy, the model of the so-called *Bürgerversicherung* (citizens' insurance) is particularly striking to the reader. The SPD is willing to establish a uniform health insurance system abolishing the dualism between statutory health insurance and private medical insurance (SPD 2013, 72 ff.). In contrast to the SPD, the CDU/CSU intends to maintain this dualism, but offers to provide premium refunds for those health insurance companies in which the effective reserves clearly exceed the legal minimum reserve (CDU/CSU 2013, 75).

Regarding traffic policies the SPD emphasizes the reliable functioning of the traffic system and therefore agrees to the provision of the necessary investment funds (SPD 2013, 33). Similarly to the SPD, the CDU/CSU wants to further invest in the traffic system and in an additional use of digital solutions (CDU/CSU 2013, 48–53).

Concerning climate, environmental and energy policy, the SPD, by outlining its main objectives, provides quantified numbers: hence, in order to fight climate change, the SPD plans to reduce CO_2 emissions by 95 per cent by 2050 compared with 1990 levels (SPD 2013, 91). Furthermore, the SPD demands the reactivation of European emissions trading and an unconditional assurance to reduce Europe's greenhouse gas emissions by 30 per cent before 2020, making a national commitment to reduce greenhouse gas emissions by 40 per cent by 2020, 60 per cent by 2030 and 80 per cent by 2040 (SPD 2013, 91). In addition, the SPD claims it will increase the share of renewable energies measured against overall energy consumption to 40–5 per cent (SPD 2013, 36), which is linked to public assistance for the socially vulnerable concerning the absorption of increasing energy prices. The CDU/CSU intends a sustainable development and, by bolstering the economy at the same time, emphasizes the development of environmental technologies (CDU/CSU 2013, 81). The SPD, like the CDU/CSU, intends to reduce greenhouse gas emissions in Europe by 30 per cent before 2020 (CDU/CSU 2013, 81), underlining that Germany, as a highly developed country, should set a good example and should therefore aim for a reduction of national greenhouse gas emissions by 40 per cent by 2020 (CDU/CSU 2013, 81–2). Furthermore, the CDU/CSU plans to increase the share of renewable energies to 20 per cent measured against overall energy consumption (CDU/CSU 2013, 82).

Regarding family policy the SPD plans to introduce family-friendly working times with partners being allowed to reduce their work time without being disadvantaged with regard to their career prospects (SPD 2013, 55). Additionally, the SPD claims it will abandon the so-called *Betreuungsgeld* (SPD 2013, 43), a compensation for parents who stay at home in order to take care of their children until the age of three. The CDU/CSU is willing to introduce an in-between model of full-time and part-time jobs with a total of about 30 working hours per week (CDU/CSU 2013, 60). Additionally, the CDU/CSU will retain the *Betreuungsgeld* (CDU/CSU 2013, 62), which allows families to autonomously choose between a day care centre or care at home.

In the sphere of domestic policy the SPD claims it will step up efforts in fighting economic, tax and cyberspace crimes (SPD 2013, 99) and partly comments on inner security policy, advocating the compatibility of civil rights and inner security (SPD 2013, 99). Regarding integration policies the SPD wants to introduce dual citizenship, which will allow immigrants to adopt German citizenship while at the same time preserving their original citizenship (SPD 2013, 58). The CDU/CSU emphasizes creating a 'safer Germany' (CDU/CSU 2013, 9) and further raising the amount of camera surveillance (CDU/CSU 2013, 110). Concerning data privacy the CDU/CSU states it will maintain high German standards, but without providing an in-depth description of how they work and how they should be maintained (CDU/CSU 2013, 102). Concerning integration policy the CDU/CSU clearly refutes the introduction of dual citizenship, referring to the problems caused by dual citizenship in terms of civil conflicts and confrontations (CDU/CSU 2013, 65).

Observing European policy, the SPD focuses on the intensification of the European Union (SPD 2013, 25) and the set-up of a European debt repayment fund which 'ensures the ability to act of all members of the monetary union' (SPD 2013, 26). In addition, the European Commission should be extended to be an institution with substantial governing functions (SPD 2013, 104). In terms of European policy the CDU/CSU promotes the traditionalism inherent to the concept of Christian Democracy, highlighting that Europe should 'acknowledge its Christian-occidental roots and the ideas of the Enlightenment and subsist on them' (CDU/CSU 2013, 11). Additionally, the CDU/CSU demands German be assigned equal status to French and English as an official language in the EU (CDU/CSU 2013, 15). Further, the CDU/CSU pledges border controls without specific occasion (CDU/CSU 2013, 117), relying on the concept of safety already employed in terms of domestic policy.

Last, with respect to the concept of democracy and representation, the SPD aims at the expansion of participatory elements in order to involve citizens during the 'planning and execution of infrastructure projects' (SPD 2013, 33) and, in addition, to introduce people's initiatives, referendums and plebiscites at the federal level (SPD 2013, 97). Furthermore, the SPD plans to reduce the voting age to 16 (SPD 2013, 57). The CDU/CSU wants to facilitate civic participation during major projects (CDU/CSU 2013, 108–9). However, its party manifesto only contains a vague description concerning desired participatory elements and in general seems to replace participation by discussion (Hildebrandt and Weichold 2013, 7).

To summarize the qualitative analysis of the party manifestos, the SPD is certainly heading towards a slightly economic state interventionism, especially in terms of the regulation of the international financial markets, the prescription of a minimum wage, the introduction of fixed quotas and the demand for equal payment laws. In addition, the SPD clearly aims at the further development of the welfare state by an increase of taxes, an introduction of the minimum wage referred to above, a minimum pension, a socially graded child benefit, a uniform *Bürgerversicherung* and family-friendly working time. In terms of a liberal, open society the SPD manifesto emphasizes gender equality, the equalization of same-sex partnerships with regard to tax and adoption rights (SPD 2013, 50), a reduction of special rights for families, the expansion of participatory elements enriching representative democracy, the reduction of the voting age to 16 and the introduction of a dual citizenship. In terms of social and welfare policy the CDU/CSU is moving to the left, too, but is emphasizing the function of the middle class as society's backbone and its substantial contribution to the national economy. Its manifesto focuses on the bolstering of entrepreneurship and the middle class by avoiding an increase in taxes, but nonetheless, concerning various aspects, it moves towards a welfare state-oriented policy, especially regarding a minimum pension, a limitation of rent increases, an increase in child benefits and a minimum wage resulting from the bargaining of the social partners. Even though the CDU/CSU points out the role of single parents, the measures listed above are clearly dominated by the traditional principles of Christian Democracy, which are the preservation and maintenance of marriage and core family structures. The orientation towards a rather authoritarian policy style accompanied by a 'typical' authoritarian value system (Niedermayer 2003, 268) is emphasized by focusing on a rather restrictive domestic policy, an increase in security measures, the maintaining of the German *Gymnasium* ('Higher Education'), scepticism regarding integrated comprehensive schools, a rather 'half-hearted' support for gender equality and the preservation of tax advantages for married couples in contrast to quasi-marital partnerships as well as the rejection of a dual citizenship. Notwithstanding the aspects listed above, the CDU/CSU still supports elements of a liberal open society such as the emphasis on renewable energies and the focus on reducing harmful effects of climate change, at least supporting a flexi-quota system and emphasizing the participation of citizens in infrastructure projects. Hildebrandt and Weichold (2013, 1) draw the conclusion that the CDU/CSU is offering a 'well-assorted convenience store' in its party manifesto, trying to serve all sections of the electorate.

Regarding the 'modernisation trap' mentioned by Wiesendahl (1992, 13; 1993, 85), a trap resulting in an attempt by the (catch-all-) parties to simultaneously attract traditional voters as well as the 'mobile middle class segment' (Wiesendahl 1993, 85), it seems that the SPD is trying to recapture both the traditionally social-democratically oriented part of the electorate (by enforcing state interventionism as a means of ensuring social safety nets) and the slightly liberal and ascending middle class (by clearly heading towards liberal societal ideas). The SPD had to face a conflict between the traditionalist and modernist factions in the party already in the 1990s (Arnim 2009, 202) and it seems that both factions have commonly developed a political concept that favours the working class in economic terms but uncouples the lower classes, which can now be considered to be the main electorate for the party 'Die Linke'. Considering that evidence can be found in the lack of attention given to the 'Arbeitslosengeld II' by the SPD, the personal responsibility demanded of the unemployed in the 'Agenda 2010' remains crucial to the policy of the Social Democrats and simultaneously shows that the left faction of the party is poorly assertive.

The CDU/CSU seems to 'walk on a thin line' by slowly but steadily accepting and supporting (to a minor degree) non-traditional styles of partnerships and families, based on the CDU policy statements of 2007 in which an acceptance of those non-traditional partnerships and same-sex unions were written down (Wiesendahl 2011, 122). Furthermore, the CDU/CSU is trying to reach the rather conservative part of the electorate, especially by emphasizing the fight against criminality and a rather restrictive view concerning immigration policies. The 'contagion by the left' that had already settled in during the time of the second grand coalition from 2005 to 2009 (Korte and Switek 2013, 5) seems to be continuing to such an extent that the CDU/CSU are cautiously willing to extend the welfare state as well as to accept certain social liberal values.

Table 7.5   Synopsis of the party manifestos of 2013

	SPD	CDU/CSU
Foreign Affairs	Pro NATO	Pro NATO
	Emphasis on Western values	Emphasis on Western values
	Foreign deployment accepted under reserve	Foreign deployment accepted under reserve
	Emphasis on national and international climate policy	Moderate emphasis on national and international climate policy, related to the preservation of jobs and domestic economy
Freedom and Democracy	Acceptance of representative democracy, widely expanded by participatory elements	Acceptance of representative democracy, only limitedly expanded by participatory elements
	Emphasis on the autonomy of the citizen	Ambivalence regarding the autonomy of the citizen
Government	Increased state orientation along with debureaucratisation and efficiency increase	State-oriented along with debureaucratisation and efficiency increase
Economy	'Re-foundation' of the social market economy	Preservation of the social market economy
	Focus on renewable energies, linked to public assistance	Focus on renewable energies
Welfare state	Extension of public assistance	Partial extension of public assistance
	Limited relevance of the market	Slightly market-oriented

Table 7.5   *Concluded*

	SPD	CDU/CSU
Structure of society	Slightly moderate liberal	Traditional/slightly liberal
	Emphasis on equal treatment policies	Moderate emphasis on equal treatment policies
Social groups	Implementation of a fixed quota	Implementation of the so-called 'flexi-quota', a flexible quota system
	Emphasis on civil rights	*No evidence in the party manifesto*
Pattern of the party manifesto	Administrative/ technocratic	Administrative/technocratic
	Detailed policies	Detailed policies
Competitors	Pronounced distinction to CDU/CSU and the FDP	Pronounced distinction to SPD/B'90/Die Grünen
State structure	Emphasis on cooperative federalism	Moderate emphasis on interstate federalism, notably concerning the inter-state fiscal adjustment
EU	Pro EU	Pro EU
Labour market and employment policy	Reduction of the current ancillary wage costs	Preservation of current ancillary wage costs
	Minimum wage of 8,50 euro	No government fixed minimum wage envisaged, but co-operative minimum wage as result of bargaining between employers and employees
Healthcare policy	National insurance scheme accompanied by a uniform official scale scheme of fees	Rejection of a uniform national insurance scheme; preservation of the status quo
Taxation system	Implementation of a property tax, increase of the top income taxes	Financial relief of the 'middle class', rejection of a property tax, no tax increases
Education policy	Emphasis on education policy as well as in R&D	Emphasis on education policy as well as in R&D

Referring to an essay by Harald Welzer published in the German news magazine *Der Spiegel* (Welzer 2013), public opinion seems to evaluate the party manifestos as indistinguishable and convergent. However, the present analysis shows – in accordance with other analyses of party manifestos (Kercher and Brettschneider 2013, 278; Merz and Regel 2013, 221; Lehmann et al. 2013) – that, even though a dominating campaign issue does not exist (Neu 2013, 24), differences between the party manifestos can be noted. In trying to offer distinctive features separating itself from the 'diffuse centrist policy' for which both the CDU/CSU and SPD were blamed in the recent past (Jun 2011, 104), the SPD moved to the left, thereby bolstering traditional social-democratic values such as freedom, (social) justice and solidarity (Reschke et al. 2013, 139). As Linhart and Shikano (2013, 437) demonstrate, the SPD and CDU/CSU both moved to the left on the social-economic axis as well as towards a liberal open society from 2005 to 2009, continuing this trend in 2013, as is shown in this qualitative analysis and also in the quantitative analysis. With regard to the finished coalition negotiations and the existing coalition agreement between the CDU/CSU and the SPD, this analysis offers the assumption that both parties are willing to further extend the welfare state but may disagree in some aspects of their conception of society.

The analysis of the manifestos shows that there are gradual differences between the CDU/CSU and the SPD. However, the number of commonalities is sufficient to build a coalition together and to ensure cooperation during a legislative period. In addition, the programmatic gap between the CDU/CSU and Bündnis'90/ Grüne is even wider than the one between the CDU/CSU and the SPD. During the election campaign, the Green Party clearly put emphasis on an increased role for the welfare state and on the libertarian ideals of its sympathizers. However, the CDU/CSU is (not yet) modernist enough to build a coalition with the Green Party on a national level. From the start it was unlikely that a coalition between the CDU/CSU and the Green Party could be built; this assumption is strengthened by the affective distance between sympathizers of the CDU/CSU and those of the Green Party (Köcher 2012; Lorenz 2007) which could not (yet) create the base of confidence necessary to build a coalition (see Köcher 2012; Bianchi et al. 2013).

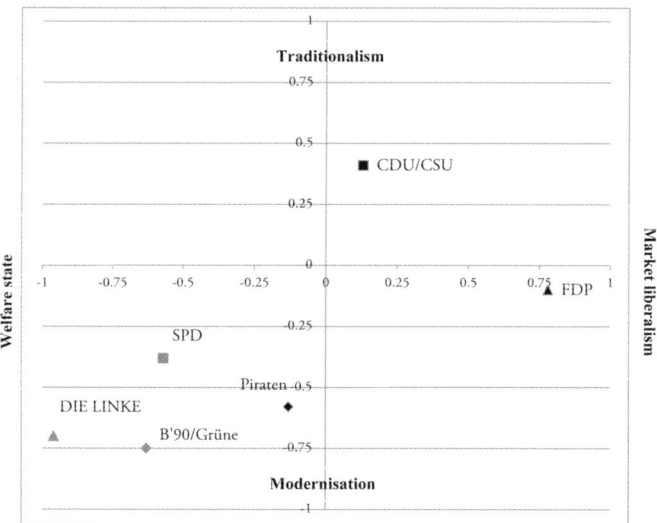

Figure 7.3   The German parties in a two-dimensional policy space
Source: Bianchi et al. (2013, 6).

Table 7.6   Scepticism concerning a coalition between the CDU/CSU and the Green Party

	Population in total (in %)	Sympathizers of the CDU/CSU (in %)	Sympathizers of B'90/Grüne (in %)
Could probably work	22	24	30
Disparities are too broad	56	56	57
Drawn; prefer not to say	22	20	13

Note: Respondents were asked the following question: 'In the recent discussion there are speculations about a coalition between the CDU/CSU and the Green Party. Do you think that such a coalition is able to function or do you think the disparities between the CDU/CSU and the Green Party are still too broad?'
Source: Allensbacher Archiv, IfD-Umfrage 11001.

A brief overview of the coalition agreement might give an insight into the changing programmatic contents of the CDU/CSU and SPD.

How to Govern: A Brief Overview of the Government Programme

Due to lack of space, this analysis cannot give a deeper insight into the coalition agreement between the CDU/CSU and the SPD, but offers a short prospect concerning the main passages that resulted in specific compromises between both parties and different factions within them. Noticeably, the coalition agreement clearly states that the grand coalition is willing to stop new indebtedness and to diminish the government debt ratio (CDU/CSU/SPD 2013, 8) without explicitly mentioning the increase in taxation or reduction of subsidies that will presumably be necessary to avoid new indebtedness. The tax policy was one of the central areas of conflict during the coalition negotiations; the CDU/CSU was able to reject the demands of the Social Democrats to increase taxes.

Concerning wage and pension policies, the three parties agreed to introduce a guaranteed minimum wage of 8.50 euro as of 2015 (with a possible deviation of two years maximum on the basis of wage agreements) and to introduce a minimum retirement pension as of 2017 (CDU/CSU/SPD 2013, 73). No statement is made in the coalition agreement regarding the unemployment benefit fixed in the Sozialgesetzbuch (SGB) II, better known as the 'Hartz-IV'-regulation, which was passed as a package of measures by the red-green government of 2003–5, and which was mainly responsible for the loss of the SPD's 'signature feature' (Oberndörfer et al. 2004, 2) and, as a further effect, the loss of a bigger part than usual of its formerly loyal voters and members (Meise 2010). It seems that the SPD indeed relies on the 'working poor' and is willing to support them by intervening in economic policies, but decouples the lower classes and the 'losers of modernisation', both in the manifesto and in the bargaining process of the coalition agreement.

Concerning the pension at the age of 63 (with the condition of at least 45 insurance years including times of unemployment), the coalition agreement clearly designates 1 July 2014 as the date from which the new pension laws will be legal, thus implementing the proposed policy of the SPD election manifesto (CDU/ CSU/SPD 2013, 72). Pensioners that reach the age of 63 and exhibit 45 years of insurance are then able to receive their pension without deduction. In addition, also according to the party manifesto of the SPD, the coalition agreement clarifies the introduction of a so-called *Lebensleistungsrente*, honouring those who worked under precarious conditions, especially regarding the wage they attained during their lifetime, but who contributed to the pension insurance for 40 years (CDU/ CSU/SPD 2013, 10; 73). These pensioners then automatically attain 30 'pension points' which are converted to an amount of money adjusted every year (in 2014 this means approximately 850 euro). Finally, the coalition agreement emphasizes the acknowledgement of the efforts involved in the raising of children, giving mothers with children born before 1992 an additional 'pension point' – times of child-rearing for children born since 1992 have already been acknowledged in past legislative periods (CDU/CSU/SPD 2013, 73).

Regarding equal treatment policy, the CDU/CSU agreed to the establishment of a fixed gender quota of 30 per cent for the management and supervisory boards of publicly listed companies, lowering the SPD's proposed quota of 40 per cent but also being willing to abandon their own proposed 'flexi-quota'. Concerning equal treatment policy in the case of same-sex unions, the coalition agreement only offers a few passages speaking of respect for and appreciation of same-sex unions in vague terms, without offering concrete policies (CDU/CSU/SPD 2013, 11; 105). This implies that the concepts of society concerning the equal treatment of homosexual couples offered by the two parties in their manifestos, as shown in the analysis below, diverge to an extent that a compromise in terms of, for instance, fiscal equalization – resulting from the CDU/CSU's conservatism and inherent even in the modernist faction – was not possible.

A compromise has been reached in the field of migration policy and dual citizenship: although the CDU/CSU vehemently refused to consider dual citizenship whereas the SPD demanded it without further restrictions, the coalition agreement states that children of foreign parents are allowed to adopt dual citizenship (CDU/CSU/SPD 2013, 105). In addition, the coalition agreement emphasizes the increase of migrants in the public service (CDU/CSU/SPD 2013, 106), and the strict movement-restricting laws (*Residenzpflicht*) for asylum seekers are loosened (CDU/CSU/SPD 2013, 109), concluding that 'Germany is a cosmopolitan country' (CDU/CSU/SPD 2013, 105). However, this rather modernist approach in migration policy is undermined by a harsh demand for immigrants to accept integration offers and the overall concept of 'demand and support'. The recent discussion concerning the feared so-called 'social benefit fraud' that Romanian and Bulgarian immigrants could commit shows the traditionalist apprehensions of the CSU especially. As much as it seems that the SPD enforced modernism in the coalition agreement, there is an explicit reliance on the Christian churches and religious communities as well as on the 'Christian background coining of our country' (CDU/CSU/SPD 2013, 113), clearly underlining the root concept of Christian Democracy.

A brief look at family policy in the coalition agreement reveals the SPD's readiness to compromise: the fiercely discussed *Betreuungsgeld* quoted above is not mentioned once in the coalition agreement although the SPD insisted on abolishing it. The coalition agreement explicitly bolsters traditional institutions such as marriage and family but simultaneously claims to fight for equal treatment of all citizens (CDU/CSU/SPD 2013, 11); this creates an unsolvable contradiction between privileging the traditional family structures and not discriminating against same-sex unions at the same time.

Even this short analysis reveals that delicate subjects do not seem to have found their way into the coalition agreement. Discussions about the *Betreuungsgeld*, equal treatment policies, especially in the area of taxation policy, and immigration policies might endure, precisely because there is no common consensus built into the coalition agreement.

Conclusion

This analysis has shown that both parties, the CDU/CSU and SPD, have diverged in the past years: whereas the CDU/CSU renewed itself while partially modifying or revising programmatic traditions and being clearly oriented towards the electorate, the SPD emphasized its etatist tradition more strongly than in 2005 or 2009 and highlighted 'social justice' as its signature feature in the party manifesto. However, the SPD does not fundamentally exclude programmatic positions of the former government policy of the Agenda 2010, which facilitated coalition-building with the CDU/CSU. In the term of office as party leader when the SPD was in opposition, Sigmar Gabriel managed to close the gap between modernizers and traditionalists in the party. Even though this move of integrating the different party factions led to intra-party consolidation, it did not help to significantly increase the amount of electoral votes for the party in the elections of 2013.

Regarding the socio-economic axis in the two-dimensional policy space, both parties moved to the left (towards state interventionism) or, in the case of the CDU, to a 'more state-centric social and economic policy' (Clemens 2013, 206). This assumption is proven by the main decisions in the coalition agreement, namely measures concerning pension policy and minimum wage policy. Concerning the socio-cultural axis, the CDU and its Bavarian partner, the CSU, remain the only established parties that tend to head towards authoritarian values even if the programmatic change of the CDU in the direction of more libertarian values in policy fields such as family policy or migration policy are clearly visible. In the future the AfD may become a relevant competitor with similarly authoritarian positions.

One can conclude that many members of the conservative wing of the party 'are also unhappy with the rather progressive policies implemented by the current government' (Debus and Müller 2013, 167), but play no major role and have been marginalized by its chairwoman, Angela Merkel. This renewal of the CDU, oriented towards the electorate, in the era of Chancellor Merkel (especially since 2005) accomplished its purpose in 2013 by gaining the support of a higher part of the population and by gaining acceptance for its policies. The popularity of Chancellor Merkel, who was clearly driven by a pragmatic style of problem-solving, crucially supported the election success. Somehow this programmatic bearing leaves enough scope for other competitors such as the national-conservative AfD or the liberal-economic FDP to evolve. At least, the coalition-building with the SPD does not restrict this scope.

In order to attract more voters the SPD will have to prove its competency in social and economic policy and at the same time will have to distance itself from the party Die Linke. The governing parties in total are going to attract – on the eve of the elections – voters who remain undecided. In consequence, this might influence the programmatic orientation: every governing party is only able to assert itself in the political competition if it manages to gain votes from its traditional voters as well as from the undecided ones. However, the grand coalition's policy is going to influence the other parties' programmatic scope as well. This leads back to the starting point: intra-party developments and party competition are interdependent, reciprocally related to one another, and interpenetrate each other. Party research is going to take a closer look at the programmatic development of the constellation of the party system as a whole after the coalition-building of the grand coalition, as well as observing whether a programmatic modernization as a consequence of practical government policy will take place with regard to the CDU as well as the SPD.

References

Arnim, Hans Herbert von. 2009. *Im Herbst der Volksparteien? Eine kleine Geschichte von Aufstieg und Rückgang politischer Massenintegration.* Bielefeld: Transcript.

Bender, Marvin; Bianchi, Matthias; Jüschke, Andreas; and Treibel, Jan. 2010. 'Der Duisburger NRW-Wahl-Index. Policy-Positionen der Parteien CDU, SPD, Grüne, FDP und Linke vor der Landtagswahl 2010 im Vergleich'. *Regierungsforschung.de*, 13 September. Available from: http://www.regierungsforschung.de/data/regierungsforschung.de__der_nrwwahlindex.pdf (accessed 15 October 2013).

Bianchi, Matthias; Bender, Steffen; Hohl, Karina; Jüschke, Andreas; Schoofs, Jan; Steitz, Susanne; and Treibel, Jan. 2013. 'Der Duisburger-Wahl-

Index (DWI) zur Bundestagswahl 2013. Policy-Positionen von CDU/ CSU, SPD, Grünen, FDP, Linke und Piraten zur Bundestagswahl 2013 im Vergleich'. *Regierungsforschung.de*, 11 September. Available from: http:// regierungsforschung.de/data/110913regierungsforschung.de_dwi_btw2013. pdf (accessed 15 October 2013).

Bösch, Frank. 2013. 'Die Christlich-Demokratische Union Deutschlands'. In *Handbuch der deutschen Parteien* (second edition), edited by Frank Decker and Viola Neu, 203–18. Wiesbaden: Springer VS.

Bräuninger, Thomas, and Debus, Marc (with Jochen Müller). 2012. Parteienwettbewerb in den deutschen Bundesländern. Wiesbaden: VS Verlag.

Bytzek, Evelyn. 2013. 'Koalitionspräferenzen, Koalitionswahl und Regierungsbildung'. In *Wahlen und Wähler. Analysen aus Anlass der Bundestagswahl 2009*, edited by Bernhard Weßels, Harald Schoen and Oscar W. Gabriel, 231–46. Wiesbaden: Springer VS.

CDU/CSU. 2013. *Gemeinsam erfolgreich für Deutschland. Regierungsprogramm 2013–2017*. Decided on 23 June.

CDU/CSU/SPD. 2013. *Deutschlands Zukunft gestalten. Koalitionsvertrag zwischen CDU, CSU und SPD*. 18. Legislaturperiode. Available from: http://www.tagesschau.de/inland/koalitionsvertrag136.pdf (accessed 15 January 2014).

Clemens, Clayton Marc. 2013. 'Beyond Christian democracy? Welfare state politics and policy in a changing CDU'. *German Politics*, vol. 22, n. 1–2: 191–211.

Debus, Marc, and Müller, Jochen. 2013. 'The programmatic development of CDU and CSU since reunification: incentives and constraints for changing policy positions in the German multi-level system'. *German Politics*, vol. 22, n. 1–2: 151–71.

Eith, Ulrich. 2010. 'Volksparteien unter Druck. Koalitionsoptionen, Integrationsfähigkeit und Kommunikationsstrategien nach der Übergangswahl 2009'. In *Analysen zur Bundestagswahl 2009*, edited by Karl-Rudolf Korte, 117–28. Wiesbaden: VS Verlag.

GLES. 2009. *Codierschema Agendafragen (2)*. GESIS-Study Materials 2011/102. Available from: http://www.gesis.org/wahlen/gles/daten_und_dokumente/ dokumente (accessed 15 October 2013).

Grabow, Karsten. 2008. 'Parteien und Parteiensystem in Mecklenburg-Vorpommern'. In *Parteien und Parteiensysteme in den deutschen Bundesländern*, edited by Uwe Jun, Oskar Niedermayer and Melanie Haas, 265–90. Wiesbaden: VS Verlag.

Hildebrandt, Cornelia, and Weichold, Jochen. 2013. *Bundestagswahl 2013: Wahlprogramme der Parteien im Vergleich*. Standpunkte 11/2013. Berlin: Rosa-Luxemburg-Stiftung.

Jun, Uwe. 2007. 'Parteiensystem und Koalitionskonstellationen vor und nach der Bundestagswahl 2005'. In *Die Bundestagswahl 2005. Analysen des Wahlkampfes und der Wahlergebnisse*, edited by Frank Brettschneider, Oskar Niedermayer and Bernhard Weßels, 491–515. Wiesbaden: VS Verlag.

Jun, Uwe. 2010. 'Die SPD in der Großen Koalition. Selbstverschuldeter Niedergang oder zwanghafte Anpassung an veränderte Ausgangsbedingungen der Politik?' In *Die Große Koalition. Regierung – Politik – Parteien*, edited by Sebastian Bukow and Wenke Seemann, 299–318. Wiesbaden: VS Verlag.

Jun, Uwe. 2011. 'Die Repräsentationslücke der Volksparteien: Erklärungsansätze für den Bedeutungsverlust und Gegenmaßnahmen'. In *Krise und Reform politischer Repräsentation*, edited by Markus Linden and Winfried Thaa, 95–124. Baden-Baden: Nomos.

Jun, Uwe. 2013. 'Sozialdemokratische Partei Deutschlands'. In *Handbuch der deutschen Parteien* (second edition), edited by Frank Decker and Viola Neu, 387–403. Wiesbaden: Springer VS.

Jun, Uwe, and Berzel, Alexander. 2014. 'Weshalb verlor die SPD die Wahl? Personal, Organisation, Programmatik, Koalitionsstrategie, Wahlergebnis'. In *Bilanz der Bundestagswahl 2013*, edited by Eckhard Jesse and Roland Sturm, 205–29. Baden-Baden: Nomos.

Kercher, Jan, and Brettschneider, Frank. 2013. 'Wahlprogramme als Pflichtübung? Typen, Funktionen und Verständlichkeit der Bundestagswahlprogramme 1994–2009'. In *Wahlen und Wähler. Analysen aus Anlass der Bundestagswahl 2009*, edited by Bernhard Weßels, Harald Schoen and Oscar W. Gabriel, 269–90. Wiesbaden: Springer VS.

Köcher, Renate. 2012. 'Gefühlte und reale Distanz'. *Frankfurter Allgemeine Zeitung*, 20 December.

Korte, Karl-Rudolf, and Switek, Niko. 2013. 'Regierungsbilanz: Politikwechsel und Krisenentscheidungen'. *Aus Politik und Zeitgeschichte*, vol. 48–9: 3–9.

Korte, Karl-Rudolf, and Treibel, Jan. 2009a. *Inhaltsanalyse 'Parteiprogrammatik und Parteirhetorik vor der Bundestagswahl 2009'*. Wahlprogramme. Available from: http://www.zdf.de/ZDFxt/module/Wortwolken/spitzentimeline/content/pdf/Wissenschaftliche_Inhaltsanalyse_zu_den_Wahlprogrammen.pdf (accessed 15 October 2013).

Korte, Karl-Rudolf, and Treibel, Jan. 2009b. *Inhaltsanalyse 'Parteiprogrammatik und Parteirhetorik vor der Bundestagswahl 2009'*. Grundsatzprogramme. Available from: http://www.zdf.de/ZDFxt/module/Wortwolken/spitzentimeline/content/pdf/Wissenschaftliche_Inhaltsanalyse_zu_den_Grundsatzprogrammen.pdf (accessed 15 October 2013).

Laver, Michael; Benoit, Kenneth; and Garry, John. 2003. 'Extracting policy positions from political texts using words as data'. *American Political Science Review*, vol. 97, n. 2: 311–31.

Lehmann, Pola; Merz, Nicolas; Regel, Sven, and Werner, Annika. 2013. 'Und sie unterscheiden sich doch! Eine Analyse der Wahlprogramme zur Bundestagswahl 2013'. *Democracy & Democratization* [blog]. Available from: http://democracy.blog.wzb.eu/2013/09/16/und-sie-unterscheiden-sich-doch-eine-analyse-der-wahlprogramme-zur-bundestagswahl-2013 (accessed 9 December 2013).

Linhart, Eric, and Shikano, Susumo. 2009. 'Ideological signals of German parties in a multi-dimensional space: an estimation of party preferences using the CMP data'. *German Politics*, vol. 18, n. 3: 301–22.

Linhart, Eric, and Shikano, Susumu. 2013. 'Parteienwettbewerb und Regierungsbildung bei der Bundestagswahl 2009: Schwarz-Gelb als Wunschkoalition ohne gemeinsame Marschrichtung?' In *Wahlen und Wähler. Analysen aus Anlass der Bundestagswahl 2009*, edited by Bernhard Weßels, Harald Schoen and Oscar W. Gabriel, 426–51. Wiesbaden: Springer VS.

Lorenz, Christian. 2007. 'Schwarz-Grün auf Bundesebene?' *Aus Politik und Zeitgeschichte*, vol. 35–6: 33–40.

Meise, Stephan. 2010. '"… wozu die Sozialdemokratie eigentlich verpflichtet wäre" – Verprellte Mitglieder, Parteiaustritte und die Vertrauenskrise der SPD'. In *Die Krise der SPD. Autoritäre oder partizipatorische Demokratie* (second edition), edited by Heiko Geiling, 113–58. Münster: LIT.

Merz, Nicolas, and Regel, Sven. 2013. 'Die Programmatik der Parteien'. In *Handbuch Parteienforschung*, edited by Oskar Niedermayer, 211–40. Wiesbaden: Springer VS.

Neu, Viola. 2013. *Wahlanalyse der Bundestagswahl in Deutschland am 22. September 2013*. Berlin: KAS. Available from: http://www.kas.de/wf/doc/kas_35530–544–1-30.pdf?131105132354 (accessed 9 December 2013).

Niedermayer, Oskar. 2003. 'Parteiensystem'. In *Demokratien des 21. Jahrhunderts im Vergleich*, edited by Eckhard Jesse and Roland Sturm, 261–71. Opladen: Leske & Budrich.

Niedermayer, Oskar. 2013. 'Die Entwicklung des bundesdeutschen Parteiensystems'. In *Handbuch der deutschen Parteien* (second edition), edited by Frank Decker and Viola Neu, 111–34. Wiesbaden: Springer VS.

Oberndörfer, Dieter; Mielke, Gerd; and Eith, Ulrich. 2004. *Die Mär von der Besonderheit des Ostens. SPD und Union kommen ihrer Aufgabe als Volksparteien nur unzureichend nach*. Available from: http://www.politik.uni-freiburg.de/forschung/awf/pdf/Sachsen_Brandenburg_2004.pdf (accessed 14 January 2014).

Pappi, Franz U., and Shikano, Susumu. 2007. *Wahl- und Wählerforschung*. Baden-Baden: Nomos.

Proksch, Sven-Oliver, and Slapin, Jonathan B. 2009. 'How to avoid pitfalls in statistical analysis of political texts: the case of Germany'. *German Politics*, vol. 18, n. 3: 323–44.

Reschke, Michael; Krell, Christian; Dahm, Jochen; Grebing, Helga; and Woyke, Meik. 2013. *History of Social Democracy*. Berlin: FES.

SPD. 2013. *Das WIR entscheidet. Das Regierungsprogramm 2013–2017*. Berlin. Decided on 14 April.

Treibel, Jan. 2010. 'Was stand zur Wahl 2009? Grundsatzprogramme, Wahlprogramme und der Koalitionsvertrag im Vergleich'. In *Die Bundestagswahl 2009. Analysen der Wahl-, Parteien-, Kommunikations- und*

Regierungsforschung, edited by Karl-Rudolf Korte, 89–116. Wiesbaden: VS Verlag.

Volkens, Andrea, and Klingemann, Hans-Dieter. 2002. 'Parties, ideologies, and issues. Stability and change in fifteen European party systems 1945–1998'. In *Political Parties in the New Europe*, edited by Kurt Richard Luther and Ferdinand Müller-Rommel, 143–67. Oxford: Oxford University Press.

Volkens, Andrea; Lehmann, Pola; Merz, Nicolas; Regel, Sven; Werner, Annika; Lacewell, Onawa Promise; and Schultze, Henrike. 2013. *The Manifesto Data Collection. Manifesto Project (MRG/CMP/MARPOR)*. Berlin: Wissenschaftszentrum Berlin für Sozialforschung (WZB).

Alemann, Ulrich Von, and Spier, Tim. 2011. 'Erholung in der Opposition? Die SPD nach der Bundestagswahl 2009'. In *Die Parteien nach der Bundestagswahl 2009*, edited by Oskar Niedermayer, 57–77. Wiesbaden: VS Verlag.

Walter, Franz; Werwath, Christian; and D'Antonio, Oliver. 2011. *Die CDU. Entstehung und Verfall christdemokratischer Geschlossenheit*. Baden-Baden: Nomos.

Welzer, Harald. 2013. 'Das Ende des kleineren Übels'. *Spiegel Online*, 27 May. Available from: http://www.spiegel.de/spiegel/print/d-96238982.html (accessed 9 December 2013).

Wiesendahl, Elmar. 1992. 'Volksparteien im Abstieg. Nachruf auf eine zwiespältige Erfolgsgeschichte'. *Aus Politik und Zeitgeschichte*, vol. 34–5: 3–14.

Wiesendahl, Elmar. 1993. 'Parteien in der Krise. Mobilisierungsdefizite, Integrations- und Organisationsschwächen der Parteien in Deutschland'. *Sowi*, vol. 22: 77–87.

Wiesendahl, Elmar. 2011. 'Ist das Strategie? Strategische Richtungssuche von CDU und SPD zwischen den Wahlen'. *Forschungsjournal Soziale Bewegungen*, vol. 24: 119–29.

Zastrow, Thomas. 2013. *Computerlinguistische Analyse der Wahlprogramme 2013*. Available from: http://www.thomas-zastrow.de/wahl13/index.html (accessed 4 December 2013).

Zolleis, Udo, and Schmid, Josef. 2011. 'Regierungswechsel statt Machtverlust – die CDU nach der Bundestagswahl 2009'. In *Die Parteien nach der Bundestagswahl 2009*, edited by Oskar Niedermayer, 37–56. Wiesbaden: VS Verlag.

Chapter 8

The Failed Struggle for Office Instead of Votes: The Greens, Die Linke and the FDP[1]

Simon T. Franzmann

Introduction

Gregor Gysi, chairman of the parliamentary group for the Left Party, expressed his satisfaction that it had emerged as the third strongest party in the German Bundestag of 2013 thus: 'Who thought in 1990 that we would be the third strongest party? Nobody!' At first glance, this comment might give the impression that, in the German parliamentary election, third place was contested. However, a direct struggle for the position did not actually occur in the election. Gysi's claim, rather, was an attempt to reinterpret the loss of approximately one-quarter of the party's votes as a victory. Indeed, all three of the smaller parties lost votes. Furthermore, not one of them – the Left, the Greens and the Free Democratic Party (FDP) – can be seen as an outright winner. A new party, the 'Alternative for Germany' (AfD), emerged and subsequently beat the FDP for the status of the second strongest bourgeois party, behind the Christian democrats (CDU). The FDP, however, did not even garner enough votes to enter parliament, as it failed to meet the five-per-cent threshold.

With this in mind, this chapter seeks to question why *all* three of the smaller parties lost votes. This seems to be particularly astonishing considering that third-place parties have traditionally been very influential in German politics. For instance, a third, smaller party normally plays a pivotal part in a coalition government, often holding the deciding vote. Although this is not a steadfast 'law' in German politics, it has a definite empirical regularity: the FDP has for instance been a member of the government longer than any other, and was also the third strongest party in the old West German republic. However, in both 1998 and 2002 the Greens emerged as the third strongest party and, as a result, became

---

1   I am grateful to Michael Angenendt, Jana Lassen and Johannes Schmitt for their research assistance. I should also like to thank the participants of the seminars on content analysis in Potsdam in 2011, and in Düsseldorf in 2013, who discussed and helped code the manifestos of the Pirate Party in 2009 and the AfD in 2013. All remaining errors are mine.

a part of the 'red-green' government led by the Social Democratic chancellor, Gerhard Schröder.[2]

There have of course been exceptions, the grand coalitions of 1966–9 and 2005–9 standing as paradigmatic. Another exception occurred in 1994, when the FDP did not receive as many votes as the Greens, but was able to continue its coalition with the CDU. This was a consequence of German electoral law: an electoral mechanism grants additional seats in the Länder for the party that wins a surplus of private districts; what is known as the Überhangmandate. Consequently, the Christian–Liberal coalition's small advantage of 0.3 per cent of the votes was translated into a ten-seat majority in parliament. In 2013, the strongest party became the Left Party. As shall be argued, however, the Left Party is ideologically too far from the common centre and too internally divided to undertake government responsibilities. Where the third-place party normally becomes a part of government, the statements of the other small parties, outlining their preferred government, can be crucial tools in understanding their collective electoral defeat.

In 2013, for instance, it was interesting to note that all three of the small parties fought against a coalition, rather than fighting in favour of a coalition: the Greens' main strategy was to undermine the Christian–Liberal coalition and they consequently fought officially as an alternative option for a 'red-green' coalition; the Left Party officially sought to form a coalition with the Greens and Social Democrats (SPD) – however, many of its members did not want to coalesce with any other party. In the last week before the elections, the liberal FDP started a campaign for a Christian–Liberal coalition, but only insofar as they were trying to 'borrow' (*Leihstimme*) votes from the CDU voters.

In order to analyse the strategies employed by the smaller parties, a theoretical framework is needed that takes into account numerous concerns. Firstly, Germany can best be characterized as an oligopoly in which the smaller political parties have to continually take into account the electoral strategies of the dominant parties. Secondly, descriptions of small parties' ideological positions need to be critically inspected. Not only can this be done during elections but also during the opinion polls that occur between the elections. One can easily recognize that, instead of searching for a pivotal position that would guarantee many coalition options, the small parties may rhetorically favour wing coalitions that necessitate that they place themselves nearer to the electoral extremes, rather than to the centre (which is already occupied by the larger party). Thirdly, particular party strategies should be inspected in more detail. It has become obvious, especially in the case of the Greens, FDP and Pirate Party (PP), that they wrongly perceived their electoral strengths, neglected vote-seeking considerations, and chose electoral strategies that were neither suitable for attracting votes nor for getting into office.

---

2   In Germany, a coalition of Social Democrats and Alliance90/Greens is commonly termed as a 'red–green' government.

Analytic Framework: German Party Politics as an Oligopoly

Searching for the best explanations as to why all the smaller parliamentarian parties lost votes in the German elections of 2013 requires a theoretical clarification of the basic assumptions underlying the argument. In formulating retrospective hypotheses about political actors' behaviour, the main analytical tool is rational choice theory. It must be remembered that, applied in political science, rational choice does not necessarily mean that parties act rationally, or that parties act as unitary actors. It simply means, rather, that, based on actors' behaviour, we can reconstruct the mechanisms that were used by them in order to fulfil their self-chosen goals (Riker 1995). With this in mind, the paradigmatic approach for explaining party competition in the tradition of rational choice theory is, without doubt, that of the economic theory of democracy outlined by Anthony Downs (1957). This is because he drafted the tools necessary for analysing party competition in a confrontational, one-dimensional space with two or more parties that adapt to a given voter distribution. Despite its popularity, this approach has received numerous criticisms. For instance, some have argued that 'valence issues' are ignored – issues on which all parties agree, such as fighting corruption and unemployment (Stokes 1963). Furthermore, the preference-shaping ability of political parties is also neglected (Bartolini 1999). Criticism has also been laid at the assumption that parties are fully informed; it has been argued, rather, that party competition works as a Hayekian 'discovery process' in which parties discover new issues, voter distributions, and only at the end successful electoral strategies (Franzmann 2011).

Finally, Downs modelled all political parties on an understanding that they are vote-maximizing actors. However, as Kaare Strøm (1990) has shown, parties have to negotiate a trade-off between at least three main goals: votes, policy and office. With regard to the first, '[v]otes have no intrinsic value for party leaders' (Strøm 1990, 573). Votes are simply a means in the pursuit of policy and/or office. The three goals are, furthermore, not mutually exclusive. For instance, a policy-seeker will also seek office in order to implement their desired policies. To do so requires votes. Moreover, the higher the uncertainty of the electoral outcome, the more likely that parties will fight for votes, rather than directly for policy or office (Strøm 1990, 588).

Referring to concrete discussions with green parties, Harmel and Janda (1994, 269) add 'intraparty democracy maximization' as a fourth possible goal. Such a goal directly contradicts vote-seeking strategies. In analysing the selection logic a party may use in choosing its electoral strategy, we can assume the following:

> Proposition 1: Small German parties choose between (a) vote-seeking, (b) policy-seeking, (c) office-seeking, (d) intra-party democracy maximizing strategies. The higher the uncertainty of the electoral outcome, the more likely that the small German parties will focus on vote-seeking, at the exclusion of the other three goals.

With this in place, it is important to identify the situational logic the parties face: in what ways can the small parties manoeuvre? Obviously, in comparison to both larger parties, small German parties are fundamentally different in their member structure and public influence. The large German parties define themselves as *Volksparteien,* who seek to integrate, both vertically and horizontally, different interests, ideas, opinions and social groups (Jun 2011). Translated into party competition terms, given sufficient size and media attention, such *Volksparteien* can shape the political market. They thus directly affect the political chances of smaller parties by defining the landscape on which they compete. Even despite a decline in recent years, the larger CDU and SPD have remained the dominant forces in the electoral market. Moreover, the last few German elections have revealed that their candidates' media performances have gained importance in the race for electoral results, and have led to a certain of 'presidentialisation' of German politics (Poguntke 2011; Poguntke and Webb 2007). In 2009, for instance, Merkel was an 'electoral asset' (Schoen 2011) for the CDU. The same can be assumed for 2013. With this in mind, the German reality of party politics is that of an oligopoly (Franzmann 2006). In this oligopoly, the two large parties set, as first movers, their strategic choices and the small parties have to adapt to these:

> Proposition 2: The German party space is best characterized as an oligopoly. The two largest parties, the CDU and SPD, define the landscape on which the smaller parties have to negotiate their electoral strategy.

> Corollary 1a: The strategies of the established smaller parties are always different from those of the larger parties.

> Corollary 1a's importance becomes clearer when it is used, in combination with proposition 1, to identify the concrete strategic choices open to the small parties.

> Corollary 1b: The small German parties have the strategic choice to choose (a) 'passive' policy/vote-seeking: adopting issues the larger parties owned previously but now neglect (for example, Die Linke since 2005 and the AfD in 2013); (b) 'active' policy/vote-seeking: find a niche adopting issues the larger parties ignore or have not yet have detected (for example, the PP in 2009 and the AfD in 2013); (c) 'passive' office/vote-seeking: campaign for a special coalition (for example, the FDP in 2002–13, the Greens in 1998–2005, the pragmatic wing of Die Linke in 2013); (d) 'active' office/vote-seeking: actively searching and fighting for the pivotal position in the party system (for example, the FDP in 1957–94, the right 'reformer' wing of the Greens in 2013);

> (e) maximizing intra-party democracy: ignoring the oligopolistic game structure, the strategic choices of the two largest parties and all other competitors (for example, the left wing of the Greens and the PP in 2013).

The examples in the brackets occurred before they were interpreted.[3] It remains to be seen, however, in which kinds of political spaces these strategies can be applied. A one-dimensional solution seems too reductive, especially since German voting behaviour has traditionally occurred along the lines of both religious beliefs and class-belonging (Pappi 1984; Huber 1989). The process of secularization and de-industrialization has, however, transformed the former, but not the latter. The economic dimension has survived, albeit with less salience. Moreover, during the same period, a social controversy about authoritarian and libertarian values became important (Kitschelt 2003). Knutsen (2009) has corroborated this view but has also added a third, regional, dimension in explaining the electoral success of the CSU in Bavaria and Die Linke in East Germany. However, this study interprets these regional dimensions as niches within the larger national electoral competition, primarily because these regional questions are not linked to ideological stances. Thus:

> Proposition 3: The German political space can best be described by using two dimensions: an economic and social one.

> Corollary 2: German party strategies and their electoral fortunes can best be understood by analyzing their two-dimensional party positions, rather than their single, ideological, positions.

German Party Position and their Success at the Opinion Polls

In analysing their strategies, it is important to understand how the smaller parties place themselves in a two-dimensional German policy space. With this in place, it will be possible to see how voters' support has developed between the two previous elections of 2009 and 2013. While their policy positions have remained relatively stable, opinion polls in Germany have revealed an increasing volatility amongst the public.

Party positions have been determined by using data from the Manifesto Projects (Budge et al. 2001; Klingemann et al. 2006; Volkens et al. 2013), now officially termed MARPOR (Manifesto Research on Political Representation). As

---

3   Please note that an understanding of German party politics as an oligopoly is not compatible with the differentiation between mainstream and niche parties. The niche party concept was developed by Meguid (2008) to analyse the electoral fate of single-issue parties acting beyond the main economic distinction between the left and right. Comparative research on party politics has made great advances in using this concept (see, for example Adams et al. 2012). However, Germany's small parties do not fit the definition of a niche party: neither the German Greens, FDP, nor Die Linke are single-issue parties. The FDP and Die Linke are clearly engaged with the economic dimension. Because of this, I refrain from using the concept of niche parties.

this argument is interested in supply-side politics, and therefore cannot rely on mass surveys, such a data source is a necessary indicator in determining policy positions. Due to the necessity of determining a two-dimensional position, this research relies on the method defined by Franzmann and Kaiser (2006). This approach uses a country-specific scheme that can be applied to as many nested dimensions as a scholar wishes. Furthermore, this method is useful at revealing reliability and validity scores (Dinas and Gemenis 2010; Franzmann 2013). An alternative would be the two-dimensional solution of Linhart and Shikano (2009), which would show very similar results to that of Franzmann and Kaiser (2006). However, its reliability is untested.

Positions in the Two-dimensional Space

The Figures 8.1a–8.1d display the two-dimensional policy space in Germany from 2002 to 2013. Perhaps the most crucial difference in explaining the dynamics of German party politics since reunification is the change in stance of the pivotal centre party – defined as 'a centre party that has no parliamentary majority to either its right or its left' (Hazan 1996, 215). Such a party forms a necessary part of an ideologically connected coalition government (Keman 1994). From 1961, until the election in 1998, the FDP was the pivot party in the German party system. In 1998, however, the SPD gained this pivotal position (Saalfeld 2002, 110–12). The SPD remained in this position until 2009, when they lost it in an electoral disaster. However, the FDP did not gain the pivotal position back; because the FDP had taken a position on the very right, the more centrally orientated CDU became the pivotal party. Indeed, in 2009, the FDP officially renounced its pivotal position by forming a coalition with the CDU/CSU, and by refusing a potential coalition with the SPD and Greens (Bieber and Roßteutscher 2011, 20).

The figures below show the two-dimensional ideological map of German party politics, and reveal the FDP's distance from the centre. The pivotal positions in the German party system currently oscillate between the two major parties, the CDU/CSU and the SPD. In 2013, the party closest to the ideological centre was the CDU/CSU. However, because the AfD, the FDP, and the PP failed to enter parliament, the SPD became a parliamentarian pivotal party despite its being positioned on the ideological left of the economic plateau. Moreover, not one of the smaller parties has really tried to undermine the SPD and CDU. Indeed, the three smaller parties have shown only slight ideological changes between 2002 and 2013. The PDS of 2002 merged, in 2005, with the offshoot of the SPD, the WASG, to form the Left Party. The newly formed 'Die Linke' became more socially radical yet more economically moderate, and as a consequence has taken the place of the PDS, remaining at the top left of the two-dimensional figures shown below. The FDP was, until the emergence of the PP, the only party in the top-right quadrant. During their time as the opposition, which ended in 2009, the FDP have become increasingly conservative. Consequently, ideologically, contestations in Germany have widened, while socio-economic concerns have become more focused. As a result, the opportunity for the emergence of an extremely conservative party has become restricted. This is because extreme right parties are more likely to occur in situations where the parliamentarian parties are in close agreement with regard to economic issues. Issues such as immigration then become important. Such a political opportunity has not occurred in Germany since reunification (Spies and Franzmann 2011). Therefore, with regard to the figures below, we can explain the emptiness of the bottom-right quadrant as a function of a lack of conservative issues. Nevertheless, in 2013, a new party emerged at the extreme right of economic concerns and with a conservative (but not extreme) consideration for social issues, the AfD). The figures below suggest that the AfD has emerged in response to the CDU's movement towards the centre. In fact, as shall be discussed below, the AfD might have profited from this move to the centre, but it profits even more from maintaining euroscepticism as a core issue. The only small party that has moved towards the centre has been the Greens, after being thrown out of the coalition government in 2005.

At the Länder level the Greens formed governments with the CDU in Hamburg and with the CDU and FDP in Saarland. Both Green coalitions collapsed before the end of the legislature. In both cases, the snap elections resulted in their exclusion from government. This might explain why the Greens have turned back, becoming more leftist in 2013. However, since the SPD has become even more economically conservative, the Greens are now placed to the right of the SPD in terms of economic issues. With regard to non-economic issues, the Greens have remained very progressive, operating a large distance from the theoretical centre and the CDU. However, this distance has become much smaller since the CDU has partly abandoned its traditional, conservative family policy prescriptions under the leadership of Angela Merkel (Poguntke 2012).

In conclusion, it can be argued that not one of the smaller parties tried to achieve the pivotal position between the SPD and CDU. It will be argued below that only the right wing of the Greens sought to take this position, but this has less intra-party power compared to the left wing. Neglecting the pivotal position might be an effect of the 2009 election against the grand coalition; the small parties have had to attract votes by signalling to the public that they prefer to remain wing coalitions. Consequently, in 2013, a fight for third place did not occur, with all attention focused on the second place. Within the left camp, this resulted in a struggle between Greens and Die Linke. Within the bourgeois camp, the FDP and the newly formed AfD have contested for a place beside the CDU/CSU.

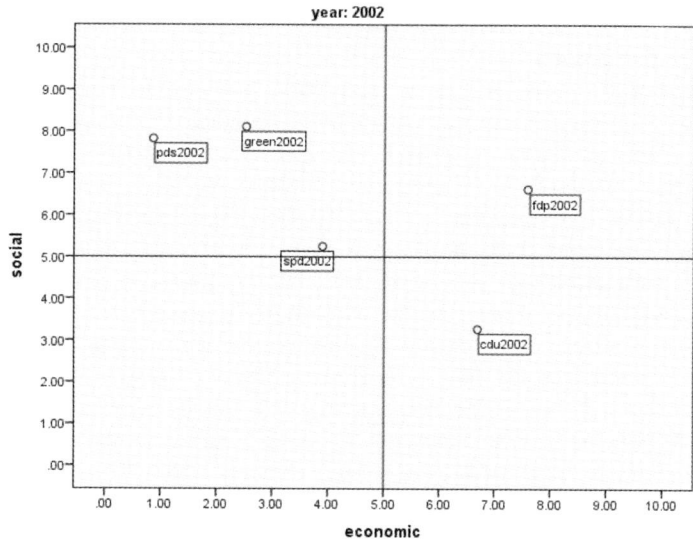

Figure 8.1a   The German policy space in 2002

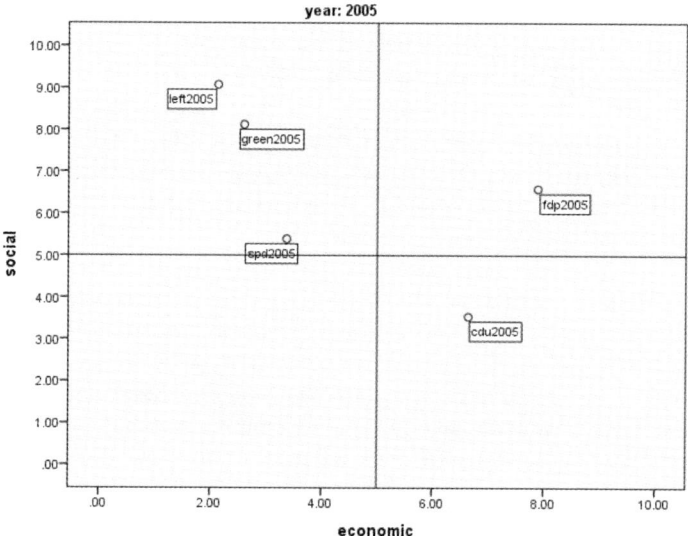

Figure 8.1b   The German policy space in 2005

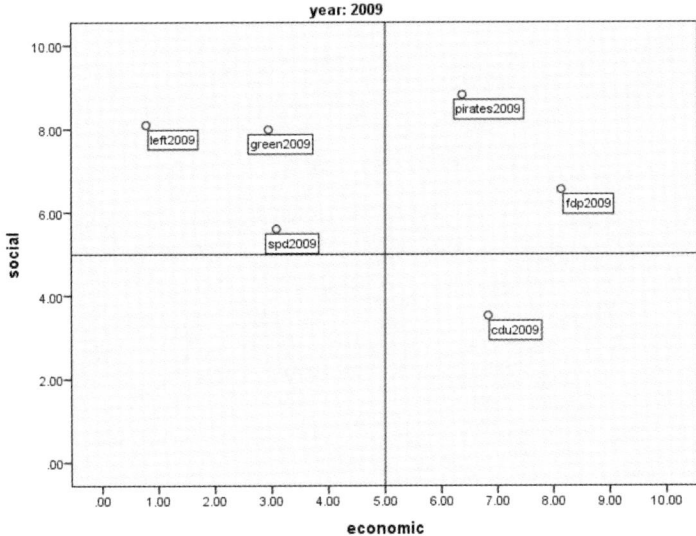

Figure 8.1c   The German policy space in 2009

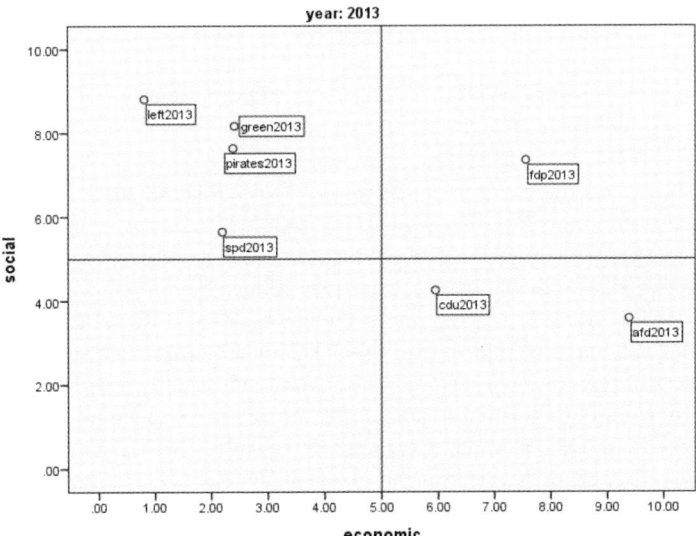

Figure 8.1d   The German policy space in 2013

Note: These diagrams are based on data from MARPOR (Volkens et al. 2013) and manifesto coding for the AfD in 2013, and the PP in 2009. Left-Right values are determined using the method of Franzmann and Kaiser (2006). The economic dimension embraces a scale from 0 (extreme left) to 10 (extreme right). The social dimension embraces a scale from 0 (extreme libertarian) to -10 (extreme authoritarian). All calculations are the author's.

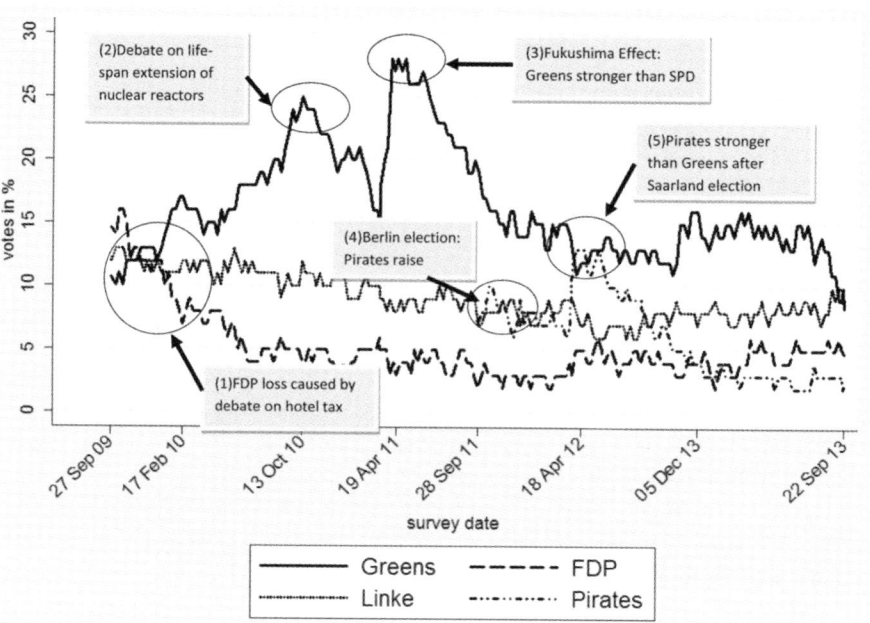

Figure 8.2   Opinion polls of small parties between the elections – 2009 and 2013

Source: author's own figure based on data from FORSA opion polls as published on wahlrecht.de, http://www.wahlrecht.de/umfragen/forsa.htm (accessed 31 March 2014).

Figure 8.2 displays the weekly results for the German small parties obtained from opinion polls conducted between the 2009 and 2013 elections.[4] The curves both fluctuate and show a high volatility. Furthermore, six remarkable peaks can be detected. The first occurs directly after the 2009 election. Support of the FDP was at its peak with over 14 per cent of the electoral vote. Those tactically voting against the grand coalition produced this large increase, as analyses derived from the 'correct voting' framework suggest (Rudi and Schoen 2013, 416–17). However, when the new Christian–Liberal government took office, electoral support for the FDP declined. One might argue that the FDP was punished for not enforcing a tax reform they had promised before the election. Furthermore, expectations of the Christian–Liberal coalition were too high, especially considering that the CDU were not officially interested in changing economic and fiscal policy (Linhart and Shikano 2013, 448). As a result, the first and only tax reform that was initiated was a reduction in value-added tax, especially with regard to hotels. At the same time, the public was informed of a campaign donation that had been given to the FDP by an important hotel manager (Mövenpickspende). The public thus interpreted the

---

4   The AfD is not displayed due to its sudden rise directly before the elections.

tax reform as an instance of nepotism and voter fraud. The FDP has never really recovered from this loss of credibility (Vorländer 2011, 121–3).

The second remarkable peaks occurred in September and October 2010, and involved the Greens. It was the very first time the Greens became electorally stronger than the SPD. This reflected the public's dissatisfaction with the policy of extending the working lifespan of nuclear reactors, which was decided by the Christian–Liberal government in September. The decision to increase the working lifespan of Germany's nuclear reactors was also in direct contrast to a former decision made by the 'red-green' government, which expressed the need to phase out nuclear reactors. The Greens, as the most credible anti-nuclear party, temporarily profited from this.

The third peak, occurring in March 2011, reveals an even higher opinion result for the Greens. Up until February 2011, public dissatisfaction with the lifespan extension of nuclear reactors had largely diminished. However, the nuclear catastrophe at Fukushima revived the anti-nuclear sentiments held by the German public. The Greens profited from this again, a gain reinforced by local protest against a large power station building project in Stuttgart. As a consequence, the Länder election that took place in Baden-Württemberg led to the formation of a German government with a Green prime minister.

The fourth and the fifth peaks both follow the PP, occurring during the Länder election. The first occurred in October 2011, and was a reaction to the success of the elections in Berlin. The fifth peak reveals that, from March to May 2012 (and after the election in Saarland), the PP became even stronger than the Greens. However, the Greens had experienced a continued decline in support, especially since their summit during the Baden-Württemberg election. The primary reason for this decline was the energy policy change of the Christian–Liberal coalition. They undermined the policy of extending the lifespan of nuclear reactors and decided to accelerate nuclear decommissioning; even more so than the previous 'red-green' coalition. As a result, the core green issue dissolved. The Greens continued to capture 11 per cent of the public support, until a few weeks before the elections when a discussion concerning their foundational policy towards paedophilia led to a further loss of voter support. The PP decline was even more dramatic. From a peak of 13 per cent, their share of support steadily declined to approximately 2 per cent, primarily due to internal factionalism.

The high volatility of electoral support might have presupposed a high level of uncertainty with regard to the electoral results. With this in mind, and in following proposition 1, the smaller parties would have had to adopt vote-seeking strategies. However, while the strategies were internally decided up to a year in advance, the politico-economic and social dynamics of the country were very different at the start of the elections. The Greens, for instance, continued to garner up to 15 per cent of the support until just two months before the election, thus perceiving themselves as in a position of strength. As a consequence they did not focus heavily on votes. One year before the national election, the PP also felt secure in obtaining seats in parliament. Die Linke had the less volatile profile, and it might therefore be suggested that they could neglect intensive vote-seeking behaviours. Finally, the FDP tended to oscillate around the five-per-cent threshold; they felt secure, however, primarily due to their parliamentarian entry point of the Länder elections in 2012 (in North Rhine-Westphalia and Schleswig-Holstein) as well as in 2013 (in Lower Saxony).

The Parties' Strategies

In this final section of the chapter, the particular strategies adopted by the various parties are inspected in more detail. A peculiarity of the 2013 election was that three ideologically liberal parties competed for votes: the FDP, the PP and the AfD. Within the liberal party family, four further divisions can be distinguished: national-liberal parties such as the former Italian PLI, economic-liberal parties such as the Dutch VVD, radical-liberal parties such as the British Liberal Democrats or the Italian PRI, and social-liberal parties such as the Dutch D66 (Fleck 2006; Franzmann 2012). Originally, the German FDP had a strong national-liberal wing. However, they transformed into a radical-liberal party in the 1970s and in the 1980s, so much so that today it is an economic-liberal party (Franzmann 2012). The Pirates can be characterized as a social-liberal party. The AfD's ideological profile is, furthermore, similar to that of a national-liberal party. However, as shown below, at times it also holds very conservative viewpoints.

Three Liberal Parties: The FDP, AfD and PP

Asked whether Germany needs a liberal party, 27 per cent of the respondents to a poll conducted after the election answered 'yes'. However, when asked whether Germany needs the FDP, only 19 per cent of the respondents answered 'yes' (Hank and Meck 2013, 29). The same survey revealed that 16 per cent of the respondents could imagine voting for the FDP, while 19 per cent thought it possible to vote for the AfD. Consequently, the FDP cannot be seen as exclusively or ideologically tied to political liberalism. This is, furthermore, the FDP's current dilemma. Economically speaking, the FDP is now a strong competitor for the AfD. The AfD is, after all, the more market-economy orientated party, a stance it combines with an anti-euro attitude. The FDP, on the other hand, is the market-orientated pro-euro party. The question of the euro thus splits each party, dividing them and making collaboration nearly impossible. In December 2010, the FDP held an internal ballot on this issue, which was ultimately won by the pro-euro faction, but only with a narrow advantage. In 2011 the former party spokesperson, Guido Westerwelle, who became a leader for the pursuit of the economic right in the FDP, was replaced by Philip Rösler. With this, Westerwelle moved on to focus on foreign policy. Combined with having to defer to the wishes of the CDU in government, the FDP has not portrayed itself as the most credible market-orientated party to the electorate. Thus, the party strategy of 2009, which presented the FDP as a stronghold of liberal market economy views in Germany, was simply not possible in 2013.

A classic alternative strategy for a German liberal party would be to emphasize their core social concerns, such as by highlighting individual civil rights. However, the PP has maintained hegemony over such topics since 2009. Despite the chaotic internal organization of the PP and the continued strengthening of left-wing factions, the PP was still attractive to approximately 2 per cent of the electorate, especially the youth. The existence of the PP and of the many social compromises made with the CDU hindered the FDP from leveraging itself away from many of its economic positions in a credible way. Table 8.1 highlights the four most salient issues in the 2013 manifestos of the FDP, AfD and PP.[5]

Table 8.1   The four most salient categories in German liberal party manifestos

FDP 2013 (economic-liberal)		AfD 2013 (national-conservative, national-liberal)		Pirates 2013 (social-liberal)	
Freedom/human rights	9.9%	Democracy	17.8%	Freedom/ human rights	18.5%
Gov-admin efficiency	8%	EU negative	13.7%	Social justice	9.5%
Infrastructure	7.4%	Gov-admin efficiency	12.3%	Democracy	8.8%
Economic orthodoxy	5.5%	Economic orthodoxy	12.3%	Market Regulation	7.3%

Source: Author's own table based on data from MARPOR (Volkens et al. 2013).

With regard to the table above, it seems that the PP has colonized liberal issues concerned with civil rights and freedoms, while the AfD has focused on economic issues. Compared to their 2009 concerns, the PP moved dramatically to the left with regard to economic issues, seeking to promote new forms of market regulation and social justice. This might partly explain the decline in their electoral support, since in the opinion polls many voters located themselves as right of the centre with regard to the economic issues supported by the PP in 2011 and 2012. However, beyond these issues the PP remains a social-liberal and radical-liberal party.

---

5   The PP manifesto for 2009 was coded together with students in a seminar on content analysis that took place at the University of Potsdam. The AfD programme was independently coded by MARPOR and by the author with students at the Heinrich-Heine University, Düsseldorf. Compared to MARPOR, the results identified even more statements on economic orthodoxy. In Table 8.1, the official MARPOR coding is reported in order to avoid coding bias. The AfD left-right scores reported in Figure 8.1d above are based on this group coding.

Classifying the AfD is even harder, despite influential newspapers such as the *Frankfurter Allgemeine Zeitung* (*FAZ*) classifying it as liberal. Beyond economic liberalism, the AfD fosters rather more conservative core issues, such as traditional forms of morality and political authority. Therefore the AfD cannot be understood only as a niche party (as a function of their resistance to issues in the politics of the euro pursued by the Christian–Liberal government). The AfD have also tried to represent themselves as the 'real' CDU by criticizing the modernization of the CDU's social policies under Merkel. Nevertheless, the AfD has become attractive for disappointed former FDP voters. However, with their anti-euro rhetoric and their social conservatism, the AfD have also become attractive for disappointed former CDU voters. By taking over the 'old' issues of the established parties, the AfD's political strategy has mirrored at the right what Die Linke has been doing on the left since 2005.

A comparison of the three liberal parties in Germany also reveals a third possible strategy for the FDP. Both the AfD and PP highlight the importance of democracy, indicating that liberal-radical ideas seem to be attractive to a number of German voters. Thus, the FDP have had the chance to rediscover and re-emphasize those radical-liberal issues. Such an active policy-seeking strategy would also have befitted an active attempt to seek election, and thus office. The theoretical opening for such a (metaphorically named) 'traffic- light coalition' with the Greens and SPD might have been a promising strategy for election. However, given the excellent result of the CDU, the FDP would have been forced to continue their Christian–Liberal coalition, in case they gained parliamentarian entry because of it. Going towards the centre, it must be remembered, is not the same as becoming leftist. However, it seems that intra-party factions, as well as the party leader Philipp Rösler, misinterpreted this strategic grouping, and instead decided to keep their (formerly successful) position at the right of the CDU. As a result, the fourth possible strategy outlined above was chosen by both the FDP chairman, Rösler, and parliamentarian leader, Rainer Brüderle: a campaign for continuing the coalition with the CDU and against a (red-)red-green coalition.[6] It must be remembered that, in 2009, 41 per cent of all FDP voters stated that they preferred the Christian Democrats (Hough 2011, 191). Such a coalition strategy therefore seemed to be rational and advantageous. However, this strategy ignored the fact that the majority of CDU voters no longer supported such a coalition. Even in 2011, a mass survey revealed that CDU voters preferred both the Greens and SPD to the FDP. In 2011 opinion polls, 53 per cent of the CDU/CSU voters preferred the SPD as a potential coalition partner, 27 per cent supported a coalition with the Greens and only 22 per cent with the FDP. On a 'sympathy scale' that measured opinions from -5 (do not like at all) to +5 (like very much) CDU voters rated a coalition with the FDP as 0.54. However, even the Greens did a little bit

---

6   FDP Wahlspot 2013, http://www.youtube.com/watch?v=qUrMdzPaBo8 (accessed 31 March 2014).

better with a mean of 0.97 and the SPD with a score of 1.53.[7] Never before in German politics had it occurred that supporters of a governing party had more sympathy for the two opposition parties than for their own party. Considering this, the FDP leaders should have already known in 2011 that closely chaining the FDP to the CDU would no longer be effective.

To conclude, one might question why all the liberal parties failed to make substantial inroads in the German election of 2013. Firstly, the AfD was probably still too young to directly enter parliament. Founded in February 2013, the AfD is, however, the most successful newcomer to German party politics in recorded history. The PP, on the other hand, focused, in a slightly eccentric way, on maximizing the outcomes of intra-party competition by taking on neglected voters and issues. Finally, the FDP continued to highlight their strategy of being the party that has focused on liberal market economy concerns, and has positioned itself at the right of the CDU. This position has, however, been fraught with difficulties. The alternative, of once more becoming a pivotal radical-liberal party, was not recognized as important.

Die Linke

While the party named 'The Left' should suggest to voters that they are located at the left of the ideological spectrum, many voters still have problems correctly placing it. Many East German voters have located Die Linke as ideologically central or even to the right of the centre (Arzheimer and Falter 2013, 131). Traditionally, the PDS has ideologically orientated itself differently in the *Landesverbände,* adopting, for example, a pragmatic position in the *Mecklenburg-Vorpommern* election and a dogmatic position in *Brandenburg* (Koß and Hough 2006). This tendency has become even stronger since its merger with the WASG led to the formation of Die Linke (Neugebauer 2011). From its origin, the West-dominated WASG has always seen itself as a protest movement, while the East-dominated PDS has portrayed itself as a democratic-socialist party with government experience (Olsen 2007). Consequently the merger of PDS and the WASG to form Die Linke positions the party as one of extremes rather than as a stable, government-orientated political party (Olsen 2007, 218). In 2013, Die Linke rhetorically opted for a 'red-red-green' government, supporting the Greens and SPD. But the SPD remained sceptical of this; the SPD leader, Sigmar Gabriel, refused such a coalition during the electoral campaign, arguing that Die Linke would be split into three parts: 'a pragmatic East part, a dogmatic communist part in the West and a GDR nostalgic part in East'.[8] After their internal elections at the *SPD Leipzig Parteitag*, the SPD officially acquiesced to such a coalition, partly due to intra-party pressure from the left wing. This is because, within the SPD, the

---

7   ZA5633, Politbarometer, 2011. Author's own calculations.

8   Statement issued by Sigmar Gabriel during a public discussion signalling the final phase of the SPD's electoral campaign (Münsterplatz Bonn, 20 August 2013).

left wing was unhappy with the process of coalition bargaining within the CDU and wished for a serious examination as to the possibility of left-camp coalition. Die Linke reacted immediately with an offer to start coalition bargaining.

However, was this a serious offer, or an offer made knowing that the SPD would not opt for it? Some indications exist that the dogmatic, West-affiliated WASG became more pragmatic in its reasoning. A justification for this can be seen in the visit of Die Linke's leader to Greece and the subsequent pledges of support by Left-Socialists and Communists in southern Europe. As sister parties, they have demanded from the German Die Linke the formation of a possible 'red-red-green' government, in order to begin to modify Germany's European austerity policies. For the pragmatic *Landesverbände*, these forms of participation fit perfectly with their possible strategies. Consequently, one can conclude that Die Linke is readying itself for its entrance into government. It remains uncertain, however, whether the SPD and Greens are really willing to participate in such a government. Die Linke applied a 'passive' policy and vote-seeker strategy by taking over SPD issues, issues that the SPD could no longer credibly represent due to their participation in government. Die Linke, furthermore, claimed that to make the SPD socially democratic one had to vote for Die Linke. In 2013, this strategy (combined with their association with formerly communist strongholds in East Germany) has resulted in a decrease in electoral support. In the future, Die Linke has to prove that it is not only a protest party, but a responsible party which is able to fulfil their political promises.

Greens

Since 2005, the Greens have been the smallest faction in the German Bundestag. However, their small size belies their importance. The Greens have had numerous and spectacular successes at the polls. In Baden-Württemberg, for instance, the Greens became stronger than the SPD. Winfried Kretschmann, moreover, was elected as the first Green prime minister at the Länder level. The former 'red-green' coalition, which existed from 1998 until 2005, was no longer possible due to the electoral weakness of the SPD. Consequently, it now seems possible to create a new version of this coalition, symbolically represented as 'green-red', with the Greens as the dominant party. Other options, such as a coalition with the CDU, were attempted in Hamburg, and a so-called 'Jamaica'-coalition of FDP, CDU and the Greens in Saarland (Bukow 2014).[9] However, both coalitions failed. Moreover, in February 2011, the snap election that ended the 'black-green' coalition in Hamburg led to an absolute majority for the SPD. In March 2012, the 'Jamaica coalition' in Saarland led to a grand coalition, primarily due to large electoral gains for both the SPD and the PP. This might explain why the Greens did not again seek or promote a coalition with the CDU in their 2013 campaign. An

---

    9   Since the German party colours equal the flag of Jamaica, a coalition of Greens, 'yellow' FDP and 'black' CDU is labelled 'Jamaica coalition'.

alternative to the possibility of a 'traffic-light coalition' with the FDP and SPD was already in place in 2009, but was refused by the respective party members (Probst 2011, 145). Consequently, the Greens started their electoral campaign by officially being seen as in favour of a 'red-green' coalition. Voices favouring a coalition with the CDU/CSU were consequently ignored (*Zeit Online* 2013a).

Interestingly, however, their concrete campaign was not fully compatible with the seeking of a 'red-green' coalition. Firstly, the Greens did not promote a 'red-green' alliance in their campaign itself. In their TV advertising campaign they blamed the Christian–Liberal coalition for nepotism and compared it with a plague of slugs that would spoil Election Day salad.[10] However, the party remains open to other coalitions that could replace this. Secondly, and perhaps more interestingly, the Greens tried to adopt social justice issues normally spoken to by the SPD and Die Linke. This is rather embarrassing considering their primary electoral concern was energy politics, with secondary concerns an alternative economy and sustainable fiscal policy (Bündnis90/Die Grünen 2013, 27–89). Ecology concerns were ranked as eighth most pressing, which is remarkably low for a Green party (Bündnis90/Die Grünen 2013, 153–68). Their fiscal policy programme, with a new tax for high-income earners was criticized by the right wing, and especially by the Baden-Württemberg prime minister, Winfried Kretschmann. In the end, however, it was unanimously decided as a party policy (*Zeit Online* 2013b). Public perception of the party, following the electoral campaign, has been dominated by concerns with the left-wing leader, Jürgen Trittin, and his economically liberal topics. His co-candidate, Katrin Göring-Eckart, who came from the right 'reformer' wing (and was surprisingly elected by left-liberal party members), did not intervene in this social democratic, rather than green, platform. This leftist-orientated programme was accompanied by discussions revolving around the introduction of a vegetarian day in all German factory canteens. The claims for such a 'veggie day' were interpreted as an anti-liberal state intervention, and provoked a disastrous response in the media (Roßbach 2013; Meier 2013). The response became even more condescending when the Green Party started to justify the idea online, under the headline 'we know better'.[11] In 2009, Blühdorn had already diagnosed the self-perception of the Greens as being the avant-garde, a perception that was no longer mirrored by societal understandings of the party (Blühdorn 2009, 49). The idea of 'veggie day' underscores Blühdorn's observation that a serious gap between perception and reality exists in the party.

The most problematic topic for the Greens was the debate concerning their attitude towards cases of paedophilia that occurred in the 1980s. The Greens were not able to prevent the resulting debate and had to concede that even their top candidate, Jürgen Trittin, was implicated (Walter and Klecha 2013). These factors

---

10   Neues aus dem schwarz-gelben Tierreich, Grüner Spot zur Wahl 2013, http://www.youtube.com/watch?v=gRpJF84byXo (accessed 31 March 2014).

11   See: http://www.gruene.de/themen/moderne-gesellschaft/gruenedewir-wissen-es-besser.html (accessed 31 March 2014).

all contributed to the Greens obtaining a 'normal' result of 8.4 per cent, which was interpreted as an electoral defeat since two months before they forecasted at least a 12 per cent result. However, even the concerns with paedophilia and 'veggie day' cannot explain the unexpectedly low electoral results, nor the Greens' policy strategy. What factors led to the decision to create a programme promoting the core issues of their officially designated coalition partner, the SPD? Such a programme seems, in fact, to be an attack on the SPD.

The indications of how this contradiction can be solved were revealed directly after the election. The two ideological wings immediately started fighting against one another. As a consequence, the former top candidate and parliamentarian spokesman, Jürgen Trittin, as well as the left-wing party spokeswoman, Claudia Roth, both resigned. The best explanation for this conflict was that during the election the programme of de facto attacking the SPD was the policy on which both wings could agree. In this sense, the Green manifesto of 2013 was a policy-seeking, as well as intra-party democratically orientated, programme. Empowered by the impression that they would soon overtake the SPD, or at least garner approximately 15 per cent of the votes, left-wing party leaders ignored the oligopolistic structure of German party politics and, as a result, ignored vote-maximizing strategies. They obviously felt so secure in their election that they even promoted higher taxes for their own voters. Boris Palmer, an influential protagonist in the reformist wing, criticized the Green left-wing leaders for simply ignoring the chance of garnering bourgeois votes. He even accused Jürgen Trittin of intentionally leading the Greens away from the 'black-green' option because of a fear of losing influence within the Green Party (Palmer 2013).

But why did the right-wing reformer camp not protest more vigorously against this programme before the election? One reason might be the inherent organizational weaknesses of the right-wing reformers. Another might be that the tactic of attacking the SPD was one the *Landesverband* Baden-Württemberg originally developed, and was thus familiar. After the disappointing Länder elections of 2001, the SPD was identified as a main opponent by the Greens in terms of potential voters. Furthermore, the Green Baden-Württemberg (GBW) *Landesverband* has sought to become a neutral party. It opted to focus on anti-nuclear politics, sustainability, guaranteeing 'the integrity of the creation', and on combining these focal points with concerns with social justice (Reiz 2001). Indeed, even in 2006, the Greens positioned themselves as socially very close to the SPD, but economically as slightly to the right (Bräuninger and Debus 2012, 227). After the election, this understanding of the Greens being seen as neutral, or as 'reformers', became obvious as the party leader, Cem Özdemir, argued that the Greens are 'not left, not right, but at the front'[12] (*Frankfurter Allgemeine Zeitung* 2013). Herbert Gruhl, a former CDU parliamentarian, who became a protagonist of the Greens' right wing in the late 1970s, early coined this motto (Mende 2011, 435). This became a code for the self-understanding of the right wing within the

---

12   'Nicht links, nicht rechts, sondern vorn.'

German Green Party. Thus, citing this motto indirectly opposes the view that the Greens' best political partner would be the SPD. A party that is neither left nor right would have the chance to position themselves as the pivotal party. This would be contrary to an understanding of the Green left wing as being a party left of the SPD (Mende 2011, 181).

We can therefore conclude that both wings of the Green Party agreed to the 2013 manifesto, but for very different reasons: the right wing had the successful Baden-Württemberg experience in mind as a means of garnering votes and obtaining a place in office by becoming a pivotal party to the larger parties. It attempted to do so by emphasizing ecological issues and attacking the SPD. Contrary to this, the left wing mistakenly felt secure of electoral success, ignored vote-seeking strategies and formulated a policy exhibiting their most preferred issues. Perhaps the left wing was also afraid of losing influence within the party by not choosing a strictly 'left wing' programme. After the election, however, these differing interpretations led to an escalation in the conflict between protagonists of both wings, symbolized by Winfried Kretschmann and Jürgen Trittin. Kretschmann was frustrated with the failed attempt to form a coalition with the CDU, stating that 'the Greens are currently out of the track' (Kretschmann cited according to *Der Spiegel* 2013). Trittin argued that the Greens had enthusiastically fought during the campaign because of their high levels of identification with the larger programme and emphasized the programmatic difference to the CDU (Bannas 2013; Trittin 2013). At the parliamentarian level, the organizational weakness of the right wing resulted in their inability to promote their economically friendly candidate, Kerstin Andreae, as co-spokeswoman. Instead, the former (and vastly weaker) electoral candidate, Katrin Göring-Eckart (who was also a member of the right wing but not their candidate for spokesperson), was elected, with the majority of the votes coming from the left wing (Roßbach and Schäfers 2013). Nevertheless, Andreae received 20 votes, signalling that a number of the right who were from the 'core' of the wing favoured a centralist course of action. However, because a potential 'red-red-green' coalition would only have a majority of ten votes, these 20 votes were enough to veto a pure left-wing government. On the other hand, the intra-party or at least intra-parliamentarian dominance of the left wing led to a (preliminary) veto against a coalition with the CDU/CSU. Consequently, the Greens, instead of theoretically having two coalition options, were, after the election, not able to participate directly in the formation of a government. In retrospect, applying a strategy more orientated towards vote-seeking, such as becoming a slightly more centrist or even a pivotal party, would have helped the left wing to use their intra-party dominance to accomplish a 'red-red-green' coalition. Most probably, these votes would have come from the bourgeois camp. This would have led to additional seats that would have raised the leftist majority in such a way that the Green right wing would no longer have the power of veto. Simply put, the Green left wing has not yet understood the paradox that can result from gaining a pivotal position, going towards the inverse direction in forming a government on the ideological left.

Conclusion

The prominent paradox for German party competition in 2013 was that, for the smaller parties, attracting votes in order to form a wing coalition should have been the result of centralist policies. The current misnomer of the German party system is that the German small parties did not understand this paradox before the 2013 election. The constant ideological jostling at the wings has led to the increased probability of a grand coalition. Instead of fighting for these pivotal positions, the smaller parties have struggled for a place besides either the SPD or the CDU. In addition, all of the small parties lost votes or did not even enter into the parliamentarian arena. The late FDP campaign of obtaining 'borrowed votes' from the CDU functioned so long as the FDP really was a pivotal party. As a result, voters could not be sure which large party the FDP would support after the election. A statement highlighting a coalition would have sent a worthy signal to the voters. However, already positioned at the ideological wing, voters did not need such a signal because they already knew which coalition was to be supported. Since the AfD, a new competitor, was obtaining votes from the right wing, the only remaining future strategy for the FDP is to reactivate their individual rights profile in order to place themselves between the two large parties.

Consequently, possible issues that need emphasis would be education and science. For liberal parties, education and science are core issues. This is also true for the FDP. With regard to these issues, liberal parties clearly outperform the Greens (Busemeyer, Franzmann and Garritzmann 2013). However, the FDP is not able to address credibly these issues during national election campaigns, primarily because, since the German federalism reform of 2006, they have been delegated exclusively to the Länder level. This has enabled cooperation between the federal and the Länder level in the field of education, as planned by the CDU and SPD. It is going back to its pivotal position by increasing the salience of education and science issues that might give the FDP a future.

The Greens, to which a similar logic applies (of going into the centre by forming a wing coalition), have already started to address liberal civil rights issues, in an attempt to replace the FDP (Kade and Gaugele 2013). Consequently, we can expect that smaller German parties have noted these movements. It is very likely that a direct fight for the pivotal position will occur in the future, between the Greens and the FDP. Even the AfD has started to attack the FDP. However, the AfD and Die Linke are 'passive' policy seekers who take over the neglected issues of the larger parties. As a result, it may be assumed that these parties will stay at the ideological wings of German party politics by following their successful strategies. As a small party closest to the centre, the Greens have the shortest route to a pivotal position. Even without a re-election, the Greens are theoretically able to enter a coalition with the CDU/CSU. A failure of the grand coalition will open a window of opportunity for the right wing, perhaps convincing the left wing to enter government.

References

Adams, James; Ezrow, Lawrence; and Leiter, Debra. 2012. 'Partisan sorting and niche parties in Europe'. *West European Politics*, vol. 35, n. 6: 1272–94.

Arzheimer, Kai, and Falter, Jürgen. 2013. 'Versöhnen statt spalten? Das Ergebnis der Bundestagswahl 2009 und die Rolle der PDS/Linkspartei in Ost-West-Perspektive'. In *Wahlen und Wähler. Analysen aus Anlass der Bundestagswahl 2009*, edited by Bernhard Weßels, Harald Schoen and Oscar W. Gabriel, 118–50. Wiesbaden: Springer VS.

Bannas, Günter. 2013. 'Brücken ins Nichts. Die Union hätte auch gerne weiter mit den Grünen reden wollen. Sagt sie. An ihr soll es nicht gescheitert sein. Nun bleibt ihr trotzdem nur noch – und wie erwartet: die SPD'. *Frankfurter Allgemeine Zeitung*, 17 October, p. 3.

Bartolini, Stefano. 1999. 'Collusion, competition and democracy, Part I'. *Journal of Theoretical Politics*, vol. 11, n. 4: 435–70.

Bieber, Ina, and Roßteutscher, Sigrid. 2011. 'Große Koalition und Wirtschaftskrise: Zur Ausgangslage der Bundestagswahl 2009'. In *Zwischen Langeweile und Extremen: Die Bundestagswahl 2009*, edited by Hans Rattinger, Sigrid Roßteutscher, Rüdiger Schmitt-Beck and Bernhard Weßels, 17–32. Baden-Baden: Nomos.

Blühdorn, Ingolfur. 2009. 'Reinventing Green politics: on the strategic repositioning of the German Green Party'. *German Politics*, vol. 18, n. 1: 36–50.

Bräuninger, Thomas, and Debus, Marc (with Jochen Müller). 2012. *Parteienwettbewerb in den deutschen Bundesländern*. Wiesbaden: VS Verlag.

Budge, Ian; Klingemann, Hans-Dieter; Volkens, Andrea; Bara, Judith; and Tannenbaum, Eric (eds). 2001. *Mapping Policy Preferences. Estimates for Parties, Electors, and Governments 1945–1998*. Oxford: Oxford University Press.

Bukow, Sebastian. 2014. 'The Green Party in Germany'. In *Green Parties in Europe. Eternal Teenagers or Maturity Ahead?*, edited by Emilie Haute. Farnham: Ashgate.

Bündnis90/Die Grünen. 2013. *Bundestagswahlprogramm 2013. Zeit für den grünen Wandel*. Available from: https://www.gruene.de/fileadmin/user_upload/Dokumente/Gruenes-Bundestagswahlprogramm-2013.pdf (accessed 31 March 2014).

Busemeyer, Marius; Franzmann, Simon; and Garritzmann, Julian. 2013. 'Who owns education? Cleavage structures in the partisan competition over educational expansion'. West European Politics, vol. 36, n. 3: 521–46.

Dinas, Elias, and Gemenis, Kostas. 2010. 'Measuring parties' ideological positions with manifesto data: a critical evaluation of the competing methods'. *Party Politics*, vol. 16: 427–50.

Downs, Anthony. 1957. *An Economic Theory of Democracy*. New York: Harper & Row.

Fleck, Hans-Georg. 2006. 'In search of a liberal identity: transition to democracy, liberal heritage, and liberal parties in Eastern Europe'. *Jahrbuch zur Liberalismus–Forschung*, vol. 18: 203–38.

Frankfurter Allgemeine Zeitung. 2013. 'Denkzettel für Özdemir?' 19 October. Available from: http://www.faz.net/aktuell/politik/inland/gruenen-parteitag-in-berlin-ein-denkzettel-fuer-oezdemir-12624373.html   (accessed   31 March 2014).

Franzmann, Simon. 2006. 'Parteistrategien auf oligopolistischen Issue-Märkten. Eine empirische Analyse der Wahlprogrammatik in Deutschland, Dänemark, Österreich und den Niederlanden mit Hilfe des Gutenberg-Modells'. *Politische Vierteljahresschrift*, vol. 47, n. 4: 571–94.

Franzmann, Simon. 2011. 'Competition, contest, and cooperation. The analytical framework of the issue-market'. *Journal of Theoretical Politics*, vol. 23, n. 3: 317–43.

Franzmann, Simon. 2012. 'Die liberale Parteifamilie'. In *Parteienfamilien – Identitätsbestimmend oder nur noch Etikett?*, edited by Uwe Jun, 155–84. Opladen: Barbara Budrich.

Franzmann, Simon. 2013. 'Towards a real comparison of left-right indices: a comment on Jahn'. *Party Politics*, forthcoming, doi:10.1177/1354068813499865.

Franzmann, Simon, and Kaiser, André. 2006. 'Locating political parties in policy space. A reanalysis of party manifesto data'. *Party Politics*, vol. 12, n. 2: 163–88.

Hank, Reiner, and Meck, Georg. 2013. 'Der Euro spaltet die Liberalen'. *Frankfurter Allgemeine Sonntagszeitung*, 11 November, p. 29.

Harmel, Robert, and Janda, Kenneth. 1994. 'An integrated theory of party goals and party change'. *Journal of Theoretical Politics*, vol. 6, n. 3: 259–87.

Hazan, Reuven. 1996. 'Does center equal middle? Towards a conceptual delineation, with application to West European party systems'. *Party Politics*, vol. 2, n. 3: 209–30.

Hough, Dan. 2011. 'Small but perfectly formed? The rise and rise of Germany's smaller parties'. *German Politics*, vol. 20, n. 1: 186–99.

Huber, John. 1989. 'Values and partisanship in left-right orientations: measuring ideology'. *European Journal of Political Research*, vol. 17, n. 5: 599–621.

Jun, Uwe. 2011. 'Volksparteien under pressure: challenges and adaptation'. *German Politics*, vol. 20, n. 1: 200–22.

Kade, Claudia, and Gaugele, Jochen. 2013. '"Claudia fehlt uns natürlich": Grünen-Chef Cem Özdemir über die Neuaufstellung der Grünen, die verpasste Koalition mit der Union, die Vergangenheit der Linkspartei – und über gefühlte Steuersenkungen'. *Die Welt*, 18 November, p. 5.

Keman, Hans. 1994. 'The search for the centre: pivot parties in West European party systems'. *West European Politics*, vol. 17, n. 4: 124–48.

Kitschelt, Herbert. 2003. 'Political–economic context and partisan strategies in the German federal elections, 1990–2002'. *West European Politics*, vol. 12, n. 21: 125–52.

Klingemann, Hans-Dieter; Volkens, Andrea; Bara, Judith; Budge, Ian; and McDonald, Michael (eds). 2006. *Mapping Policy Preferences II. Estimates for Parties, Electors, and Governments in Eastern Europe, European Union and OECD 1990-2003*. Oxford: Oxford University Press.

Knutsen, Oddbjørn. 2009. 'Regions, social structure and value orientations: a comparative study of 15 West European countries'. *European Political Science Review*, vol. 1, n. 3: 401–34.

Koß, Michael, and Hough, Dan. 2006. 'Between a rock and many hard places: the PDS and government participation in the eastern German Länder'. *German Politics*, vol. 15, n. 1: 73–98.

Linhart, Eric, and Shikano, Susumo. 2009. 'Ideological signals of German parties in a multi-dimensional space: an estimation of party preferences using the CMP data'. *German Politics*, vol. 18, n. 3: 301–22.

Linhart, Eric, and Shikano, Susumu. 2013. 'Parteienwettbewerb und Regierungsbildung bei der Bundestagswahl 2009: Schwarz-Gelb als Wunschkoalition ohne gemeinsame Marschrichtung?' In *Wahlen und Wähler. Analysen aus Anlass der Bundestagswahl 2009*, edited by Bernhard Weßels, Harald Schoen and Oscar W. Gabriel, 426–51. Wiesbaden: Springer VS.

Meguid, Bonnie. 2008. *Party Competition between Unequals: Strategies and Electoral Fortunes in Western Europe*. Cambridge: Cambridge University Press.

Meier, Albrecht. 2013. 'Im BLICK: Alles "Veggie" oder was? Albrecht Meier über die Banalisierung des Bundestagswahlkampfs'. *Der Tagesspiegel*, 11 August, p. 3.

Mende, Silke. 2011. 'Nicht rechts, nicht links, sondern vorne'. In *Eine Geschichte der Gründungsgrünen*. München: Oldenbourg.

Neugebauer, Gero. 2011. 'Als Quo vadis? Wie die LINKE versucht, sich als Partei und für sich eine Position im Parteiensystem zu finden. Interne Konsolidierungsprozesse und Orientierungssuche im Fünf-Parteien-System'. In *Die Parteien nach der Bundestagswahl 2009*, edited by Oskar Niedermayer, 107–30. Wiesbaden: VS Verlag.

Olsen, Jonathan. 2007. 'The merger of the PDS and WASG: from Eastern German regional party to national radical left party?' *German Politics*, vol. 16, n. 2: 205–21.

Palmer, Boris. 2013. 'Gabriel hat die Grünen genial abgefischt'. *Cicero Online*, 20 December. Available from: http://www.cicero.de//berliner-republik/boris-palmer-gabriel-hat-die-gruenen-genial-abgefischt/56727 (accessed 25 March 2014).

Pappi, Franz U. 1984. 'The West German party system'. In *Party Politics in Contemporary Western Europe*, edited by Stefano Bartolini and Peter Mair, 7–26. London: Frank Cass.

Poguntke, Thomas. 2011. 'Conclusion. Governing under conditions of uncertainty'. *German Politics*, vol. 20, n. 1: 223–6.

Poguntke, Thomas. 2012. 'Towards a new party system: the vanishing hold of the catch-all parties in Germany'. *Party Politics* (doi: 10.1177/1354068812462925).

Poguntke, Thomas, and Webb, Paul (eds). 2007. *The Presidentialization of Politics: A Comparative Study of Modern Democracies*. Oxford: Oxford University Press.

Probst, Lothar. 2011. 'Bündnis90/Die Grünen auf dem Weg zur "Volkspartei"? Eine Analyse der Entwicklung der Grünen seit der Bundestagswahl 2005'. In *Die Parteien nach der Bundestagswahl 2009*, edited by Oskar Niedermayer, 131–56. Wiesbaden: VS Verlag.

Reiz, Gabriele. 2001. '"Nicht rechts, nicht links, sondern vorn" Baden-Württembergs Grüne wollen sich nach dem Wahldebakel als 'Wertkonservative' neu bestimmen'. *Frankfurter Allgemeine Zeitung*, 12 April. Available from: http://www.faz.net/aktuell/politik/buendnis90-die-gruenen-nicht-rechts-nicht-links-sondern-vorn-122304.html (accessed 31 March 2014).

Riker, William H. 1995. 'The political psychology of rational choice theory'. *International Journal of Political Psychology*, vol. 16, n. 1: 23–44.

Roßbach, Henrike. 2013. 'Ein Veggie-Day wäre unverschämt'. *Frankfurter Allgemeine Zeitung*, 5 August. Available from: http://www.faz.net/aktuell/wirtschaft/fleischverbot-ein-veggie-day-waere-unverschaemt-12397865.html (accessed 31 March 2014).

Roßbach, Henrike, and Schäfers, Manfred. 2013. 'Die Angst der Grünen vor dem Regieren. Partei auf Profilsuche'. *Frankfurter Allgemeine Zeitung*, 11 October. Available from: http://www.faz.net/aktuell/wirtschaft/wirtschaftspolitik/partei-auf-profilsuche-die-angst-der-gruenen-vor-dem-regieren-12613983.html (accessed 31 March 2014).

Rudi, Tatjana, and Schoen, Harald. 2013. 'Verwählt? Eine Analyse des Konzepts "korrektes Wählen" bei der Bundestagswahl 2009'. In *Wahlen und Wähler. Analysen aus Anlass der Bundestagswahl 2009*, edited by Bernhard Weßels, Harald Schoen and Oscar W. Gabriel, 407–25. Wiesbaden: Springer VS.

Saalfeld, Thomas. 2002. 'The German party system: continuity and change'. *German Politics*, vol. 11, n. 3: 99–130.

Schoen, Harald. 2011. 'Merely a referendum on Chancellor Merkel? Parties, issues and candidates in the 2009 German federal election'. *German Politics*, vol. 20, n. 1: 92–106.

Spiegel Online. 2013. 'Grüner Ministerpräsident Kretschmann: "Die Partei ist aus der Spur"'. 13 Octobert. Available from: http://www.spiegel.de/politik/deutschland/gruener-ministerpraesident-kretschmann-a-927609.html (accessed 31 March 2014).

Spies, Dennis, and Franzmann, Simon. 2011. 'A two-dimensional approach on the political opportunity structure of extreme right parties in Western Europe'. *West European Politics*, vol. 34, n. 5: 1044–69.

Stokes, Donald E. 1963. 'Spatial models of party competition'. *American Political Science Review*, vol. 5, n. 2: 368–77.

Strøm, Kaare. 1990. 'A behavioral theory of competitive political parties'. *American Journal of Political Science*, vol. 34, n. 2: 565–98.

Trittin, Jürgen. 2013. *Sondierung. Bewertung der Ergebnisse. Letter to the Regional Conference of Alliance 90/Greens in South Lower Saxony*. Available from: http://www.trittin.de/trittin/texte/reden/20131101_Sond.pdf (accessed 31 March 2014).

Volkens, Andrea; Lehmann, Pola; Merz, Nicolas; Regel, Sven; and Werner, Annika. 2013. *The Manifesto Data Collection. Manifesto Project (MRG/CMP/MARPOR)*. Version 2013a. Berlin: Wissenschaftszentrum Berlin für Sozialforschung (WZB).

Vorländer, Hans. 2011. 'Als Phönix zurück in die Asche? Die FDP nach der Bundestagswahl 2009'. In *Die Parteien nach der Bundestagswahl 2009*, edited by Oskar Niedermayer, 107–30. Wiesbaden: VS Verlag.

Walter, Franz, and Klecha, Stephan. 2013. 'Die fatale Schweigespirale'. *Die Tageszeitung*, 16 September, p. 9.

Zeit Online. 2013a. 'Schwarz-gelb ist nicht erneuerbar'. 26 April. Available from: http://www.zeit.de/politik/deutschland/2013–04/gruene-parteitag-bundestagswahl (accessed 31 March 2014).

Zeit Online. 2013b. 'Grüne beschließen höhere Abgaben für Besserverdienende'. 27 April. Available from: http://www.zeit.de/politik/deutschland/2013–04/gruene-parteitag-beschluss (accessed 31 March 2014).

Chapter 9

So Similar, Yet So Different: Alternative für Deutschland and the Pirate Party

Gianfranco Baldini and Silvia Bolgherini

Introduction[1]

Political parties are facing serious challenges in Europe, as more generally in advanced democracies. Decreasing party identification, increasing anti-party sentiments, fragmentation and personalization, rise of fringe parties: the catalogue is long and well known by now (Webb 2011). Although some recent works point to more mixed evidence on the crucial matter of party decline (Norris 2011; Dalton et al. 2011), parties nonetheless are in trouble. This is particularly evident in countries where the global economic crisis, which started in 2007–8, has hit hard, like in Southern Europe (Verney and Bosco 2013). These challenges include decreasing electoral turnout and high mobilization of social movements – such as the *Indignados* in Spain 2011 – but also the breakthrough of new political parties – for instance, Golden Dawn in Greece 2012 and the Five Star Movement (M5S) in Italy, which gained 25 per cent in the 2013 polls. Turnout decline is part of a longer trend that involves most European countries (Franklin 2004), including those where parties are still deemed to command a reasonable amount of trust. On this topic, we now have a rich literature. On the other side, new parties have only recently started to attract a great deal of scholarly attention (Lucardie 2000; Deschouwer 2008; Litton 2013). True, the two latest party families that rose to national prominence in many European countries during the 1980s – Green parties and, especially, radical-right populists, henceforth RRP – have been widely researched (Müller-Rommel and Poguntke 2001; Mudde 2013). However, the situation is different for more recently born parties (defined here as parties born in the past decade).

Many of these new parties tend to share a sentiment of hostility towards the political establishment. However, some of them are difficult to locate along the left-right spectrum, for example, the Italian M5S (Baldini 2013). Moreover, in many countries Euroscepticism has become a persistent phenomenon, with increasing

1   For research assistance we would like to thank Ludovica Barozzi, Giorgia Fontana, Irian Schropp, and Filippo Triola. Gianfranco Baldini is also most grateful to the DAAD (German Academic Exchange Service) for granting him, in September 2013, a one-month research fellowship at the University of Frankfurt. We dedicate this chapter to the memory of our colleague and friend Aldo Di Virgilio.

implications for the nature of the party system (Usherwood and Startin 2013). The Austrian case shows that this is by no means confined to the European Parliament (EP): merely a week after Germany voted, a brand new, highly personalized anti-euro party (led by businessman Frank Stronach) entered the Austrian parliament with 5.7 per cent.

Generally, analyses on new parties tend to focus on parties that have entered the national parliaments at least once (Bolleyer and Bytzek 2013; Krouwel 2012). This literature disregards cases where new parties emerge either at sub-state level, or at state level, but without entering national parliaments. Why should one care about such parties? In his seminal contribution, Giovanni Sartori defined the *relevance* of parties along two dimensions: the coalition and the blackmail potential. Accordingly, a party is relevant when it either has to be considered as a potential coalitional partner or when it can affect the direction and content of the policies decided (Sartori 1976, 122–3). However, when analysing new parties, these elements need to be complemented by a focus on their genesis, which gives key insights into their potential for institutionalization (Panebianco 1982). This allows the combination of systemic and organizational approaches.

In Spring 2013, most opinion polls put the Pirate Party (*Piraten*) and the Alternative für Deutschland (AfD) on a 3–5 per cent level, forecasting their possible entry into the German Bundestag. Moreover, the AfD was deemed to be able to affect – during the electoral campaign, but also during post-electoral coalition talks – Angela Merkel's position on the controversial German role in the management of the Eurozone crisis.[2] Therefore, despite not entering the Bundestag, we argue that both parties have channelled two different – yet somehow complementary – forms of political challenge to the established party system. The Pirates have mobilized a young and internet-based electorate very critical of the traditional means of representative democracy. The AfD, while capturing a slightly older and more dispersed electorate, has provided a new political platform for Eurosceptic sentiments hitherto expressed more latently.

The chapter compares the two parties' electoral constituencies (in terms of voters' profile and electoral geography), and looks at some organizational aspects of their founding phase. It argues that the two parties display a very different profile. Yet, they have both attracted voters usually weary of traditional political parties, also attracting a cross-party consensus. In the EP 2014 election they both showed some potential of becoming relevant parties in the longer run (especially the AfD).

Challenges to the German Party System

New parties can pose different challenges to established party systems. They can have anti-establishment positions (Abedi 2004) or act as anti-system parties

---

2   See Greven and Uken (21 October 2013, 'Die AfD bestimmt den Europa-Kurs', http://www.zeit.de/wirtschaft/2013–10/grosse-koalition-europapolitik).

(Sartori 1976; Capoccia 2002). The rise and success of both the Greens and RRP in the 1980s and 1990s was largely accounted for by 'the mobilization of the electorate along the "libertarian–authoritarian" cleavage' (Ennser 2012, 153). In other words, no matter how much new parties in Europe could differ in terms of leadership and organization, or indeed voter profile, most of them emphasized issues on the libertarian/authoritarian dimension. This scheme also applies to the first two waves of party system change in Germany.

Post-WWII Germany is usually deemed to be 'protected' against the most radical challenges thanks to the combined effect of the shadows of the Nazi past and a thorough legislation on the role of political parties – both in society as well as on their internal democratic procedures. This resulted in a constitutional ban on the descendants of Nazi and Communist parties in the early 1950s. More generally, this also resulted from the fact that the 'German Basic Law was one of the earliest cases of what could be called the positive constitutional codification of political parties in postwar Europe, attributing to political parties a constructive role in the democratic system' (Van Biezen 2012, 195–6). However, Germany was not immune to the periodic rise of right-wing radical parties, which sporadically gained representation in some regional parliaments (as well as in the EP in 1989).

Most recent works on the German party system have focused on national cross-time rather than cross-national comparisons (Jun 2011; Lees 2010; Poguntke 2014). To be sure, all these works portrayed a general decline on many aspects of party health (increasing volatility and number of parties, decline of party membership and electoral turnout, rise of *Politikverdrossenheit* [Arzheimer 2002; Poguntke 2014]). This leaves open the question about whether, and to what extent, the German case is (or has ever been) unique or peculiar.

In Table 9.1 we update an assessment on the 'health' of some European party systems, as constructed by Paul Webb and collaborators (2002), in two steps. We first define the challenges to the party system as the cumulated impact of the different indicators listed in the table (whose overall level is then defined in three categories: Low, Medium, High). Then, we assess the significance of the parties that have appeared in the last decade, or indeed the possible increasing potential of older challenger parties (such as the French National Front). Two observations are in order. First, a decade ago Germany was part of a big group of countries witnessing challenges to the party system (defined as medium-level in the table), in practically all dimensions except for the first one (volatility). In other words, German peculiarities were more visible in aspects related to the constitutional role of parties – and patterns of stability and alternation as conveyed by the *Kanzlerdemokratie* model (Niclauß 2004) – than in any form of party system 'solid-rock' stability.[3] Second, by looking at what happened in the last decade, one can detect the emergence of a possible 'third wave' of party system change in

---

3   Yet, Germany has the lowest number of new parties on a 1945–2010 Western Europe comparative perspective (Krouwel 2012, 52).

Table 9.1 Party system change indicators: Germany and other West European cases compared

Country	Total Net Volatility	Eff. N. Elect. Parties	Turnout	Partisan identification	Absolute membership	Anti-party sentiment (APS)	Dealignment + APS	Level of systemic change around 2000	New Parties since 2000, rise in RRP	Trend of systemic change since 2000
UK	Fluctuates 0	Up ('74) 1	Fluctuates 1	Down ('74) 0	Down ('64) 1	Significant 1	Yes 0	4 M	1 Green Mp Westminster, UK Independence. Party in EP	+
Italy	Up ('92) 1	Up ('92) 1	Down ('79) 1	Down ('89) 1	Down ('79) 1	Critical 1	Yes 1	7 H	M5S	++
Germany	**Fluctuates 0**	**Up ('87) 1**	**Down '87 1**	**Down ('76) 1**	**Down ('87) 1**	**Significant 1**	**Yes 0**	**5 M**	**Pirates & AfD**	**+**
France	Up ('81) 1	Up ('78) 1	Down ('81) 1	Down ('80) 1	Down ('81) 1	Significant 1	Yes 0	6 H	various anti-capitalist lists, Front National	=
Belgium	Up ('81) 1	Up ('68) 1	Down ('95) 1	Down ('80) 1	Down ('90s) 1	Critical 1	Yes 1	7 H	Various RRP parties, party system 'duplication'	=
Nederland	Up ('67) 1	Up ('71) 1	Down ('71) 1	Down ('81) 1	Down ('80) 1	Significant 1	Yes 0	6 H	Fortuyn List- Party for Freedom	+
Sweden	Up ('91) 1	Up ('88) 1	Down ('98) 1	Down ('64) 1	Down ('91) 1	Significant 1	Yes 0	6 H	Sweden Democrats; Pirates in EP	+
Denmark	Up ('73) 1	Up ('73) 1	Stable 1	Down ('80) 0	Down ('66) 1	Significant 1	Yes 0	5 M	Danish People's party	-
Norway	Up ('73) 1	Up ('89) 1	Down ('93) 1	Down ('90) 1	Down ('90) 1	Significant 1	Yes 0	6 H	none, rise Progress Party	+
Finland	Up ('91) 1	Fluctuates 0	Down ('75) 0	No data 0	Down ('90) 1	Significant 1	no data 0	3 M	True Finns	+
Ireland	Up ('87) 1	Up ('87) 1	Down ('82) 1	Down ('79) 1	Down ('90) 1	Significant 1	Yes 0	6 H	None	=
Spain	Down ('86) -1	Down ('82) -1	Fluctuates 0	No data 0	Up ('82) 0	Low -1	No -1	-4 L	None	=

Note and *Source*: columns on systemic indicators, as assessed around 2000, are derived from Webb (2002, 439); assigned values (-1, 0, 1) after each column are then summed up to assess level of systemic change (Low, L; Medium, M; High, H; EP= European Parliament.

Germany (to which we shall come back in the conclusion). Let us briefly see the first two (see also Table 9.3 below).

In the early 1980s, the party system had first seen the emergence of *Die Grünen* (the most successful Green party in Europe to date), which transformed what had hitherto been defined as a two-and-a-half party system into a two-bloc system, leading to alternation between red-green – Social Democratic Party (SPD) and Greens – and black-yellow – Christian Democratic Union/Christian Social Union and Free Democratic Party (CDU/CSU–FDP) – coalitions.[4] Then, it evolved again after 1990 and the reunification elections with the entry of the Party of Democratic Socialism (PDS) (later to merge with the *Arbeit und soziale Gerechtigkeit – Die Wahlalternative*, WASG, to form *Die Linke*) and the transformation of the two-bloc system into a fluid five-party system (Niedermayer 2008). Since then, no new party has been able to enter the German Bundestag. But in order to assess the stability of the system one should also consider that Germany – like Belgium and Spain (and to some extent the United Kingdom) – has a multilevel party system. Considering that Germany has no relevant regionalist party, the consolidation of different coalitional patterns between federal and Länder level, occurring particularly since 1990, provides a further indicator of party system change (Poguntke 2014). An example today is *Die Linke* being accepted as a coalition partner by the SPD in several Länder, on a dynamic which in 2013 has again been ruled out (like in 2009) at the federal level.

Party system changes – that Germany shares with other European countries (see Table 9.1, last column) – are now related to the emergence of the Pirates and the AfD. These two new parties channel new challenges: old demands for more direct democracy have acquired new meaning by intersecting the discontent towards the political establishment and the end of the 'permissive consensus' in public opinion for the European Union. This peculiar blend can be read as a sign of democratic stress, as defined, in general, by the combined pressures of socio-economic crisis, multiculturalism and cultural change, and political disenchantment (Painter 2013). Although the global economic crisis hit Germany much less than other European countries, signs of stress are nonetheless evident – one can just point to the debate that followed the publication of Thilo Sarrazin's book (Sarrazin 2010). On these issues, we argue that these two parties are acquiring a potential for relevance even without entering the Bundestag.

---

4   Taking Sartori seriously, one should refrain from defining the German system as a two-and-a-half party system (see, among others, Jeffery 1999). Indeed, the FDP, being in government for almost 50 years in the period 1949–2005 retained a clear coalition potential which makes counting it as a 'half-party' rather misleading, even considering its limited electoral success when compared to the CDU/CSU and SPD.

Pirates Entering (Some) Regional Ships, AfD Aiming for Berlin

Despite both conveying new political messages, the two parties have a different genesis and a rather different profile. First appearing in Sweden at the beginning of 2006, the Pirates were formed in Germany a few months later and obtained 2 per cent at the 2009 federal elections. The real breakthrough came with the regional elections in Berlin in 2011 (8.9 per cent and 15 seats), and the party also gained entrance to regional parliaments of Saarland (7.4 per cent), North-Rhine Westphalia (7.5 per cent) and Schleswig Holstein (8.3 per cent) in 2012. After having been put on a 6–8 per cent level by many opinion polls in 2012, the party faced a disappointing result in the Lower Saxony regional election in January 2013 (2.1 per cent) and entered into a spiral of internal dissent, losing momentum. Indeed, the genesis of the party – and especially the open participation model of internal organization – bears some of the seeds of its difficult institutionalization. The latter term is notoriously a very slippery concept in the literature on political parties. The classical reference is the work of Panebianco (1982), which starts from the genetic model, as defined by two polar dynamics: diffusion and penetration. The first is typical of parties that emerge as a result of the initiatives of local elites, activists and groups that arise through a spontaneous process. On the contrary, the second model implies the presence of a strong, centralized and cohesive leadership group from the very beginning of the party's life. While mixed instances are clearly possible, the idea behind this framework is that institutionalization is stronger in the second model. Panebianco, however, further considers the deviant case of charismatic leadership. A charismatic leader, especially when s/he is also the party founder, might just want to slow down such a process as it threatens the strict identification between the leader and the party.

Interestingly, the Pirates resemble very closely the first model: they grew out of a process of germination, with the spontaneous activity of computer-user native digitals (Blumberg 2010). As membership grew, the party got embroiled in endless internal discussions on whatever aspect of policy was being considered – or indeed on which procedures to follow, lacking any real coordination in issue management and decision-making (Zolleis et al. 2010, 22). Great importance was given to the 'many-to-many' enlarged participation principle and to the liquid-feedback platform as key elements of a new, more direct and un-mediated means of doing politics. However, since early 2013, the image of the party was increasingly associated with endless quarrels, and press coverage on the Pirates grew more and more hostile. Until then, the party had gained visibility (and votes) thanks to the copyright reform issue, and other related topics such as free download and personal data protection. The 2013 electoral campaign was mainly focused on the NSA scandal, which, however, the party failed to capitalize on.[5] On economic

---

5   Meiritz and Reinbold, 'Pirate party fails to capitalize on NSA scandal', *Der Spiegel*, 19 September 2013 (http://www.spiegel.de/international/germany/pirate-party-fails-to-capitalize-on-nsa-scandal-a-923303.html).

policy, the main proposal was centred on the basic income grant (*Bedingungsloses Grundeinkommen*), together with other policies targeted at youth, such as those related to housing (for instance, a cap on rents).

AfD's birth and initial consolidation was very different. Generally, the party benefited from the convergence of different initiatives, which pre-dated the Eurozone crisis. These included forums and groups such as *Zivile Koalition, Bündniss Bürgerwille, Bund Freier Bürger*, and *Plenum der Ökonomen*. Led by neo-liberal economists, intellectuals and entrepreneurs, since 2010 these groups have developed a critical view of the management of the European bailout policy, as concerted by the European Central Bank and the EU Commission, with the crucial support of the German government. Then they gathered together in 2012 to give birth to *Wahlalternative 2013*, the true core of the future party (Häusler 2013, 27). According to Häusler, a key turning point for the creation of *Wahlalternative* (and then for the AfD as such) came after Angela Merkel's volte-face[6] in March 2010 on the crucial issue of the first-aid package to Greece. Hence, a mixed genetic model seems to fit this case best.

On charismatic leadership, the parties differ a lot. The Pirates have a sort of ideological hostility to the principle of charismatic leadership, which is clearly in conflict with the horizontal democracy participatory model. The AfD soon acquired a collegial structure in which Hamburg economics professor Bernd Lucke emerged as the main leader, but without ever acquiring strong charismatic traits. The party's dominant coalition came also from long-time single-currency sceptics, some of whom had resorted to the Federal Constitutional Court against the introduction of the euro and the abolition of the Deutsche Mark in January 1998. The founding party conference took place in April 2013. The decision to run at the federal elections was built on a favourable climate of opinion, as an opinion poll revealed that 26 per cent of the electorate would consider voting for a party proposing the exit from the euro.[7] After some ups and downs, however, most opinion polls then put the AfD at 2–3 per cent for the duration of the May-August period. As elections approached, support for the party seemed to surge to 4–5 per cent and beyond.[8]

---

6   On 25 March 2010, Merkel solemnly ruled out any direct financial help to Greece at the German Bundestag in the morning, while signing up at the EU summit in Brussels on the evening of the same day to the first package for Greece (*Die Freie Welt*, 11 April 2013, 'Ausführliche Infos zu AfD in der "Welt"', http://www.freiewelt.net/nachricht/ ausfuhrliche-infos-zu-afd-in-der-welt-22340/). *Die Freie Welt* is the *Zivile Koalition*'s online magazine, close to the AfD.

7   See Emnid survey published by *Focus* (Randenborgh et al., 'Der Euro in der Zange', 11 March 2013).

8   Lucke had an argument with the pollster Forsa about the party's alleged under-estimation (see Lachmann, *Die Welt*, wondering why the AfD was scoring so bad in the polls despite its alleged appeal (5 June 2013, http://www.welt.de/politik/deutschland/ article116837815/Warum-die-AfD-so-schlechte-Umfragewerte-hat.html). Forsa then won the court case (see *Süddeutsche Zeitung*, 17 September 2013, 'AfD verliert Rechtsstreit mit

One would think that the party was built on an increasing level of Euroscepticism, which in Germany had for a long time remained at a latent level (Lees 2008). However, even if the crisis of the Eurozone revealed a potential of contestation for the controversial German role in Europe,[9] data on support for the euro currency, as well as for European institutions in general, are not clear-cut. According to Eurobarometer data, in Germany, trust for the EU suffered a serious decline in the last five years (see Table 9.2), like in many other member states. However, two clarifications are in order: firstly, distrust is particularly strong vis-à-vis the European Central Bank (ECB, see Table 9.2 again), but much less so for the EU in general and for both the EP and the European Commission. Regarding the euro, the situation is indeed rather ambiguous: net trust remains in the positive and almost unchanged since 2008 (with the exception of 2011). Secondly, other data reveal a different picture, one in which the majority of German citizens do not just still appear to support the euro, but do increasingly trust European institutions more in general (Gros 2013).

Table 9.2   Changes in Germans' net trust in national and European institutions in comparison to net support for the euro

	2008	2011	2012	2013	diff 13–08
Net trust ECB	36	8	-7	-9	**-45**
Net trust EU	-1	-20	-31	-32	**-31**
Net trust EP	18	1	1	1	**-17**
Net trust EC	7	-9	-9	-11	**-18**
Net support EURO	41	31	35	37	**-4**
Net Trust NG	-21	-15	-17	-6	**15**
Net Trust NP	-11	-2	-3	1	**12**

Notes: ECB = European Central Bank; EU = European Union; EP = European Parliament; EC = European Commission; NG = National Government; NP = National Parliament
Source: Authors'own update on Gros and Roth (2011, 5) with data from Standard EB79 (2013).

Forsa', http://www.sueddeutsche.de/politik/vorwurf-der-verfaelschten-umfragedaten-afd-verliert-rechtsstreit-mit-forsa-1.1772865).

9   Germany was famously defined as a 'reluctant hegemon' for its reluctance to be seen as an assertive leader because of its controversial role in twentieth-century Europe (Bulmer and Paterson 2013; see also *Economist*, 15 June 2013).

Moreover, data in Table 9.2 show an increasing level of trust in the national institutions (government and parliament). Similar data could be found in several German opinion polls, which revealed a constant increase in satisfaction with regard to Merkel's government (*Regierungszufriedenheit*), from January to July 2013. Over a longer time span, it is interesting to note that satisfaction towards the government was at its nadir right after the first-aid package to Greece in June 2010 (Infratest-Dimap Bundesweit *Regierungszufriedenheit*). Nonetheless, being uncertain on the effective threat coming from the AfD, in general Merkel chose to downplay the euro issue, and to build the campaign on her reliability as a leader, as proven by the increasing confidence on her persona.[10]

But how did these two new challenger parties present themselves to the electorate?

Professors and Computer-addicts? *Spitzenkandidaten* and Organization of the AfD and the Pirate Party

The two parties had a rather clear-cut image in the media. The AfD was seen as a party built up by economics professors and entrepreneurs mainly drawn from the CDU's ranks. On the other side, the Pirates came under close scrutiny as a group of young amateurs (with most of the press referring to them as 'nerds'), with no structured political platform.[11]

Looking at the socio-demographic and political profile of the top candidates on the 16 regional lists (*Spitzenkandidaten*) one can indeed spot many differences between the two parties. Four main features have been considered: age, gender, profession and previous political careers. Data on age show a striking gap (almost 17 years) between the average for the Pirates' top candidates (35.6) and for those of the AfD (52.4). Gender balance is equally different, as the Pirates had twice as many female candidates as the AfD – four for the Pirates, only two for the AfD. Both parties' professional backgrounds are indeed consistent with their respective public images: one-quarter of the Pirates have web- or ICT-related occupations, while 6 out 16 of the AfD's are economics professors or economists.

---

10   As argued by Denkler in the *Süddeutsche Zeitung* (3 August 2013, 'Merkel macht die Meinung', http://www.sueddeutsche.de/politik/rekordwerte-fuer-schwarz-gelb-merkel-macht-die-meinung-1.1736974) and confirmed also by Infratest-Dimap surveys (http://www.tagesschau.de/multimedia/bilder/uvotealbum118.html) where she scored 71 per cent on 'happiness' against 51 per cent of the government.

11   See, for instance, Meiritz and Reinbold's article on *Spiegel Online* (13 May 2013, 'Kandidaten für den Bundestag: Das letzte Aufgebot der Piraten', http://www.spiegel.de/politik/deutschland/piraten-kandidaten-fuer-den-bundestag-voller-krampf-voraus-a-899397.html), which point to their very amateurish style; and the article by Jacobsen on *Zeit Online* (29 June 2103, 'Wo sind die Piraten?', http://www.zeit.de/politik/deutschland/2013–06/Ueberwachung-Prism-Piraten), which points to the rather hostile press attitudes towards them as a problematic aspect of their campaign.

The rest are mostly employees and white-collar for the Pirates, and high civil servants or highly ranked self-employed for the AfD.[12] An overwhelming majority of the Pirates are new to politics, as only 3 out of 16 had previous experiences in other parties; by contrast, those with experience are as many as six in the AfD.[13] In brief, the Pirates' top candidates for 2013 federal elections were much younger, more gender-balanced, less politically experienced and with lower to medium status occupations when compared to those of the AfD.

More generally, organizational traits of the two parties are also different. Both parties organized territorially through the traditional regional associations (*Landesverbände*), implemented from 2006 to 2009 for the Pirates (Niedermayer 2013a, 82) and in just three months (March–May 2013) for the AfD (Häusler 2013, 49). Although in both parties sub-regional bodies are organized along the existing administrative tiers, the Pirates also make use of less conventional formats such as 'crews' and free discussion tables (*Stammtische*). Concerning party organs, both parties have a mix of traditional and new structures (or procedures), which, however, turn out to be very different. In the AfD the relation between Lucke – emerged as main party leader in the campaign – and the other two official co-speakers[14] remains somehow unclear, and this is also the case for the role of the Scientific Council of the party, in which other important economics professors – and the party's co-founders – sit. While this might resemble the collective leadership structure of the Greens, it remains difficult to judge whether this model can persist. The first party conference adopted a rather hierarchical approach (Korte 2013). However, in 2014 the party first turned from the 'one man one vote' (OMOV) system to a traditional delegate system for selecting the EP election *Spitzenkandidaten* in January, then went back to an all-member conference in March to define the *Europawahl* manifesto.[15]

The Pirates are clearly more innovative. First, they have already held as many as 14 party conferences since 2006, at least one per year being compulsory. Then they also have very open rules in terms of participation and voting procedures (open participation for the party programme, which has been formulated on a thematic rolling basis, and a OMOV system). Membership grew from 360 in 2006 (Blumberg 2010, 13) to 29,180 in December 2013 (but down from 31,093

---

12 Seven non-web-related Pirates candidates were employees and public or private white-collar, while the other five were self-employed or precarious workers (student, babysitter). AfD non-economist candidates were instead two high civil servants, two self-employed (entrepreneur, architect/designer), two white-collars and four other professionals (including one detective and a radio speaker).

13 One Pirate candidate came from the Greens, one from the CDU and another from the FDP; among the AfD candidates one came from the SPD, four from the CDU and another one from the FDP.

14 Together with Lucke, the founding conference in April 2013 elected Frauke Petry and Konrad Adam as party speakers.

15 See official party website: www.alternativefuer.de. Accessed 20 February 2014.

just before the general election).[16] This makes them the seventh largest party in Germany. However, the party conference held in January 2014 saw the emergence of new patterns. First, attendance fell from an average of 6.8 to 2.7 per cent of members.[17] Second, this trend is related to the emergence of a more elitist pattern of party leadership, as made up by more well-off members (Klecha 2014). All these could possibly be seen as early signs of a shift towards more traditional party models.

In an interesting parallel with the party's *Spitzenkandidaten*, the 17,250 AfD members[18] are also aged 52 on average.[19] Although assessments of the AfD are obviously still premature, it may be claimed that, unlike the Pirates – devoted to openness, participation and liquid feedback as decision-making platforms – the party seems prone towards a more classical hierarchical leadership. Hence, the fact that for the 2013 federal elections the AfD also chose its federal and regional leadership through open membership-based procedures should not mislead. This was probably due to lack of time (or to a still 'manageable' party size). On the contrary, for the Pirates this procedure can be referred to a sort of ideological principle.[20] Moreover, only after the 2011 Berlin regional election did the Pirate Party shift from 'an amorphous faceless mass' (Hensel et al. 2012) to an organization with recognizable leaders and prominent candidates, while the AfD started from the beginning with a group of eminent members, later to form the party leadership.

A Catch-all Appeal?

In the 2009 federal elections, 2 per cent of the German voters put their cross next to the Pirate Party's symbol. This result brought the party to be the talk of the town and to rise to the attention of the national media. Both survey data and specific electoral data – that is, data separated from what normally in Germany

---

16   Data available on http://wiki.piratenpartei.de/Mitglieder#Mitgliederentwicklung.

17   All members having paid fees have the right to attend and vote (about 7,000 as of February 2014). See *Ibidem*.

18   The party claimed 14,000 members in August 2013 (Korte 2013). Newspaper sources indicated a rise to 17,250 by the end of the year (http://www.abendzeitung-muenchen.de/inhalt.parteien-spd-wieder-mitgliederstaerkste-partei.f6813aad-6ed4–4daa-b76f-86849953b42d.html).

19   See interview with AfD's prominent member J. Starbatty in *Stuttgarter Zeitung* (11 September 2013, 'Werden nicht von rechts unterwandert', http://www.stuttgarter-zeitung.de/inhalt.interview-mit-afd-experte-starbatty-das-wird-eine-weltsensation-page1.a9c7c3df-f0a4–4a35-b1e7–7649ff961945.html). Instead the average member of the Pirates is aged 38.9 (http://wiki.piratenpartei.de/Mitglieder).

20   See the article by Götze in the *FAZ* (24 September 2013, 'Professoren und Protestwähler', http://www.faz.net/aktuell/politik/bundestagswahl/die-afd-und-ihre-anhaenger-professoren-und-protestwaehler-12589732.html).

is subsumed under the *Sonstige* label (Niedermayer 2013b, 63) – on the Pirates started to be collected after the party's success in Berlin in 2011. These data allow us to single out some recurrent features which will be presented here, also drawing on the 2013 federal elections. A parallel scrutiny will be attempted also for the AfD, this time on the basis of the sole 2013 data. The analysis focuses on three dimensions: cross-partisanship (the capacity of a party to attract votes across the political spectrum), socio-demographic voters' profile, and geography of the vote.

Cross-partisanship

Several works emphasize the Pirates' capacity to attract a cross-party consensus (Hensel and Klecha 2013; Hensel et al. 2012). This would mostly come from the left – the Greens, but also the Social Democrats and *Die Linke* – which would usually provide the biggest vote switching in their favour, but the party also attracts votes from other minor parties (Hirscher 2011; Infratest 2012b; Onken and Schneider 2013, 619–20). Smaller – but not irrelevant – switching would come from governing parties (CDU/CSU and FDP) (Infratest-Dimap 2012b; Haas and Hilmer 2013). Also, first-time voters often vote for the Pirates, who, however, seem to have a specifically strong appeal for non-voters, who represent one of the highest sources of their electorate (Niedermayer 2013b, 65). These patterns, first detected in 2009, have not substantially changed since then, and have also been confirmed at the 2013 elections. The first 2013 post-electoral surveys allow for the claim that, presumably, on this occasion also, the Pirates collected votes above all from former non-voters[21] and first-time voters.[22] Data on vote switching for the Pirates from and to other parties are, however, still unavailable.

Since its foundation, AfD's potential electorate has a larger base (Häusler 2013, 44), also with a cross-partisan appeal, this time more skewed towards the centre-right, in particular Christian Democrat and Liberal voters, leading one pollster to define it as a 'clear bourgeois party with center-right oriented voters'.[23] Research on vote switching confirmed these expectations:[24] out of the 2 million

---

21   Pirates were still considered by 50 per cent of the interviewees an interesting option for those who otherwise had not voted (Infratest-Dimap survey: http://wahl.tagesschau.de/wahlen/2013–09–2-BT-DE/umfrage-aussagen.shtml).

22   Pirates obtained around 10 per cent of their votes from these electors, although significantly less than what the CDU, with 31 per cent, and even the Greens, with 11 per cent, did (22 September 2013, *Süddeutsche Zeitung*, 'Wer Union wählte', http://www.sueddeutsche.de/politik/waehlerwanderung-und-statistiken-woher-die-union-millionen-waehler-bekam-1.1777776).

23   INSA-Chief Hermann Binker's declaration reported on *Focus* (22 April 2013, 'Die Anti-Euro-Partei gefährdet Merkels Macht', http://www.focus.de/politik/deutschland/bundestagswahl-2013/tid-30948/alternative-fuer-deutschland-die-anti-euro-partei-gefaehrdet-merkels-macht_aid_966678.html).

24   Vote switching analysis by Infratest-Dimap (http://wahl.tagesschau.de/wahlen/2013–09–2-BT-DE/analyse-wanderung.shtml#11_Wanderung_UNION).

votes obtained, more than 20 per cent were cast by former FDP voters and around 15 per cent by former CDU voters. A remarkable transfer also came from former non-voters (10.5 per cent) as well as from *Die Linke* (17 per cent). Summing up on this dimension, both Pirates and AfD show a high level of cross-partisanship. Both drew votes from former abstainers and both cover practically the whole political spectrum, thus displaying an interesting catch-all potential.

Voter Profile

The evidence on the average Pirate voter provides a rather distinctive profile: a male, young (mostly under 25 and, anyway, younger than 45), often first-time voter, high-school educated, self-employed (or employee in private sector) or indeed student (Hensel and Klecha 2013, 62 ff.; Niedermayer 2013b; Onken and Schneider 2013; Brähler and Decker 2012). And, most of all, a new-technology and media-user. Along with these features, other works show that a high number of Pirate voters have low incomes (Onken and Schneider 2013), while they don't appear to have a distinguished confessional profile (coming one-third each from Catholic, Protestant and non-confessional background, on a proportion achieved by no other party: Brähler and Decker 2012). Overall, data from 2013 are consistent with this pattern. The only exception was that the party seemed to have scored better among unemployed (5 per cent) rather than workers (4 per cent) or employees (3 per cent).[25]

The average AfD voter is also male and relatively young, but the reversal correlation between age and vote is weaker than in the Pirates (Forschungsgruppe Wahlen 2013; Infratest-Dimap 2013): 73.7 per cent of the Pirate voters are under 45 as against 39 per cent of the AfD voters, with 34.3 per cent in the 45–60 cohort (Bundeswahlleiter 2014). What is more striking, however, is that AfD voters have a lower education level (mostly *Mittlere Reife*) and lower job status (including many unemployed) than expected.[26] This would contradict the common idea that AfD 'support comes from a particular segment of voters, whose core is the radicalized middle-class', that means, an average highly-educated and medium-high income voter.[27]

---

25   See Infratest-Dimap survey on election day (http://wahl.tagesschau.de/wahlen/2013–09–2-BT-DE/umfrage-job.shtml).

26   According to Forschungsgruppe Wahlen (2013), 6 per cent of those holding a middle school degree (*Mittlere Reife*) voted for AfD against 5 per cent of those with high school (*Hochschulreife*) or graduate degrees (*Hochschulabschluss*). As for job status, 7 per cent of unemployed voted AfD against 5 per cent of employed and 4 per cent of retired (*ibidem*), while Infratest-Dimap showed an AfD preference among the 3 per cent of unemployed, while among those holding a job, votes came mostly from workers (6 per cent) rather than from employees and self-employed (both at 5 per cent).

27   Forsa-Chief Manfred Güllner's declaration, reported on *Deutsche Wirtschafts Nachrichten* (18 August 2013, 'Forsa-Chef widerspricht eigenen Umfragen: AfD hat

Despite some of the differences hinted at above, the two parties seem to delve into similar basins: young men often with high-school education. As for job status, voting preferences of the unemployed are not really clear-cut, as data from different pollsters (see footnote 25) contradict each other. All in all, these surveys point to the likely appeal of both these parties for a rather marginal electorate, with precarious life and uncertain job conditions. That is partially confirmed when one considers that around 13 per cent of voters with low incomes declared that they were considering voting for an 'other' party.[28] Hence both parties' catch-all potential seems to have been even higher than expected, beyond the core constituencies made up by new technologies' experts (Pirates) or highly educated professionals (AfD).

Geography of the Vote

In the 2009 federal elections, the Pirates had a rather homogeneous vote distribution all around Germany. No strongholds as well as no significant difference between urban and rural areas (Brähler and Decker 2012) emerged, although the Pirates scored better in the three city-states as well as in some Eastern Länder like Brandenburg, Thuringia, and Saxony Anhalt. No major concentration was to be found in the Western Länder. In 2013 no relevant change occurred. The East was confirmed as a good electoral basin for the Pirates. Building on their success in the 2012 regional elections, they also fared well in Saarland and North-Rhine Westphalia. In any event, all the variations were within a 0.5 percentage point (except in Saarland with +1.1 per cent).

AfD also showed a homogeneous distribution in the whole country with 14 Länder (all but Bremen and Hamburg) in which it conquered 5 per cent in at least one district (*Wahlkreis*). The vote was higher along a kind of dragon-shaped area, which slithers from Mecklenburg-West Pomerania towards Brandenburg, then left to Saxony and Thuringia, finally bending south-west to very affluent areas in Hessen, Baden-Württemberg and south-east Bavaria. To sum up, both parties obtained better results in the east, in particular in Saxony, Thuringia and Brandenburg where, along with Berlin, their cumulated score was above 8 per cent. This 'far-East' feature could help when trying to explain the success of these two parties in areas where political dissatisfaction and social alienation are traditionally very high and where support for protest and even anti-system parties is disproportionally higher compared to the West (Conradt and Langenbacher

Chance auf den Bundestag', http://deutsche-wirtschafts-nachrichten.de/2013/08/16/forsa-chef-widerspricht-eigenen-umfragen-afd-hat-chance-auf-den-bundestag/).

28   According to a pre-electoral survey by Infratest-Dimap on 13 September and analysed by Bundeszentrale für politische Bildung (http://www.bpb.de/fsd/werwaehltwas/). Low income means less than 1,500 euro per month.

2013, 48). But it is not enough to define the profile of the voters, as we need to see why people turned to them.

Why Vote for these Parties?

Data availability also affects our knowledge of voting motivations. As for the Pirates, for which more data are available, three main elements stand out. First, Pirate voters define themselves as 'unconventional' and looking for transparent politics (Niedermayer 2013b), eager to bring 'fresh air' into politics (Infratest-Dimap 2012a). To be unconventional is not equal to being an anti-system party. Pirates are by no means perceived to be an anti-system or extremist party (Niedermayer 2013b, 72–3). Rather, they portray themselves as actors struggling for a renewal of democracy through new personnel and a focus on new left-libertarian issues (Hensel and Klecha 2013, 64; Debus and Faas 2013). One can argue that Pirates gain consensus in a 'monitory democracy', defined as 'the age of surveys, focus groups, deliberative polling, online petitions and audience and customer voting' (Keane 2011, 214), by striving for more participation and openness in democratic procedures (Hensel and Klecha 2012, 48). In this sense, they recall the initial phase of the Green surge with their focus on alternative politics (Poguntke 1993).

Second, the Pirates appeal to dissatisfied and frustrated voters. This is done both by providing alternative avenues to voters unsatisfied with traditional parties and by channelling the protest against social changes attributed to the welfare reforms introduced by the Schröder governments in 1998–2005 (such as the Hartz reforms), as well as from the implications of the Europeanization and globalization processes on the rights of the individuals (Falter 2010, 38). Many surveys also show that the Pirates are often seen as 'the only force (to …) vote for', thus confirming the party's capacity to attract non-voters mentioned above.

Third, being mostly concerned with web-related issues (for instance, free download and file sharing, reform of the copyright laws, protection of personal data on the internet), they have to deal with constraints (and not just opportunities) proper to a niche party (Meguid 2008). Experts have detected early signs of self-awareness on this issue (Niedermayer 2013b, 64; Hensel and Klecha 2012, 43). However, they were clearly unable to benefit from the NSA scandal during the electoral campaign. On 2013 election day, still 50 per cent of the people interviewed by a polling institute[29] defined the Pirates as an alternative for people who otherwise would abstain.[30] In the same survey, almost three-quarters of the

---

29   Infratest-Dimap survey (http://wahl.tagesschau.de/wahlen/2013–09–2-BT-DE/umfrage-aussagen.shtml).

30   This was still true (albeit with a 15 per cent decrease from six months before). Plus, the party was also hit by internal controversies during 2013. Just to mention two: the controversial figure of former managing director (*Geschäftsführer*) Johannes and the alleged

voters defined the Pirates as a party lacking in credibility. Nonetheless, over 40 per cent of the respondents were still convinced that this party could give voice to the young generations.

As far as the AfD is concerned, some analyses refer to its electorate as made up of three components: liberals, conservatives and right-wing populists.[31] Data on voting motivations do not allow for the assessment of the actual weight of each component. However, in the aftermath of the elections, Lucke ruled out any possible cooperation with parties such as the French National Front and the Dutch Party for Freedom (PVV).[32] On polling day, the party was considered as a valuable option for non-voters by almost 40 per cent, but also as a party 'not-to-be-taken-seriously' by almost 60 per cent. Yet, as many as 44 per cent thought the AfD 'could not solve any problem' but had 'the courage to name things straight'; and 21 per cent thought that 'it was good that a party argued against the euro'.[33]

Considering that for more than 30 per cent of the respondents[34] (and more than 50 per cent among AfD voters)[35] the future of the euro was the third most important issue in vote choice, one can infer that the party was seen as a potential channel for expressing concern on this topic.[36] However, given that voters expressing disappointment – rather than conviction – as their main voting motivation peaked

---

nepotism in the Pirates' Berlin parliamentary group. See respectively, among others, the articles by Beitzer in the *Süddeutsche Zeitung* (10 May 2013, 'Alles außer Drama', http://www.sueddeutsche.de/politik/neue-politische-geschaeftsfuehrerin-nocun-alles-ausser-drama-1.1670102) and by Meiritz and Reinbold in *Spiegel Online* (18 May 2013, 'Berliner Fraktion in der Krise: Piraten unter Amigo-Verdacht', http://www.spiegel.de/politik/deutschland/vorwurf-der-vetternwirtschaft-gegen-fraktion-der-berliner-piraten-a-900685.html).

31   See right-wing movements' analyst Alexander Häusler's evaluation in an interview for *WDR* (10 October 2013, 'AfD zeigt rechtspopulistische Tendenzen', http://www1.wdr.de/themen/politik/afdstudie100.html). See also the controversial support coming from a fringe party like *Die Freiheit*, which claimed their platform to be 90 per cent the same as that of the AfD (Häusler 2013, 88).

32   See the article by Busse in *FAZ* (13 November 2013, 'Rechtes Bündnis gegen Brüssel',   http://www.faz.net/aktuell/politik/europaeische-union/le-pen-und-wilders-rechtes-buendnis-gegen-bruessel-12662825.html).

33   Infratest-Dimap   survey   (http://wahl.tagesschau.de/wahlen/2013–09–2-BT-DE/umfrage-aussagen.shtml).

34   This percentage was 31 per cent according to an Infratest-Dimap survey (http://wahl.tagesschau.de/wahlen/2013–09–2-BT-DE/umfrage-wahlentscheidend.shtml),   and 39 per cent according to Forschungsgruppe Wahlen (http://www.forschungsgruppe.de/Umfragen/Politbarometer/Archiv/Politbarometer_2013/August_II_2013/).

35   As reported in the *Süddeutsche Zeitung* (22 September 2013, 'Wer Union wählte', http://www.sueddeutsche.de/politik/waehlerwanderung-und-statistiken-woher-die-union-millionen-waehler-bekam-1.1777776).

36   Data from an Infratest-Dimap post-electoral survey also point to this: 47 per cent declared the EU/foreign policy as the decisive issue when voting for the AfD (http://www.infratest-dimap.de/bundestagswahl-2013/wahlentscheidende-themen/).

at 57 per cent for the AfD (the highest percentage among the six most voted parties),[37] the protest potential of the party should not be underestimated. More specifically, 37 per cent of AfD voters also named disappointment against the established parties as their main voting motivation.[38]

As we have seen, the AfD was mainly built around the anti-euro issue and a critique of Eurozone crisis' management. While this meant that the party could be considered a one-issue party, this did not appear to damage it. The reason the one-issue label hampered the Pirates much more than the AfD is probably related to the different breadth and the perceived salience of the conveyed issues. Broadly speaking, these parties seem to have collected the votes of disaffected people, as well as of those disappointed or worried by the course of German politics. In addition, one can also argue that some citizens normally not interested in voting, or in politics at large, would probably have deserted the polls had the Pirates and the AfD not been there.

Conclusion

Over the last three decades, many European countries have witnessed a deteriorating relationship between citizens and the political system, and a growing sense of disenchantment of the former with the latter. Representative democracy faces important challenges, also by means of increasing requests for direct democracy and un-mediated political participation. The nature and the meaning of the challenges vary from country to country. Germany, among the countries witnessing increasing challenges, was less used to coping with new parties. The rise of the two parties analysed here might prove to be an early sign of an emerging third wave of party system change in the 2010s (Table 9.3), as triggered by the complex dynamics of democratic stress mentioned above.

Interestingly, ingredients of previous waves (as respectively framed by the post-materialist rise of the Greens and the success in the East of the PDS-*Die Linke*) can also be found at the roots of the emergence of the Pirates and the AfD as current main challenger parties. As we have seen, a more open and less mediated way of doing politics was a key element in the emergence of the Pirates. On a parallel route, the AfD brought to light the possible consequences of the end of the permissive consensus on the European issues, faring particularly well in the most disaffected Länder (Saxony and Thuringia).

---

37   Infratest-Dimap survey (http://wahl.tagesschau.de/wahlen/2013–09–2-BT-DE/umfrage-mobilisierung.shtml).

38   *Süddeutsche Zeitung*, 22 September 2013, 'Wer Union wählte' (http://www.sueddeutsche.de/politik/waehlerwanderung-und-statistiken-woher-die-union-millionen-waehler-bekam-1.1777776).

Table 9.3   Waves of party system change in Germany

Waves	Trigger(s)	Party	Potential of institutionalization	
			Systemic (coalition/ blackmail potentials) at federal/Land Level	**Organizational (genetic model; role of leadership)**
I (1980s)	Post-materialism	Greens	H on both levels	Genesis by diffusion; no charismatic leader ('Realos' prevailing over 'Fundis' normalizes party organization)
II (1990s)	Reunification	PDS-*Die Linke*	M-H at federal level H at Land level	PDS heir of a party born by penetration (externally legitimated); WASG splinter group from SPD (elite); parties merge in 2005 to form *Die Linke*, some charismatic elements (O. Lafontaine; G. Gysi)
III (2010s)	Democratic stress	AfD Pirates	AfD: M at federal level/ not applicable at Land level Pirates: L at federal level/ M at Land level	AfD: mixed genetic model; low charismatic traits Pirates: genesis by diffusion; anti-charismatic

Note: L: Low, M: Medium, H: High.
Source: Authors' own compilation.

The dissimilar programmatic inspiration has been clearly matched also by the different profile of the parties' *Spitzenkandidaten*. However, lack of data on vote motivations make it difficult to assess whether the vote for both parties was related more to a protest against the way traditional parties deal with the public than an effective appeal of their programmatic platforms.

The differences between the two parties are clearly more important than the similarities, some of which this chapter has nonetheless shown. The former can help in explaining their different potential for institutionalization.

One can argue that the AfD seems capable of achieving a higher level of institutionalization. This results from the combination of a higher systemic relevance due to the blackmail potential already displayed on the euro issue, a mixed genetic model leading to more secure lines of consolidation and, finally, a higher electoral salience of its programmatic core issues. On the contrary, post-electoral developments inside the Pirates confirm their organizational problems (as also conveyed by their weak genetic model), as the party looks still to be absorbed in a self-referential debate,[39] which makes their future very uncertain. All

39   Press analysis of the main German magazines shows an ongoing internal debate following the poor electoral results and the leadership's stepping down, mainly centred on (re)

in all, institutionalization is a long process, often marked by setbacks. The 2014 EP elections have been an important turning point after which the relevance of both parties can be better assessed.

References

Abedi, Amir. 2004. *Anti-Political-Establishment Parties: A Comparative Analysis.* London: Routledge.

Arzheimer, Kai. 2002. *Politikverdrossenheit. Bedeutung, Verwendung und empirische Relevanz eines politikwissenschaftlichen Begriffes.* Wiesbaden: Westdeutscher Verlag.

Baldini, Gianfranco. 2013. 'Don't count your chickens before they're hatched: the 2013 Italian parliamentary and presidential elections'. *South European Society and Politics*, vol. 18, n. 4: 473–97.

Blumberg, Fabian. 2010. *Partei der 'digital natives'? Eine Analyse der Genese und Etablierungschancen der Piratenpartei.* Berlin: Konrad Adenauer Stiftung.

Bolleyer, Nicole, and Bytzek, Evelyn. 2013. 'Origins of party formation and new party success in advanced democracies'. *European Journal of Political Research*, vol. 52, n. 6: 773–96.

Brähler, Elmar, and Decker, Oliver. 2012. *Die Parteien und das Wählerherz.* Berlin: Meinungsforschungsinstitut USUMA.

Bulmer, Simon, and Paterson, William E. 2013. 'Germany as the EU's reluctant hegemon? Of economic strength and political constraints'. *Journal of European Public Policy*, vol. 20, n. 10: 1387–405.

Bundeswahlleiter. 2014. Repräsentative Ergebnisse der Männer und Frauen nach Altersgruppen. Available from: http://www.bundeswahlleiter.de/de/ bundestagswahlen/BTW_BUND_13/veroeffentlichungen/repraesentative (accessed 11 November 2014).

Capoccia, Giovanni. 2002. 'Anti-system parties: a conceptual reassessment'. *Journal of Theoretical Politics*, vol. 14, n. 9: 9–35.

Conradt, David P., and Langenbacher, Eric. 2013. *The German Polity* (tenth edition). Lanham: Rowman and Littlefield.

Dalton, Russell J.; Farrell, David M.; and McAllister, Ian. 2011. *Political Parties and Democratic Linkage.* Oxford: Oxford University Press.

organization needs. Among others, see the article by Jacobsen in *Zeit Online* (24 September 2013, 'Was von den Piraten bleibt', http://www.zeit.de/politik/deutschland/2013–09/ Piraten-Abschied-Thesen). Before the elections, the possibility of the Pirates going back to being a protest movement was also spoken of (see the article by Schulz in *FAZ*, 6 September 2013, 'Letzte Ausfahrt ohne Enterhaken', http://www.faz.net/aktuell/feuilleton/piraten-vor-den-wahlen-letzte-ausfahrt-ohne-enterhaken-12561255.html).

Debus, Marc, and Faas, Thorsten. 2013. 'Die Piratenpartei in der ideologisch-programmatischen Parteinekonstellation Deutschlands'. In *Die Piratenpartei*, edited by Oskar Niedermayer, 189–212. Wiesbaden: Springer VS.

Deschouwer, Kris (ed.). 2008. *New Parties in Government: In Power for the First Time*. London: Routledge.

Ennser, Laurenz. 2012. 'The homogeneity of West European party families: the radical right in comparative perspective'. *Party Politics*, vol. 18, n. 2: 151–71.

Falter, Juergen. 2010. 'The development of a multiparty system in Germany: a threat to democratic stability?' In *Political Parties and Democracy. Volume II: Europe*, edited by Kay Lawson, 27–46. Westport: Praeger.

Forschungsgruppe Wahlen Mannheim. 2013. Wahlanalyse Bundestagswahl 2013. 22 September. Available from:http://www.forschungsgruppe.de/Wahlen/ Grafiken_zu_aktuellen_Wahlen/Wahlen_2013/   Bundestagswahl_2013/ (accessed 12 November 2014).

Franklin, Mark N. 2004. *Voter Turnout and the Dynamics of Electoral Competition in Established Democracies Since 1945*. Cambridge: Cambridge University Press.

Gros, Daniel. 2013. 'The myth of German Euroskepticism'. 9 October. Available from: http://www.project-syndicate.org/commentary/daniel-grosthe-wrong-conventional-wisdom-on-germans--trust-in-europe (accessed 11 November 2014).

Gros, Daniel, and Roth, Felix. 2011. 'Do Germans support the euro?' CEPS Working document no. 359 (December).

Haas, Stefanie, and Hilmer, Richard. 2013. 'Backbord oder Steuerbord: Wo stehen die Piraten politisch?' In *Die Piratenpartei*, edited by Oskar Niedermayer, 75–9. Wiesbaden: Springer VS.

Häusler, Alexander. 2013. *Die 'Alternative für Deutschland' – eine neue rechtspopulistische Partei?* FORENA Report. Düsseldorf: Heinrich Böll Stiftung.

Hensel, Alexander, and Klecha, Stephan. 2013. *Die Piratenpartei. Havarie eines politischen Projekts?* Frankfurt am Main: Otto Brenner Stiftung.

Hensel, Alexander; Klecha, Stephan; and Walter, Franz. 2012. *Meuterei auf der Deutschland*. Berlin: Suhrkamp.

Hirscher, Gerhard. 2011. *Die Wählerschaft der PIRATEN-Partei*. München: Hanns-Seidel-Stiftung.

Infratest-Dimap. 2012a. ARD-DeutschlandTREND – Piratenwähler. April. Available from: http://www.infratest-dimap.de/umfragen-analysen/ bundesweit/ard-deutschlandtrend/2012/piratenwaehler-aus-protest (accessed 11 November 2014).

Infratest-Dimap. 2012b. ARD-DeutschlandTREND – 'Kurs Backbord!' – aus Sicht der Wahlberechtigten segeln die Piraten im linken Parteienspektrum. Eine Verortung im Links-Rechts-Kontinuum. April. Available from: http://www.infratest-dimap.de/umfragen-analysen/bundesweit/ard-deutschlandtrend/2012/verortung-der-piraten (accessed 11 November 2013).

Infratest-Dimap. 2013. Bundestagswahl 2013. Available from: http://wahl.tagesschau.de/wahlen/2013–09–2-BT-DE/index.shtml (accessed 11 November 2013).

Jeffery, Charlie. 1999. 'Germany: from hyperstability to change?' In *Changing Party Systems in Western Europe*, edited by David Broughton and Mark Donovan, 96–117. London: Pinter.

Jun, Uwe. 2011. 'Volksparteien under pressure: challenges and adaptation'. *German Politics*, vol. 20, n. 1: 200–22.

Keane, John. 2011. 'Monitory democracy?' In *The Future of Representative Democracy*, edited by Sonia Alonso, John Keane and Wolfgang Merkel, 212–35. Cambridge: Cambridge University Press.

Klecha, Stephan. 2014. 'Perspektivlos mit offener Zukunft'. Göttinger Institut für Demokratieforschung [blog]. Available from: http://www.demokratie-goettingen.de/blog/perspektivlos-mit-offener-zukunft (accessed 11 November 2014).

Korte, Karl-Rudolf. 2013. *Wer steht zur Wahl? Alternative für Deutschland (AfD) Parteiprofil*. Report for Bundeszentrale für politische Bildung, 29 August. Available from: http://www.bpb.de/politik/wahlen/wer-steht-zur-wahl/bundestag-2013/165526/afd (accessed 11 November 2014).

Krouwel, André. 2012. *Party Transformations in European Democracies*. Albany: SUNY Press.

Lees, Charles. 2008. 'The limits of party-based Euroscepticism in Germany'. In *Opposing Europe? The Comparative Party Politics of Euroscepticism. Volume I*, edited by Aleks Szczerbiak and Paul Taggart, 16–37. Oxford: Oxford University Press.

Lees, Charles. 2010. 'Rule makers and rule takers: on Volkspartei adaptation and strategy'. *German Politics*, vol. 19, n. 1: 89–104.

Litton, Krystyna. 2013. 'Party novelty. Conceptualization and measurement of party change'. *Party Politics*, forthcoming.

Lucardie, Paul. 2000. 'Prophets, purifiers and prolocutors. Towards a theory on the emergence of new parties'. *Party Politics*, vol. 6, n. 2: 175–85.

Meguid, Bonnie. 2008. *Party Competition between Unequals: Strategies and Electoral Fortunes in Western Europe*. Cambridge: Cambridge University Press.

Mudde, Cass. 2013. 'Three decades of populist radical right parties in Western Europe: so what?' *European Journal of Political Research*, vol. 52, n. 1: 1–19.

Müller-Rommel, Ferdinand, and Poguntke, Thomas (eds). 2001. *Green Parties in National Governments*. London: Frank Cass.

Niclauß, Karlheinz. 2004. *Kanzlerdemokratie. Regierungsdemokratie von Konrad Adenauer bis Gerhard Schröder*. Paderborn: Schöningh.

Niedermayer, Oskar. 2008. 'Das fluide Fünfparteiensystem nach der Bundestagwahl 2005'. In *Die Parteien nach der Bundestagswahl 2005*, edited by Oskar Niedermayer, 9–35. Wiesbaden: Springer VS.

Niedermayer, Oskar. 2013a. 'Organisationsstruktur, Finanzen und Personal der Piratenpartei'. In *Die Piratenpartei*, edited by Oskar Niedermayer, 81–99. Wiesbaden: Springer VS.

Niedermayer, Oskar. 2013b. 'Die Wähler del Piratenpartei: wo kommen sie her, wer sind sie und was bewegt sie zur Piratenwahl?' In *Die Piratenpartei*, edited by Oskar Niedermayer, 63–73. Wiesbaden: Springer VS.

Norris, Pippa. 2011. *Critical Citizens Revisited.* Cambridge: Cambridge University Press.

Onken, Holger, and Schneider, Sebastian H. 2013. 'Entern, kentern oder auflaufen? Zu den Aussichten der Piratenpartei im deutschen Parteiensystem'. Zeitschrift für Parlamentsfragen (ZParl), Heft 3/2012: 609–25.

Painter, Anthony. 2013. *Democratic Stress, the Populist Signal and Extremist Threat.* London: Policy Network.

Panebianco, Angelo. 1982. *Modelli di partito.* Bologna: Il Mulino.

Poguntke, Thomas. 1993. *Alternative Politics. The German Green Party.* Edinburgh: Edinburgh University Press.

Poguntke, Thomas. 2014. 'Towards a new party system: the vanishing hold of the catch-all parties in Germany'. *Party Politics, vol. 20, n. 6: 950-. .*

Sarrazin, Thilo. 2010. *Deutschland schafft sich ab: Wie wir unser Land aufs Spiel setzen.* Stuttgart: Deutsche Verlags-Anstalt.

Sartori, Giovanni. 1976. *Parties and Party Systems. A Framework for Analysis.* Cambridge: Cambridge University Press.

Usherwood, Simon, and Startin, Nick. 2013. 'Euroscepticism as a Persistent Phenomenon'. *Journal of Common Market Studies*, vol. 51, n. 1: 1–16.

Van Biezen, Ingrid. 2012. 'Constitutionalizing party democracy: the constitutive codification of political parties in post-war Europe'. *British Journal of Political Science*, vol. 42, n. 1: 187–212.

Verney, Susannah, and Bosco, Anna. 2013. 'Protest elections and challenger parties: Italy and Greece in the economic crisis'. *South European Society and Politics (Special Issue)*, vol. 18, n. 4.

Webb, Paul. 2002. 'Conclusion: political parties and democratic control in advanced industrial societies'. In *Political Parties in Advanced Industrial Democracies*, edited by Paul Webb, David M. Farrell and Ian Holliday, 438–60. Oxford: Oxford University Press.

Webb, Paul. 2011. 'Political parties, representation and politics in contemporary Europe'. In *Developments in European Politics*, edited by Paul M. Heywood, Erik Jones, Martin Rhodes and Ulrich Sedelmeier, 65–80. Basingstoke: Palgrave Macmillan.

Zolleis, Udo; Prokopf, Simon; and Strauch, Fabian. 2010. *Die Piratenpartei. Hype oder Herausforderung für die deutsche Parteienlandschaft?* München: Hanns-Seidel-Stiftung.

Chapter 10

Coalition Formation and Coalition Governance after the Election of 2013

Thomas Saalfeld

Introduction

The study of coalition has traditionally focused on three main questions: 'Will it last?' as well as 'Who gets in?' and 'Who gets what?' (Laver and Schofield 1990). More technically, the key concerns relate to the composition of the coalition, portfolio allocation and the stability and conflict management in the coalition once it has been formed. The German general election of 22 September 2013 led to the formation of the third cabinet under Federal Chancellor Angela Merkel and, after 2005–9, the second 'grand coalition' headed by her. This coalition of Christian Democrats (CDU/CSU) and Social Democrats (SPD) reflected the preferences of many German voters surveyed immediately before the election (Hilmer and Merz 2014), although the coalition was not the preferred option for either of the two parties. The coalition formed in November 2013 was intensely disputed within the SPD, highlighting the importance of the intra-party dimension of coalition bargaining. And the CDU/CSU could have secured more portfolios and, most likely, more policy influence in a coalition with the Greens. So, why did this coalition form despite the reservations on both sides?

It will be attempted to answer this question by drawing on recent theories of coalition formation and governance, which seek to model the (rational) actors' expectations about the number and attractiveness of portfolios they may receive in a coalition, the expected ideological and electoral costs of all available options for coalitions and the transaction costs of governing in future coalitions. Neither the allocation of portfolios nor the policy distance between the governing parties is sufficient to explain (a) the formation of a particular coalition and (b) the type of coalition agreement and governance structures the actors create at the beginning of their political cooperation. Coalition agreements, in particular, have become a focus for the study of coalition governance (Moury and Timmermans 2013; Müller and Meyer 2010). Therefore, the length and nature of the 2013 coalition agreement will be treated as an important part of this governance structure as it contains

> … policy intentions endorsed by the party organizations before government inauguration. Because they are often drafted under conditions that facilitate compromise, party leaders can agree on more policy deals than they would

otherwise, and by producing broad packages the results also become more acceptable to the MPs, the rank and file and the voters of the coalition parties. ... The specific conditions under which coalition agreements are drafted – behind closed doors, in a limited time, addressing multiple issues in parallel – ... facilitates making compromises and policy packages (Moury and Timmermans 2013, 118–19).

Coalitions are temporary forms of cooperation between competing political parties. In other words, they are characterized by a mixture of cooperative and competitive motives. If no single party has an overall majority of votes in the chamber, a coalition of parties may have incentives to work together. Only cooperation in a coalition will allow them to deliver benefits to voters and receive electoral rewards at the next election. Despite these benefits of coalition, the parties remain competitors for scarce and limited resources such as votes, government offices and policies. A party's willingness to join a coalition and bear the cost of the necessary compromises in policy and office terms depends on (a) the ideological proximity of the parties (which is inversely related to the policy cost of cooperation);[1] (b) the number of important offices (especially positions in the cabinet) the party can secure for its own members; and (c) mutual expectations about the behaviour of the other partners once a coalition has been formed (transaction costs). This includes expectations about the other parties' leaderships to generate, maintain and deliver the support of their parliamentary backbenchers and rank-and-file members in the country for the coalition and its policies. In this sense, coalition politics resembles a two-level game in international diplomacy with the risk of 'involuntary defection' when negotiators at the upper level reach a deal which may fail to be ratified by some representative body or group at the lower level following domestic (here: intra-party) bargaining (Putnam 1988).

Coalition agreements between parties as collective actors are attempts credibly to commit to a deal negotiated by their leaderships. They can be seen as incomplete contracts, in which government parties delegate policy-making to a cabinet. The government is headed by the Federal Chancellor and includes cabinet ministers and junior ministers. Due to her constitutional power to formulate the guidelines of government policy, the Federal Chancellor has considerable agenda-setting powers (*Kanzlerprinzip*). In addition, the organization and reorganization of government departments requires a proposal from, and the consent of, the Federal Chancellor. The German Basic Law also gives significant agenda-setting and policy-making powers to individual ministers (*Ressortprinzip*). When the preferences of government parties are not perfectly aligned, the head of government and the individual ministers are able to exploit their agenda-setting powers in order to formulate (or influence) government policy in line with their

---

1   In formal models this cost is usually expressed as the squared negative amount of the ideological difference between an individual party p and a coalition compromise c, namely: $-\|y_C - y_p\|^2$. See Linhart (2013).

own preferences. Martin and Vanberg (2004) describe this risk as 'ministerial drift', if individual ministers use their informational advantage and agenda-setting powers (for instance, proposal powers) to move a government policy closer to their own ideal point than envisioned in the coalition agreement. Martin (2004, 445) describes the problem as follows:

> ... coalition parties may differ substantially on important policy issues. Naturally, these differences can make it very tough for coalition partners to agree to an acceptable compromise in the negotiations preceding government formation, but even if they are able to do so, it is not a foregone conclusion that any of the resulting agreements can be enforced successfully. In particular, parties usually have incentives to renege on the terms of the coalition bargain, especially where the issues involved demand they make large policy concessions to their allies. Parties also have ample opportunity to renege, afforded by the fact that they are forced to delegate important policy-making powers to one another through the allocation of cabinet ministries.

It is relatively uncontentious that 'forming a government is not the end of politics but the beginning' (Laver and Shepsle 1990, 873). Expectations about the future play an important part in the parties' reasoning prior to the formation of a coalition. First, the choice of coalition partner may be influenced by uncertainty about the transaction costs of governing with one another: parties will consider the other potential coalition partner's record in the past in terms of trustworthiness or ability to deliver on their side of a coalition agreement. Second, the next elections play a significant role in the actors' thinking. Indeed, electoral considerations increase as the legislative term approaches its end (Lupia and Strøm 1995). How is cooperation feasible under such circumstances, especially towards the end of a legislative term when their own electoral incentives may become overwhelmingly important to the parties? What are the key mechanisms of coordination in the absence of complete agreement and in the presence of strong competitive motives?

Formalized theories of coalition formation have largely neglected issues of coalition governance (including the expectations of the future coalition partners regarding the transaction costs of governing together). They have done so for different reasons arising from their respective models: from the perspective of veto-player theory (and most other cooperative game-theoretic accounts), the *process* of governing in coalitions after their formation is not very interesting as all parties have a veto over government policy.[2] They have full information on their partners' intentions and will simply not agree to any policies proposed by a coalition partner, if this proposal is outside the 'winset' of the legislative status quo. In other words, each demand for a policy change made by a coalition partner will be evaluated. If the partner's proposal offers an improvement over the legislative

---

2   I am leaving aside issues arising from the wider veto-player framework developed by Tsebelis (2002). The focus here is on the partisan veto players forming a coalition.

status quo, or if the other (partisan) veto player is at least indifferent about this proposal, all parties will agree to change the policy. If only one coalition party prefers the status quo to a legislative change proposed by its partner (for example, a minister from a different party), its leaders will veto it (Tsebelis 2002). Issues of governance between the formation and termination of a cabinet do not arise for the purpose of modelling cabinet formation, termination or policy-making as the key events of concern.

Laver and Shepsle's (1990; 1996) portfolio-allocation model develops a different rationale and deals with a coalition partner's non-preferred policy proposals in a different way. Like veto-player theory, the portfolio-allocation model also does not place a great deal of emphasis on the transaction costs of governing in coalitions. The specific reason is that policy-making powers in a particular ministerial jurisdiction are assumed to be delegated to a minister who effectively dictates policy, if his or her party controls the median legislator on this policy dimension. Policy coordination is effectively restricted to the point in time when parties agree on a distribution of portfolios in the cabinet.

Both models were criticized for being empirically unrealistic or for failing to account for important aspects of the process of governing in coalitions (Müller and Meyer 2010). In recent years, authors such as Müller and Meyer (2010), Martin and Vanberg (2011) or Falcó-Gimeno (2014) sought to improve on these perspectives by including information about the institutions constraining the process of coalition governance after the coalition's formation. Martin and Vanberg (2011) have focused on formal parliamentary institutions, whereas Falcó-Gimeno (2014) attempted to explain the extent to which parties rely on coalition agreements and mutual monitoring rather than delegating to ministers in the sense of Laver and Shepsle (1996). Based on non-cooperative game theory, these authors sought to open the 'black box' of events between the formation and termination of a coalition.

The present contribution relies on the fundamentals of the models developed by Martin and Vanberg (2011) and Falcó-Gimeno (2014) to generate some intuitive expectations of, and explanations for, the nature and result of coalition bargaining in 2013. Martin and Vanberg (2011) argue that legislative institutions such as plenary debates and the legislative process can provide coalition government MPs with information about the intentions and policy proposals of their coalition partners. They will use these legislative institutions to subject another party's minister and his or her policy proposals to detailed scrutiny, if the minister's policy proposals are poorly aligned with their own. The larger the ideological distance, the more aggressively government backbenchers will use legislative institutions to scrutinize this minister's policy proposals. For example, CDU/CSU backbenchers could be expected to use the Bundestag's committees to monitor legislative proposals tabled by SPD ministers and vice versa. The committee stage of bills that are contentious between the two coalition partners should be longer than the committee stage of bills that enjoy unanimous support from both parties. Martin and Vanberg (2011) show this is indeed the case. In a similar vein, Kim and Loewenberg (2005) found that coalition partners have an above-average propensity to chair committees shadowing the ministries controlled by the other party. In other words, if the finance ministry is controlled by the Christian Democrats, the Social Democrats could be expected to control the agenda of the Bundestag's finance committee. This could be achieved, at least partially, if the committee is chaired by a Social Democrat.

Falcó-Gimeno's (2014) argument is slightly different. He argues that coalition partners will formulate lengthy and detailed coalition agreements, if (a) their policy preferences are not closely aligned; (b) their preferences in the relevant policy areas are not only conflicting but also 'overlapping' rather than 'tangential' (tangentiality exists where a policy area is salient for one, but not for the other coalition partner[s]; when preferences are 'overlapping' at least two coalition parties are competitors in a particular policy area); and (c) the coalition partners do not value long-term cooperation with one another very highly – that is, beyond a single legislative term. Partners that wish to form a long-term coalition and value future cooperation highly will have strong incentives to see all coalition parties' common longer-term interests and are more likely to refrain from unilateral opportunistic action. In these cases, the coalition agreement will be self-enforcing, and elaborate coalition-governance institutions are unnecessary. In the following, it will be argued that the coalition negotiations were protracted and led to a very comprehensive and detailed coalition agreement, because the partners were wary of the other side's incentives to defect in the course of the legislative term (the 18th Bundestag, 2013–17).

Bargaining Power Redistributed? The Election of 22 September 2013

Elections are the point at which bargaining power is (re-)distributed between the parties insofar as bargaining power depends on their parliamentary strength. The latter is usually conceived of as a vector of (a) the number of seats controlled by the parties and (b) the ideological position of the parties on key policy dimensions. This section will focus on the sheer size of the parties in terms of the seats controlled in the Bundestag elected in 2013.

The Bundestag election of 22 September 2013 resulted in a small earthquake as far as the options for coalition formation are concerned. The CDU/CSU grew in strength. With 41.5 per cent of the votes it won 49.3 per cent of the seats (311 seats) and nearly missed an overall majority of the seats in the Bundestag. The SPD, Left Party and Greens, by contrast, stagnated with 193, 64 and 63 seats, respectively. Most importantly, however, the liberal FDP failed to overcome the five-per-cent hurdle of Germany's electoral law and narrowly failed to secure any seats in the Bundestag (see the contribution of Mader and Schoen to this volume). Not only had this party been represented in the Bundestag uninterruptedly since 1949, it had held a pivotal position in the German party system for many years

(Pappi 1984) and, hence, had been in government for 49 out of the 64 years of German history since the foundation of the Federal Republic in 1949.

The demise of the FDP had a number of consequences for coalition formation: first, the continuation of a 'bourgeois coalition' of CDU/CSU and FDP was no longer feasible. When this 'black-yellow' coalition was formed in 2009, this was very much seen as a return to the 'normality' of centre-right coalitions during the Kohl years. As the traditional coalition patterns prevalent since 1982 were no longer available, any new coalition formed in 2013 would have to straddle the boundaries of the traditional German centre-right and centre-left 'camps' (Lager). Secondly, as the CDU/CSU failed to win an overall majority and the SPD had made a very explicit pre-electoral pledge to refuse any formal or informal coalition with the Left Party, there were only four options left: (a) a minority government of CDU and CSU; (b) the renewal of the 'grand coalition' of Christian Democrats and Social Democrats as in 1966–9 and 2005–9; (c) a coalition of CDU/CSU and Greens; or (d) new elections.

Table 10.1   Banzhaf power index for all Bundestag parties for a 50%+1 majority, 2005 and 2013

	2005		**2013**	
	Seats	**Banzhaf power index**	**Seats**	**Banzhaf power index**
CDU/CSU	239	0.75	311	0.75
SPD	146	0.25	193	0.25
FDP	93	0.25	–	–
Greens	76	0.25	63	0.25
Left Party	68	0.00000	64	0.25
Total	*622*		*631*	

Source: Author's own calculation based on the distribution of seats.

Intuitively, this seems to have put the CDU/CSU into a very strong bargaining position as Chancellor Merkel had a whole range of choices. This was recognized by both the Social Democrats and the Greens. The latter pulled out of preliminary coalition talks with the Christian Democrats very quickly. The former announced that any coalition agreement would have to be ratified not by a party conference of delegates, but by a referendum of the entire membership. As a result, the 'red lines' drawn by the SPD leadership in the negotiations had more credibility in the face of the Christian Democrats' strategic advantage (Sturm 2014).

Looking at the bargaining power of the parties from a mathematical point of view, however, the CDU/CSU was not stronger in 2013 than it had been four years earlier. Table 10.1 presents values of the Banzhaf power index. When computing this power index, all (theoretically) possible winning coalitions are listed in a first step. In a second step, the 'critical voters' (or parties) are counted. A 'critical voter' is one that would turn a winning coalition into a minority. Note that each party is treated as a single 'voter' with a particular 'bargaining weight' determined by the number of seats it controls in the legislature. A party's power is then calculated as the fraction of all critical 'swing votes' it could cast over the total number of 'swing votes' (for an explanation see Straffin 1996). A comparison of the power index values demonstrates that, in purely mathematical terms, the CDU/CSU's bargaining power in 2013 was exactly equal to its bargaining power in 2005, the Bundestag election after which the first grand coalition under Merkel was formed: the Christian Democrats were the 'decisive voter' (or, rather, party) in three out of four possible cases (0.75). The other parties' bargaining power, by contrast, was one-third of that of the CDU/CSU (0.25). In other words, despite its poor electoral performance, the SPD's bargaining power had not changed, if mathematical power indices are applied. This may explain to an extent why the SPD came out of the 2013 coalition negotiations with a relatively good 'deal'.

Payoffs

Most formal theories of coalition formation assume that parties will form coalitions that maximize their expected utility, although there is no agreement what, precisely, the 'currency' of their expected utility is. It is generally assumed that parties care about office payoffs (positions in the executive), policy payoffs (reducing the policy costs of coalition compromises with partners whose preferences differ) and their parties' chances at the next elections. Party leaders also care about maintaining the support of their rank and file, which assures their chances to maintain their leadership positions (Luebbert 1986).

In addition to these motivations, coalition formation in Germany tends to be constrained by pre-electoral commitments that can be interpreted as signals the parties send to voters about their intentions after the election (Schubert 2013; 2014). These signals can take the form of statements by leading members or even by bodies of the relevant parties, or they can be made in the form of (real) coalitions at the state level, which are sometimes seen as a test bed for new patterns of collaboration (Decker 2013). The party leaders' choices in the autumn of 2013 were constrained by negative pre-electoral commitments the parties had made in the run-up to the election: both the CDU/CSU and SPD leaderships had – explicitly or implicitly – ruled out any cooperation with the Left Party. The latter had repeatedly emphasized its willingness to form a coalition with the Social Democrats and the Greens, but these offers were rejected unequivocally by the SPD leadership (Decker 2013, 93). Only after the election of 2013 did the Social Democrats end their refusal in principle to consider coalitions with the Left Party in the future. However, policy differences would remain substantial, especially in foreign and security policy.

Office Payoffs

William Riker's (1962) seminal theory is based on the assumption that political parties can be modelled as if they predominantly cared about government office combined with the game-theoretic notion of minimal-winning coalitions that was prominent in the formal literature at the time (Von Neumann and Morgenstern 1953). What would this mean for coalition formation in the aftermath of the election of September 2013? Based on the norm of a proportional allocation of cabinet portfolios, a coalition with the Greens would have been far more attractive to the CDU/CSU than a coalition with the Social Democrats, had it been motivated solely by office goals. With the 311 Bundestag seats it won in 2013, the CDU/CSU would have contributed 83.2 per cent to the combined seat share of a potential CDU/CSU–Green coalition as the latter had only 63 seats. In a grand coalition of the two major parties, by contrast, it would have contributed merely 61.7 per cent to the combined seat share of a potential coalition of Christian Democrats and Social Democrats as the latter controlled 193 parliamentary seats in the 2013 Bundestag. Given a norm of proportionality and assuming 16 cabinet-level ministerial positions (like in 2005–9), the CDU/CSU could have expected at least 13 cabinet positions in a coalition with the Greens whereas it could hope for only nine to ten seats around the cabinet table in a coalition with the SPD.

The distribution of seats in the Bundestag placed the CDU/CSU in a decisive position during the coalition negotiations following the election of September 2013 (see Table 10.1). Although a continuation of the CDU/CSU-FDP coalition was no longer possible, it was able simultaneously to start discussions with the SPD and the Greens. The CDU/CSU leadership under Chancellor Merkel and Bavarian Minister President Horst Seehofer invited both Greens and Social Democrats to preliminary talks between 4 and 17 October 2013. For the first time, the Christian Democrats considered a coalition with the Greens at the national level. Exploring such a coalition did not seem to be hopeless anymore after the CDU/CSU-FDP government Merkel II (2009–13) had decided to phase out all nuclear power plants following the Fukushima disaster (Huß 2014). Nevertheless, the first rounds of preliminary talks and a number of background conversations quickly led to the conclusion that a coalition between Christian Democrats and Social Democrats was the Christian Democrats' preferred option. This conclusion was largely based on the potential policy costs both CDU/CSU and Greens would have faced in a coalition, despite the fact that a number of more left-leaning Green leaders (for example, Jürgen Trittin and Petra Roth) had stepped down after the disappointing election result. The relatively swift withdrawal from preliminary talks by the Green leadership fronted by Cem Özdemir and Kathrin Göring-Eckardt was regretted by more conservative Greens such as Winfried Kretschmann, the Green minister president of Baden-Württemberg. Yet, within the CDU/CSU a third round of preliminary discussions with the SPD leadership under Sigmar Gabriel had already led to a clear preference of most Christian Democratic leaders for a grand coalition. Formal negotiations between CDU, CSU and SPD started on 23 October

2013 and were completed on 27 November 2013. After internal ratification in all parties, which involved a membership vote in the SPD (see below), the three party leaders formally signed the coalition agreement in Berlin on 16 December 2013.

Policy Payoffs and Potential Costs

The Christian Democrats' decision to open formal talks with the Social Democrats largely reflects the perceived policy costs of a grand coalition, which were considered to be lower than with the Greens. Especially, the radical turnaround in the Federal Republic's energy policy (the so-called *Energiewende*), one of the crucial issues on the new government's agenda, could have been expected to lead to significant differences between the CDU/CSU and Greens. But how do we get a sense of policy differences and associated costs? Formal analyses of party competition tend to consider party competition and cooperation as taking place in an ideological 'space'. In its simplest form, this space may consist of a single dimension (usually a line from 'left' to 'right'). In the German case (like in most other advanced democracies), there is little disagreement that this socio-economic left-right dimension is by far the most important dimension when it comes to distinguishing between the different parties' ideological position in the policy space. It is also the most important dimension in the voters' perception. On the left end of this socio-economic continuum, voters and parties would favour a strong state using taxation in order to redistribute income from the rich to the poor and to expand the welfare state with a view to protecting those in need. On the right, there would be voters and parties giving clear priority to free enterprise, low taxation and a minimal welfare state functioning as a safety net.

Nevertheless, patterns of cooperation and competition between the parties are also shaped by at least one further dimension in Germany. There is some disagreement concerning the nature of the second dimension. Some would argue that this second dimension is best represented by a continuum ranging from 'cosmopolitanism' to 'nationalism' (Kriesi et al. 2006). More frequently, however, authors use a 'social-liberal' dimension as the second most important dimension in Germany (Hornsteiner and Saalfeld 2014). Here, persons and parties with individualist, libertarian, socially liberal values would be located at one end of the spectrum, and those with political views favouring law and order, religion and conservative family values on the other.

The data on which Figure 10.1 is based were prepared to capture the policy distances between all 'relevant' (Sartori 1976) parties in the German Bundestag during the 2005 and 2013 election campaigns. These two elections are compared to assess the different spatial locations of the relevant Bundestag parties prior to the formation of the grand coalitions of 2005 (Merkel I) and 2013 (Merkel III). The Wordfish scaling model (Slapin and Proksch 2008) was used to derive estimates of the parties' policy positions from their manifestos in 2005 and 2013. The analysis includes the manifestos of the CDU/CSU, the SPD, the FDP, the Greens and the Left Party. Each party's positions in 2005 and 2013 are represented by an arrow. The arrow's origin provides information about the party's position

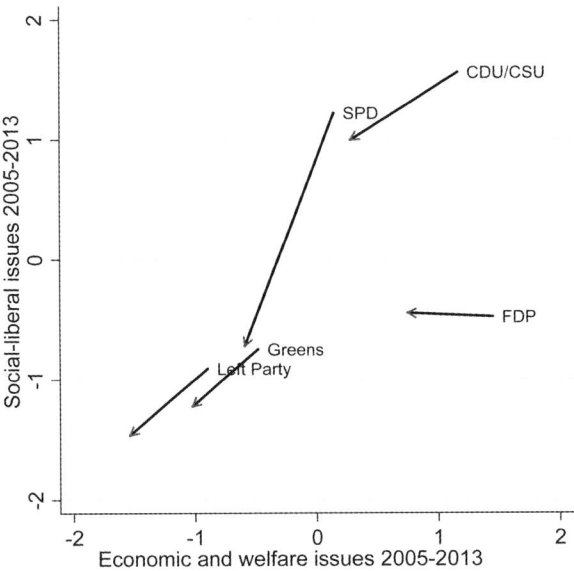

Figure 10.1   The Bundestag parties' changing ideological positions on two key issue areas, 2005 and 2013

Sources: Election manifestos of CDU/CSU, SPD, FDP, Greens and Linke 2005 and 2013. Parties' positions are estimated using word frequencies and reported, with further sources, in Hornsteiner and Saalfeld (2014). For a detailed description of the method see Slapin and Proksch (2008). Absolute values are not comparable across dimensions.

on the relevant policy dimension in its 2005 election manifesto. The arrowhead denotes the party's position in its 2013 manifesto.

The first, most striking observation from Figure 10.1 is that all parties moved to the economic left and (less prominently) towards social liberalism between 2005 and 2013. The SPD's move is unsurprising as it sought to recapture some of the electoral ground lost to the Left Party since 2005 due to Chancellor Gerhard Schröder's welfare reforms in the 2002–5 Bundestag. After the party's turn to the centre between 1994 and 1998, its 2005, 2009 and 2013 manifestos reveal a move back to more traditional Social Democratic policies. Nevertheless the distance from the CDU/CSU did not increase on the socio-economic dimension as the Christian Democrats also moved to the left. After its unsuccessful emphasis on a relatively neo-liberal position in the 2005 election, the Christian Democrats returned to more centrist positions in their economic and welfare policies. In addition, the party's gradual modernization under Angela Merkel's leadership extends to policy areas captured by the second dimension in Figure 10.1 and was reflected in legislation between 2009 and 2013 to tackle discrimination against women, immigrants and disabled or gay persons. These changes from 2005 were moderate but are clearly reflected in Figure 10.1. Thus the policy cost for both parties in the grand coalition formed in 2013 increased more strongly on the social-liberal dimension where the Social Democrats had moved sharply towards the social-liberal end of the spectrum. Since the social-liberal dimension is clearly less important in terms of its salience (Benoit and Laver 2006), the odds for the grand coalition to form in 2013 were thus relatively favourable.

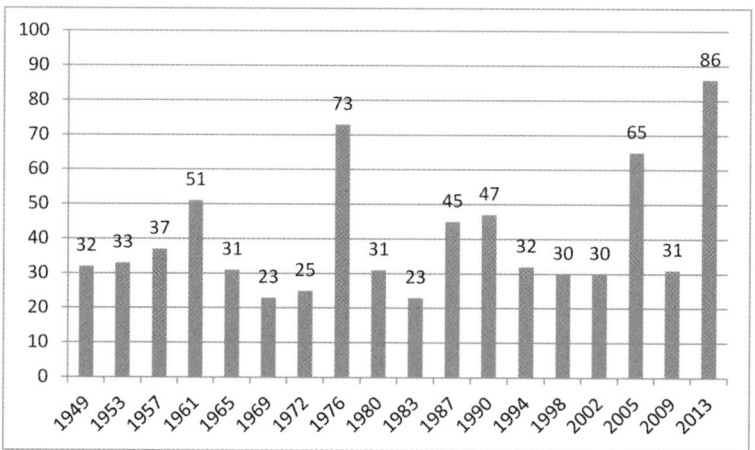

Figure 10.2   Duration of cabinet formation, 1949–2013 in Days
Sources: 1949-1987: Saalfeld (2000: 49); 1990-2013: Datenhandbuch zur Geschichte des Deutschen Bundestages, online edition (http://www.bundestag.de/dokumente/datenhandbuch/06, accessed 15 May 2014).

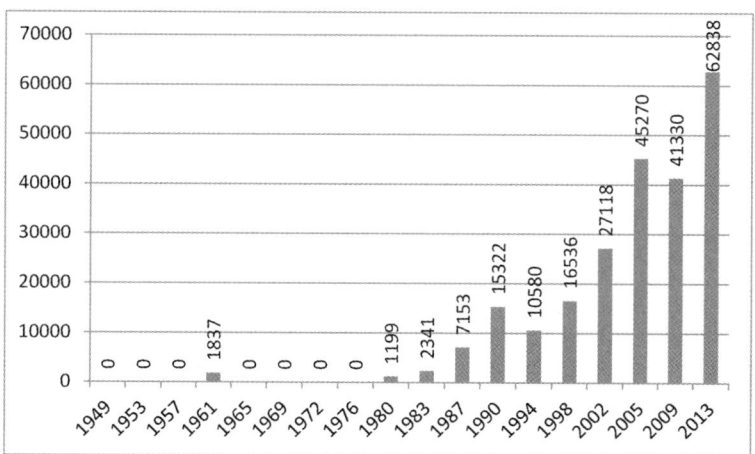

Figure 10.3   Length of Coalition agreements in Words, 1949–2013
Sources: Coalition Agreements 1961, 1980-2013. Until 1976, formal written agreements were exceptional. For further references see Saalfeld (2000) and Hornsteiner and Saalfeld (2014).

The general proximity of the parties is reflected in a consensus between their leaders – Merkel (CDU), Gabriel (SPD) and Seehofer (CSU) – who demonstrated a willingness to compromise from the very beginning. Nevertheless, the duration of the bargaining process was relatively long and drawn-out (see Figure 10.2), reflecting a number of distinctive issues: first, the negotiations were conducted in 12 specialized working groups (four of which had sub-committees). These working groups included 259 politicians from all parties concerned (Sturm 2014, 213). They were dominated by the parliamentary parties' policy experts and, in some cases, also by representatives from the federal states. Second, the prospective coalition partners were keen to avoid too many vague compromises and sought to draw up a relatively precise coalition agreement defining the future government's agenda. In other words, the coalition partners relied less on vague, 'implicit' compromises delegating the power to work out compromises to cabinet ministers (this risking 'ministerial drift'), and sought to constrain the government from the very beginning by writing a relatively precise document. This led, third, to a relatively long coalition agreement, the longest in the history of the Federal Republic (see Figure 10.3). Fourth, the length of the negotiations and the precision of the agreement helped to secure intra-party acceptance of the deal. Especially, the SPD grassroots had been reluctant to join the grand coalition, a fact that was exploited by the party's leadership in the coalition negotiations when they thought to extract further concessions from the CDU/CSU.

The negotiations in 2013 appeared tougher than many previous negotiations. Party leaderships on both sides wanted to signal to their members and voters that they were not giving in too quickly. The Social Democrat leadership was particularly concerned to ensure that the party would not, as they saw it, repeat mistakes made in the 2005–9 grand coalition where the CDU/CSU seemed to have benefited electorally in 2009 and the SPD felt that it had been penalized for its government role during the 2005–9 Bundestag. In addition, Sigmar Gabriel and the SPD leadership were in a very vulnerable position within their own party. After all, the 2013 election resulted in the party's second weakest performance since 1949, and many members attributed the poor showing to the Schröder government's (1998–2005) labour-market and pensions policies (Agenda 2010) – the party's leadership around Sigmar Gabriel, Frank-Walter Steinmeier and Peer Steinbrück (until 2013) having been closely associated with Schröder's policies, which seemed to have contributed to the rise of the Left Party and the SPD's strong decline. Angela Merkel and Horst Seehofer, by contrast, seemed to be without serious challenges to their political authority.

From the outset, there was strong opposition against the grand coalition in the SPD. This opposition was articulated openly by Hannelore Kraft, the party's popular minister president of Northrhine-Westfalia. Therefore, the leadership had to seek the endorsement of a convention of party delegates on 20 October in order to commence formal negotiations. It also had to commit to a membership vote on the coalition agreement after the conclusion of the negotiations. This was a first in the Federal Republic's history. Coalition agreements are normally ratified by conferences of party delegates (Saalfeld 2000). Apart from gaining intra-party acceptance, this move strengthened the SPD leadership's bargaining position vis-à-vis the Christian Democrats. Nevertheless, its continued vulnerability was highlighted at the SPD Annual Conference in Leipzig (14/15 November 2013) when the leadership was re-elected with disappointing results.

Partly as a result of the SPD's pre-commitment to a membership vote, all three parties went into the negotiations with a number of non-negotiable 'red lines': the Social Democrats demanded a statutory general minimum wage of 8.50 euro; a partial reversal of the Schröder government's pension reforms (by demanding that people with 45 years of service could retire at the age of 63 with a full pension); a curtailing of the trend towards temporary employment through agencies; dual nationality for the descendants of immigrants born in Germany; equal rights of marriage for homosexual couples; and a gender quota in the supervisory boards of companies listed on the stock markets. The CDU's 'red lines' were no increases in taxation; an increase in the pensions for mothers with children born before 1992 (*Mütterrente*); and the continuation of tax privileges for married couples (*Ehegattensplitting*). The non-negotiable demands placed in the public domain by the CSU were similar to the CDU's plus an insistence on the extension of state subsidies received by parents of pre-school children for crèches and kindergartens to parents looking after their children at home (*Betreuungsgeld*) and a toll system for foreign cars (Sturm 2014, 219). Given the strong public pre-commitment the parties had issued on these demands, they were all included in the coalition agreement with strong indications of log-rolling as an important mechanism to reach agreement (Stratmann 1997).

Apart from formulating 'red lines', the parties issued public threats. The successful negotiations between Christian Democrats and Greens to form a coalition in Hesse (rather than forming a regional grand coalition with the Social Democrats) was seen as an indication that the CDU/CSU was willing to consider alternatives even in a state where relations between CDU and Greens had been fraught with bitter personalized disputes in the past. Equally, the Social Democrats passed a resolution at their Leipzig Conference that, in the future, coalitions with the Left Party should be considered in principle, subject to certain conditions in fiscal, foreign and defence policy. The Christian Democrats saw this move as an indication that the SPD leadership might withdraw from the grand coalition before 2017 with a view to leading a left-wing coalition including Social Democrats, Greens and the Left Party. The membership vote in the SPD was seen as a further attempt of the party's leadership to extract more concessions from the CDU/CSU under Chancellor Merkel than they could have hoped for given their weak electoral performance. After the completion of the coalition negotiations, the leadership campaigned hard for a majority of SPD members to support the coalition agreement negotiated in October and November. In the end, 77.8 per cent of the party's members voted, of which 76 per cent supported the coalition agreement (Sturm 2014, 224).

Although the length of the negotiations met with some public criticism, the SPD leadership succeeded in getting its key demands agreed in the coalition agreement. It was seen to have defended the party's core policies and asserted its issue ownership by capturing some key portfolios in the new government. More importantly, Sigmar Gabriel's authority was strengthened within and beyond his own party through his commitment and effectiveness in the vigorous debates within the SPD and the result of the membership vote. On 17 December, the Bundestag majority elected Angela Merkel to become German Federal Chancellor for the third time. In line with the Bundestag's Standing Orders, Members cast their vote secretly. The CDU leader received 462 out of 631 votes and was duly elected Federal Chancellor. Nevertheless, the result suggests that 42 members of the majority parties refused to support her. Nominally, her new government had a majority of 504 out of 631 seats in the Bundestag (just under 80 per cent), causing concern about the viability of a vigorous opposition, which consisted of the Left Party (64 seats) and the Greens (63 seats).

Portfolio Allocation and Coalition Governance

It could be argued that portfolio allocation is the most important parameter of coalition governance (Laver and Shepsle 1996). Beyond the mere number of seats around the cabinet table and the traditional preferences particular political parties have for particular portfolios (for example, the Social Democrats have a strong preference for the social affairs portfolio in whatever coalition they are in), the *precise pattern* of portfolio allocation is crucial.

In purely quantitative terms, the portfolio allocation in the cabinet Merkel III follows the proportionality norm that has been observed across modern parliamentary democracies time and again: cabinet positions are allocated in proportion to the contribution each government party makes to the size of the government (in terms of the number of seats it controls in the legislature), with a slight overrepresentation of smaller parties (see Table 10.2). The CDU, contributing just over 50 per cent of the parliamentary seats held by the new government, was allocated the Chancellorship (Angela Merkel) and six further portfolios. These seven seats around the cabinet table constituted 43.75 per cent of the cabinet seats, including the Federal Chancellorship. The SPD, contributing just over 38 per cent of legislative seats, received six portfolios (37.5 per cent of cabinet seats). Contributing approximately 11 per cent of legislative seats, the CSU secured three (18.75 per cent of portfolios). In short, both major parties, particularly the CDU, were willing to make some concessions to the CSU as far as the number of positions in the cabinet is concerned.

Table 10.2   Portfolio allocation in the cabinet Merkel III and Bundestag committee chairs (2013)

Portfolio	Name	Party	Committee chair
Federal Chancellor	Angela Merkel	CDU	–
Finance	Wolfgang Schäuble	CDU	**SPD**
Home Affairs	Thomas de Maizière	CDU	CDU/CSU
Defence	Ursula von der Leyen	CDU	**SPD**
Health	Hermann Gröhe	CDU	**SPD**
Education and Research	Johanna Wanka	CDU	CDU/CSU
Minister without Portfolio in the Chancellor's Office	Peter Altmaier	CDU	–
Agriculture and Food	Hans-Peter Friedrich (Christian Schmidt from 17 February 2014)	CSU	CDU/CSU
Transport and Digital Infrastructure	Alexander Dobrindt	CSU	**SPD**
Economic Cooperation and Development	Gerd Müller	CSU	CDU/CSU
Economic Affairs and Energy (and Deputy Federal Chancellor)	Sigmar Gabriel	SPD	**CDU/CSU**
Foreign Affairs	Frank-Walter Steinmeier	SPD	**CDU/CSU**
Justice and Consumer Protection	Heiko Maas	SPD	Greens
Work and Social Affairs	Andrea Nahles	SPD	SPD
Families, Senior Citizens, Women and Youth	Manuela Schwesig	SPD	**CDU/CSU**
Environment, Nature, Construction and Reactor Safety	Barbara Hendricks	SPD	Greens

Sources: http://www.bundesregierung.de/Webs/Breg/DE/Bundesregierung/Bundeskabinett/bundeskabinett and http://www.bundestag.de/bundestag/ausschuesse18/ (both accessed 15 May 2014).

Although this chapter will not provide any precise measurements of portfolio salience for the government parties, the distribution of portfolios suggests that the CDU received a number of portolios with the highest general 'salience' in German politics (Druckman and Warwick 2005). In addition the partners achieved a degree of 'tangentiality' in Luebbert's (1986) and Falcó-Gimeno's (2014) sense. Apart from the Chancellorship, the CDU secured the Federal Ministries of Finance, Home Affairs and Defence. Not only are these amongst the most salient portfolios in general, but they are particularly important to the Christian Democrats. The CSU lost defence as one of the 'classical' portfolios, but retained the Federal Ministries of Agriculture and Transport. Although the party was not able to retain control of any of the 'classical' portfolios, it secured those that have always had particular importance for it to deliver targeted benefits to its constituency in Bavaria. The SPD leader, Sigmar Gabriel, received the newly created Ministry of Economic Affairs and Energy. This portfolio was crucial for the radical change of Germany's energy policy. The Ministry of Work and Social Affairs was allocated to the Social Democrats as well. This department is clearly the one ministry the SPD cared about in particular. After all, it is responsible for the delivery of some of the SPD's key electoral pledges such as a statutory minimum wage.

Although the mere numerical balance of portfolios and variations in their salience is interesting, these data conceal a large number of important changes to the jurisdictions of individual federal ministries, which are of great significance for policy-making but tend to be neglected in the literature on portfolio allocation. In 2013, the role of Sigmar Gabriel as leader of the SPD and Deputy Federal Chancellor was underlined by combining the Ministry of Economic Affairs with the responsibility for energy policy – a major, powerful role after the decision to phase out nuclear power taken in 2011.[3] The responsibility for consumer protection was removed from the Federal Ministry of Agriculture (controlled by the CSU) and incorporated in the Ministry of Justice (controlled by the SPD). One ministry led by the CSU gained in powers, however: the Ministry of Transport was given responsibility for the development of Germany's digital infrastructure. The responsibility for (public) construction, which had belonged to the jurisdiction of the Ministry of Transport (led by a CSU minister), was moved to the Ministry of the Environment (led by an SPD politician).

Thus, the new government was reconfigured beyond the level of cabinet positions. Like in previous governments, the cabinet Merkel III is not characterized by a widespread practice of using of junior ministers as 'watchdogs' to monitor 'ministerial drift' (see Thies 2001). In other words, the combination of a cabinet minister of one party with a junior minister of a different coalition

---

3   The Federal Ministry of Economic Affairs does not have an extensive jurisdiction in itself. In the past it has been combined with the Federal Ministry of Work and Social Affairs to reflect the status of Wolfgang Clement (2002–5), or with the Finance Ministry in the case of Karl Schiller (1971–2).

partner was exceptional. Rather, the coalition used the familiar practice of allocating portfolios with a high level of mutual policy coordination to different coalition partners: for example, the Ministry of Foreign Affairs (Steinmeier, SPD) was 'shadowed' by the Ministry of Defence (von der Leyen, CDU) and the Ministry of Economic Cooperation and Development (Müller, CSU). The Minister of Finance (Schäuble, CDU) was paired up with Sigmar Gabriel's Ministry of Economic Affairs and Energy on the one hand and the Ministry of Agriculture (Schmidt, CSU) on the other. The Ministry for Home Affairs was controlled by the CDU (de Maizière), whereas the Ministry of Justice was headed by a Social Democrat (Maas). The ministries in charge of welfare policy were shared amongst the parties with the SPD controlling the Ministry of Work and Social Affairs (Nahles) and the Ministry for Families, Senior Citizens, Women and Youth (Schwesig), whereas the CDU was in charge of the Ministry of Health (Gröhe).

Authors such as Martin and Vanberg (2011) or Kim and Loewenberg (2005) placed strong emphasis on the use of parliamentary institutions (such as the allocation of committee chairs) as monitoring devices in the management of potential ministerial drift between coalition partners. Like in previous governments, there is some evidence of a practice where legislative committee chairs are chosen in such a way as to ensure that the minister of one coalition party is 'shadowed' by a committee chair from the other main governing party – at least when the government (rather than the opposition) parties were allocated the relevant Bundestag committee chair. Table 10.2 demonstrates that this pattern, first observed by Kim and Loewenberg (2005), was also in evidence in the 2013 Bundestag, at least to a certain extent. Such a 'shadowing' is observable in 7 out of 12 possible cases, which have been highlighted in bold in Table 10.2. However, the ministers and committee chairs in home affairs and work and social affairs, two crucial portfolios of high salience, were exceptions to this pattern and were drawn from the same party.

In short, there is some evidence that the two parties relied heavily on ex-ante controls of the risk of 'ministerial drift' by drawing up a very extensive coalition agreement. It is possible that the grand coalition, therefore, felt it less necessary than its predecessors to shadow ministers with committee chairs from the other party.

Conclusion

The election of 2013 brought a radical change to the German postwar party system as the FDP disappeared from the Bundestag. In the end, a grand coalition seemed the only feasible option for a stable majority cabinet. Thus, there was an air of inevitability about the formation of this coalition. The main protagonists – Merkel, Schäuble, Seehofer, Steinmeier, Gabriel and many others – had governed reasonably efficiently together in the grand coalition of 2005–9, and they knew each other and trusted each other to the extent that this is possible. Moreover, there was considerable popular support for the formation of a grand coalition, at least initially (Hilmer and Merz 2014).

Nevertheless, negotiations in the run-up to the formation of the third national grand coalition in the Federal Republic's history (after 1966–9 and 2005–9) were protracted. There are several reasons for this seemingly paradoxical course of events: The strategic situation was new as the voters had thrown out the FDP after 64 years of uninterrupted membership of the Bundestag. The voters' verdict did not allow for the formation of a centre-right (CDU/CSU–FDP) or centre-left (SPD–Green) coalition, a pattern that German politicians and voters had become accustomed to since the 1980s. Given the Social Democrats' unequivocal pre-electoral commitment against any cooperation with the Left Party, the range of options was severely constrained. It was necessary to form a coalition across the traditional divide between the centre-left and centre-right parties. The CDU/CSU did not occupy the ideological median in the Bundestag (this position was occupied by the SPD), but it appeared to be in the comfortable position of being able to choose its coalition partner amongst the two parties across the traditional divide between the centre-left and centre-right: the SPD on the one hand and the Greens on the other. It may have been precisely this strategic advantage enjoyed by the CDU/CSU, with its near-overall majority in the Bundestag, that led to particular sensitivities amongst all potential coalition partners.

The SPD leadership's attitude was influenced by the perception that the previous grand coalition had only benefited the Christian Democrats and Angela Merkel – and damaged their own party's electoral credibility. In addition, the grand coalition was met with deep scepticism amongst the SPD rank-and-file members. Especially the left wing of the party wanted a clear revision of the policies initiated by the SPD-Green Schröder government between 1998 and 2005. Such revisions towards a more left-wing, welfarist position were unlikely to be successful in a coalition with the CDU/CSU. The Greens, too, feared the overwhelming strength of the CDU/CSU in a potential 'black-green' coalition led by the experienced Chancellor Angela Merkel.

In order to secure a beneficial bargaining result in the face of a very strong CDU/CSU, the SPD leadership drew a number of 'red lines' and – for the first time in the Federal Republic's history – committed to a vote of all party members for the ratification of the bargaining result. This tactic was relatively successful as the SPD negotiators secured control of those ministries whose jurisdictions were crucial to the party's attempt to reclaim issue ownership in classical areas of SPD strength such as social and welfare policies. At the same time, the CDU/CSU secured control of a number of key portfolios such as finance, home affairs and defence. Under the circumstances, the bargaining result looked like a reasonable approximation of a deal built on tangential preferences as modelled by Luebbert (1984; 1986) and Falcó-Gimeno (2014).[4]

The longer the coalition negotiations went on, the more scepticism became noticeable in the media, reinforcing the sense of electoral risks amongst the parties involved. There was an expectation that any grand coalition with an overwhelming majority in the Bundestag (around 80 per cent of the seats) and a numerically weak parliamentary opposition could only be justified under particular circumstances (for the 2005–9 coalition see Gross 2011, 74). It could be justified, it was argued, if the new government used its majority to tackle big issues of national importance and initiated major reforms that would have been far more difficult to realize under conditions of intense competition between the two major parties. The grand coalition of 2005–9, for example, had agreed to carry out a reform of German federalism with a view to reducing the mutual interdependence between federation and states and generating clearer lines of accountability for both tiers. However, the deal the parties agreed on in 2013 seemed more like a package of small if socially costly policy measures reminiscent of the collective result of log-rolling in the US congress (Stratmann 1997). Nevertheless, the length of the coalition negotiations and the detail of the coalition agreement are in line with the predictions made by Falcó-Gimeno (2014). Since both parties did not value a long-term collaboration (they clearly saw the grand coalition as an exceptional necessity), they negotiated the most extensive and detailed coalition agreement so far. Whether the coalition will last its entire term (until 2017) will depend on a number of factors, especially any 'exogenous shocks' that it may be subjected to. In particular, however, it will depend on the parties' constant evaluation of the electoral risks arising from the coalition (Lupia and Strøm 1995).

References

Benoit, Kenneth, and Laver, Michael. 2006. *Party Policy in Modern Democracies*. London: Routledge.

Decker, Frank. 2013. 'Koalitionssignale – ein von der Koalitionstheorie zu Unrecht vernachlässigter Faktor?' In *Die deutsche Koalitionsdemokratie vor der Bundestagswahl 2013*, edited by Frank Decker and Eckhard Jesse, 75–96. Baden-Baden: Nomos.

---

4   This point should not be overstated, however. The business wing of the CDU/CSU did express reservations about the welfarist outlook of the coalition agreement (for instance, in the area of pensions and the way the statutory minimum wage was to be implemented) immediately after the completion of the negotiations. In other words, competition on the socio-economic dimension persisted, at least between the more 'extreme' wings of both major parties ('extreme' being defined in spatial terms).

Druckman, James N., and Warwick, Paul V. 2005. 'The missing piece: measuring portfolio salience in Western European parliamentary democracies'. *European Journal of Political Research*, vol. 44, n. 1: 17–42.

Falcó-Gimeno, Albert. 2014. 'The use of control mechanisms in coalition governments: the role of preference tangentiality and repeated interactions'. *Party Politics*, vol. 20, n. 3: 341–56.

Gross, Martin. 2011. *Große Koalition, Große Folgen? Die Auswirkungen schwarz-roter Regierungsbündnisse auf die Parteiensysteme in Bund und Ländern 1946 bis 2009*. Marburg: Tectum.

Hilmer, Richard, and Merz, Stefan. 2014. 'Die Bundestagswahl vom 22. September 2013: Merkels Meisterstück'. *Zeitschrift für Parlamentsfragen*, vol. 45, n. 1: 175–206.

Hornsteiner, Margret, and Saalfeld, Thomas. 2014. 'Parties and the party system'. In *Developments in German Politics 4*, edited by Stephen Padgett, William E. Paterson and Reimut Zohlnhöfer, 78–102. Basingstoke: Palgrave Macmillan.

Huß, Christian. 2014. 'Durch Fukushima zum neuen Konsens? Die Umweltpolitik von 2009 bis 2013'. In *Politik im Schatten der Krise: Eine Bilanz der Regierung Merkel, 2009–2013*, edited by Reimut Zohlnhöfer and Thomas Saalfeld, 521–54. Wiesbaden: VS Verlag.

Kim, Dong-Hun, and Loewenberg, Gerhard. 2005. 'The role of parliamentary committees in coalition governments. Keeping tabs on coalition partners in the German Bundestag'. *Comparative Political Studies*, vol. 38, n. 9: 1104–29.

Kriesi, Hanspeter; Grande, Edgar; Lachat, Romain; Dolezal, Martin; Bornschier, Simon; and Frey, Timotheos. 2006. 'Globalization and the transformation of the national political space: six European countries compared'. *European Journal of Political Research*, vol. 45, n. 6: 921–56.

Laver, Michael, and Schofield, Norman. 1990. *Multiparty Government: The Politics of Coalition in Europe*. Oxford: Oxford University Press.

Laver, Michael, and Shepsle, Kenneth A. 1990. 'Coalitions and cabinet government'. *American Political Science Review*, vol. 84, n. 3: 873–90.

Laver, Michael, und Shepsle, Kenneth A. 1996. *Making and Breaking Governments: Cabinets and Legislatures in Parliamentary Democracies*. Cambridge: Cambridge University Press.

Linhart, Eric. 2013. 'Does an appropriate coalition theory exist for Germany? An overview of recent office- and policy-oriented coalition theories'. *German Politics*, vol. 22, n. 3: 288–313.

Luebbert, Gregory. 1984. 'A theory of government formation'. *Comparative Political Studies*, vol. 17, n. 2: 229–64.

Luebbert, Gregory. 1986. *Comparative Democracy: Policymaking and Governing Coalitions in Europe and Israel*. New York: Columbia University Press.

Lupia, Arthur, and Strøm, Kaare. 1995. 'Coalition termination and the strategic timing of parliamentary elections'. *American Political Science Review*, vol. 89, n. 3: 648–65.

Martin, Lanny W. 2004. 'The government agenda in parliamentary democracies'. *American Journal of Political Science*, vol. 48, n. 3: 445–61.

Martin, Lanny W., and Vanberg, Georg. 2004. 'Policing the bargain: coalition government and parliamentary scrutiny'. *American Journal of Political Science*, vol. 48, n. 1: 13–27.

Martin, Lanny W., and Vanberg, Georg. 2011. *Parliaments and Coalitions: The Role of Legislative Institutions in Multiparty Governance*. Oxford: Oxford University Press.

Moury, Catherine, and Timmermans, Arco. 2013. 'Inter-party conflict management in coalition governments: analyzing the role of coalition agreements in Belgium, Germany, Italy and the Netherlands'. *Politics and Governance*, vol. 1, n. 2: 117–31.

Müller, Wolfgang C., and Meyer, Thomas. 2010. 'Meeting the challenges of representation and accountability in multi-party government'. *West European Politics*, vol. 33, n. 5: 1065–92.

Pappi, Franz U. 1984. 'The West German party system'. *West European Politics*, vol. 7, n. 4: 7–26.

Putnam, Robert B. 1988. 'Diplomacy and domestic politics: the logic of two-level games'. *International Organization*, vol. 42, n. 3: 427–60.

Riker, William H. 1962. *The Theory of Political Coalitions*. New Haven: Yale University Press.

Saalfeld, Thomas. 2000. 'Coalitions in Germany: stable parties, chancellor democracy and the art of informal settlement'. In *Coalition Government in Western Europe*, edited by Wolfgang C. Müller and Kaare Strøm, 32–85. Oxford: Oxford University Press.

Sartori, Giovanni. 1976. *Parties and Party Systems. A Framework for Analysis*. Cambridge: Cambridge University Press.

Schubert, Thomas. 2013. 'Vorstufe der Koalitionsbildung oder strategisch-taktische Wahlkampfinstrumente? Koalitionsaussagen vor Bundestagswahlen'. In *Die deutsche Koalitionsdemokratie vor der Bundestagswahl 2013*, edited by Frank Decker and Eckhard Jesse, 97–113. Baden-Baden: Nomos.

Schubert, Thomas. 2014. 'Politikfloskeln oder Bündnissignale? Koalitionsaussagen zwischen Wahlkampfstrategie und Bündnispolitik'. In *Bilanz der Bundestagswahl 2013: Voraussetzungen, Ergebnisse, Folgen*, edited by Eckhard Jesse and Roland Sturm, 75–94. Baden-Baden: Nomos.

Slapin, Jonathan B., and Proksch, Sven-Oliver. 2008. 'A scaling model for estimating time-series party positions from texts'. *American Journal of Political Science*, vol. 52, n. 3: 705–22.

Straffin, Philip D. Jr. 1996. *Game Theory and Strategy*. Washington, DC: Mathematical Association of America.

Stratmann, Thomas. 1997. 'Logrolling'. In *Perspectives on Public Choice: A Handbook*, edited by Dennis C. Mueller, 322–41. Cambridge: Cambridge University Press.

Sturm, Roland. 2014. 'Die Regierungsbildung nach der Bundestagswahl 2013: lagerübergreifend und schwierig'. *Zeitschrift für Parlamentsfragen*, vol. 45, n. 1: 207–30.

Thies, Michael F. 2001. 'Keeping tabs on partners: the logic of delegation in coalition governments'. *American Journal of Political Science*, vol. 45, n. 3: 580–98.

Tsebelis, George, 2002. *Veto Players: How Political Institutions Work*. New York: Rand Corporation/Princeton: Princeton University Press.

Von Neumann, John, and Morgenstern, Oskar. 1953. *Theory of Games and Economic Behavior*. Princeton: Princeton University Press.

Name Index

Subject Index